TOWARD SUSTAINABLE COMMUNITIES

Revised Edition

TOWARD SUSTAINABLE COMMUNITIES

Revised Edition

RESOURCES FOR CITIZENS AND THEIR GOVERNMENTS

Mark Roseland

with Sean Connelly, David Hendrickson, Chris Lindberg,
and Michael Lithgow

Foreword by Jeb Brugmann

NEW SOCIETY PUBLISHERS

Cataloguing in Publication Data:
A catalog record for this publication is available from the National Library of Canada and the Library of Congress.

First published by Canada's National Round Table on the Environment and the Economy as *Toward Sustainable Communities: A Resource Book for Municipal and Local Governments*, by Mark Roseland, 1992. Revised and updated, 1998. This is a completely revised and updated edition.

Cover design by Diane McIntosh.

Graphics credits: Grahame Arnould, pp. 31, 46, 101, 109, 111, 113, 213; City of Vancouver, pp. 118, 119; Greater Vancouver Regional District, p. 131; *RAIN Magazine*, p. 137; Recycling Council of British Columbia, p. 71; Eva Riccius, pp. 49, 58, 72; Mark Roseland, p. 61; David Rousseau, pp. 132-134; Christopher Small, p. 114; Ray Straatsma, p.171; Denise Taschereau, pp. 42, 43, 45, 47, 48, 115, 150, 173; Heather Wornell, pp. 55, 60, 90.

Printed in Canada. Third printing December 2009.

New Society Publishers acknowledges the support of the Government of Canada through the Book Publishing Industry Development Program (BPIDP) for our publishing activities.

Paperback ISBN 13: 978-0-86571-535-6

Inquiries regarding requests to reprint all or part of *Toward Sustainable Communities* should be addressed to New Society Publishers at the address below.

To order directly from the publishers, please call toll-free (North America) 1-800-567-6772, or order online at www.newsociety.com

Any other inquiries can be directed by mail to:

New Society Publishers
P.O. Box 189, Gabriola Island, BC V0R 1X0, Canada
1-800-567-6772

New Society Publishers' mission is to publish books that contribute in fundamental ways to building an ecologically sustainable and just society, and to do so with the least possible impact on the environment, in a manner that models this vision. We are committed to doing this not just through education, but through action. We are acting on our commitment to the world's remaining ancient forests by phasing out our paper supply from ancient forests worldwide. This book is one step toward ending global deforestation and climate change. It is printed on acid-free paper that is 100% old growth forest-free (100% post-consumer recycled), processed chlorine free, and printed with vegetable based, low VOC inks. For further information, or to browse our full list of books and purchase securely, visit our website at: www.newsociety.com

NEW SOCIETY PUBLISHERS   www.newsociety.com

Contents

Preface to the Third Edition

Many of our most critical global environmental issues are rooted in local, day-to-day problems. Atmospheric and potential climate change, for example, can be altered by local citizens and government officials making enlightened decisions about local traffic congestion and inefficient land-use patterns. Local decisions about such issues benefit all of us globally.

While global environmental change is accelerating, there is a wealth of important and exciting information that can help us set the planet on a sustainable course. Unfortunately, most of this information is not available through the mainstream media. I have endeavored to make these ideas, tools and resources accessible. Those concerned citizens, elected officials, and municipal staff who prompted me to write this book are the people for whom it is written.

Toward Sustainable Communities: A Resource Book for Municipal and Local Governments was originally published in 1992 and distributed by the government of Canada's National Round Table on the Environment and the Economy. Over 12,000 copies were distributed internationally, and the book was also used as a textbook in several university courses.

The book received much critical and popular acclaim. Jeb Brugmann, then Secretary General of the International Council for Local Environmental Initiatives, called it "a rare compendium of tested, practical suggestions, helpful contacts, and essential references to use in setting community planning and development on a sustainable course." Doreen Quirk, President of the Federation of Canadian Municipalities, said it "will assist your municipality in developing an integrated approach to sustainable development for the 21st century."

The second edition, published in 1998 by New Society, differed in several important ways. First, the orientation changed slightly, as reflected in the new subtitle: *Resources for Citizens and Their Governments*. Second, the conceptual framework was revised and more explicit. Third, that edition was completely revised and updated, and included numerous internet and e-mail resources. Fourth, the chapters were written in a more narrative style, although tools, initiatives, and useful resources were emphasized as before. Fifth, the sequence of the chapters differed significantly from the original edition. Sixth, some chapters were added and some dropped or incorporated into other chapters. And an appendix of organizations and publications was added to provide general resources on sustainability. Finally, that edition was longer than the original and had a much more appealing design.

This new edition has been completely updated, and has been revised significantly as well. In particular, the conceptual framework in the opening chapters is an exciting leap forward, and has been shown to resonate with diverse audiences in several different parts of the world. Another significant revision is that the Centre for Sustainable Community Development at Simon Fraser University will be hosting an up-to-date Resources section for the book on its web site, www.sfu.ca/cscd. To summarize, *this edition is even better than the last one.*

The book is designed to be both stimulating and useful. Part 1 explores the meaning of sustainable development and its implications for communities, and develops a framework for sustainable community development. It concludes with a chapter on thinking strategically, which examines policy instruments for sustainable community development.

Part 2 is a set of sustainable community "building blocks." Each chapter provides an overview explaining the topic and its relevance to sustainable communities, followed by a set of "Tools and Initiatives" and "Resources." These building blocks are a set of planning tools, practical initiatives, and associated resources that have helped citizens and their governments move toward sustainable communities. While not every tool will fit every community, many of them will fit quite well. Each chapter is accompanied by bibliographic references

Part 3 focuses on mobilizing citizens and their governments toward sustainable communities. It concentrates on governing sustainable communities and tools for managing community sustainability, and concludes with some lessons for designing effective sustainable community development policies and thoughts for the challenge ahead. It is followed by an appendix of additional sustainable community resources.

The book is not intended to be comprehensive; rather, it attempts to identify and document the current range of initiatives toward sustainable communities. Dozens of tools, initiatives and resources are presented in these pages, accompanied by hundreds of references to aid interested readers in their own research. Certain tools and initiatives may be missing because we didn't know about them, but many others were omitted because of space and budget limitations. We have presented those that seemed most readily transferable to other communities.

The term "North America" in this book refers primarily to communities in the developed countries of North America, in other words, those in the US and Canada. The term "community" refers to a group of people bound by geography and with a shared destiny, such as a municipality or a town.

The mixed use of Canadian and US spellings throughout the book (e.g., centre versus center, neighbour versus neighbor) is due to keeping the original spellings intact in all excerpts from the literature of Canada, the US, and other countries. As well, measurement units are original in these excerpts, while the equivalents of SI and Imperial units are provided throughout the text (with the exception of an equivalent for "ton," as the unit is nearly equal in both forms of measurement).

This volume is part of a larger, ongoing research project. If you are aware of sustainable community initiatives and resources other than those described here, or are involved in developing your own sustainable community initiatives, please send your information and/or documentation to me at the Centre for Sustainable Community Development, Simon Fraser University, Burnaby, BC, Canada V5A 1S6, or via the internet at www.sfu.ca/cscd.

This book is dedicated to the citizen activists and local government officials around the world who have developed the wide array of initiatives that make it possible. Your efforts to create a sustainable future have sustained me as well.

Mark Roseland, Vancouver, British Columbia

Foreword

By Jeb Brugmann

For generations, environmentalists in North America have fought to protect "nature," but have been ambivalent in the struggle to create healthy, equitable and economically sustainable communities for the human family. *Toward Sustainable Communities* confronts this major contradiction and shortcoming in the North American environmentalist tradition with practical, hopeful guidance.

The intellectual roots of the North American environmental movement in the Anglo-Romantic traditions of the 19th century inspired many battles to protect a pure and wild nature, but they failed to guide humankind on a course that is sustainable. While we have tended to nature's ecosystems, we have permitted our cities and towns to become engines of resource extraction and exploitation, waste generation and release.

During the period that environmentalism has become a force in North American public life, our cities and communities have sprawled without consideration for resource efficiency. Infrastructure has been constructed — housing, roadways and sewage systems, for instance — in a way that encourages disregardful resource consumption. Water resources have been depleted or polluted. The design of built environments has altered microclimates and promoted photochemical smog formation. Environmental services, such as public transit systems, have been left without public support. Our settlements have not only become less and less sustainable, but they are less and less "livable"— so much so that, globally, organizations now campaign for "livable communities." At the same time, our cities and towns have developed into the primary geographic point sources of contintental and global environmental problems, threatening even the most distant wild areas and species that were saved through the landmark campaigns of the environmental movement.

During recent decades, a new, more humanistic tradition has developed in the environmental movement, which focuses attention directly on the state, form and management of human communities. It includes the Habitat movement, the Healthy Cities movement, and the more recent "sustainable communities" and eco-cities movements. These movements share the perspective that the most direct and effective means to protect the environment is to redevelop, retrofit and redesign our own communities — in other words, to make them sustainable communities.

The evolution of *Toward Sustainable Communities* from its first printing in 1992 to this current edition chronicles the evolution of thinking and practice in this movement. At the start, the notion of sustainable communities focused primarily on environmental considerations. The most important paradigm shift introduced into practice at this early stage has arguably been the understanding of cities as ecosystems in their own right. The ecosystem framework has helped practitioners to understand the energy and resource flows in their communities, and how these can be made more efficient, for instance through "cascading" designs. The urban ecosystem concept has also helped us to understand how cities shift their environmental burdens to distant places and to different scales, such as to communities in developing countries or to the global climate, sometimes even as a result of their local environmental improvements. As a result, urban environmentalism has become imbued with a sense of responsibility and responsiveness both to the local community, to distant partner communities, and to the global commons. "Globalisation" has empowered the development of local responses to all of these scales.

Subsequent editions of *Toward Sustainable Communities*, culminating in this new edition, have chronicled the maturing of sustainable community theory to include the social and economic dimensions of urban or "human ecosystems" development. This maturing has been driven by lessons from practice, which Mark Roseland has so carefully chronicled over the years. Practitioners found that their plans and strategies for eco-efficient urban development and environmental health, when advanced through siloed environmental policies and regulatory regimes, were falling short in the face of social imperatives and market-based economic forces. This new edition of *Toward Sustainable Communities* therefore applies a new framework, based on the concept of "community capital," to understand city development as a process of developing and managing natural, social and economic capital— not just of natural resource management.

This community capital framework opens up new horizons for practice, and as can be expected from Mark Roseland and this book, he offers us a compendium of practical cases, models and tools to indicate the way.

The overarching message that I take away from Roseland's new approach is that we need a period of innovation and experimentation in the use of enterprise-based approaches, not only of policy and public investment approaches, to pursue our sustainable community strategies. This requires our final abandonment of the traditional environmentalist predisposition to view enterprise and the market as a problem that we hope will go away. The politics of our time have made the futility of that hope entirely apparent. Now we need to find ways, at the community level, to become masters of the market forces that drive the unsustainable and inefficient development of our settlements, in spite of our accumulated environmental "best practices." This will inevitably lead us into new kinds of alliances and partnerships, new models of organization, and new frameworks for understanding how our communities fit into a globally networked society and ecosystem.

Fortunately, Mark Roseland has persisted in tracking the development of our community of practice. This book holds up a mirror, which I am sure will embolden us to refresh our mental models and to persist in our commitments.

— Jeb Brugmann founded and was the first secretary general of Local Sustainability — The International Council for Local Environmental Initiatives. He presently serves as president of Globalegacy Group, and is a partner in The Next Practice management consulting firm.

ACKNOWLEDGMENTS

In the years since the first edition of this book appeared, interest in sustainable communities has exploded (due at least in part to the impact of the book). What was a difficult but possible task for one person to accomplish in 1992 is no longer possible today. Fortunately, many people helped directly or indirectly in making it possible to complete this edition.

First and foremost, this book came together with the assistance of Sean Connelly, David Hendrickson, Chris Lindberg, and Michael Lithgow, researchers at the SFU Centre for Sustainable Community Development. I could not have been more fortunate than to have these talented and capable people working with me, and they were instrumental particularly in producing Part 2 of this edition. Maureen Cureton and Heather Wornell were essential contributors to the second edition of the book, and much of their efforts are still reflected in this edition.

Thanks also to my colleagues in the Department of Geography at Simon Fraser University for allowing and encouraging me to teach courses on sustainable communities. My students used the first and second editions as a text and provided valuable feedback as well as new material for this edition. My students in the Centre for Sustainable Community Development at Simon Fraser also provided valuable research assistance, much of which made its way into the chapter, "Community Economic Development." Additional researchers who contributed substantially to this effort include Karen Asp, Denise Taschereau, Zane Parker, Gavin Davidson, Angela Smailes, Irene Gannitsos and Kelly Vodden.

It is extremely heartening to work with a bright new generation of thinkers and future leaders who will be making important contributions to sustainable communities for many years to come.

Several other individuals also deserve specific mention for their contributions. I am delighted that Jeb Brugmann wrote the foreword. Jeb's work with Local Sustainability — The International Council for Local Environmental Initiatives and with Globalegacy has inspired me, and I am honored to have his thoughts on these pages. My thanks also to Chris and Judith Plant at New Society Publishers for encouraging this revised and updated edition.

I am also obliged to Joan Fletcher, Gavin Davidson, Ryan Hill, Dorli Duffy, and Jay Lambert for research assistance. I am grateful to Christina Lai, SFU Centre for Sustainable Community Development, for unwavering administrative support.

Related research support for this edition came from the Social Sciences and Humanities Research Council, Canada Mortgage and Housing Corporation, the Canadian International Development Agency, and the Simon Fraser University work-study program. I gratefully acknowledge financial support for the second edition from the President's Research Fund at Simon Fraser University, and from the Science Council of British Columbia for research on policy instruments. Support for the original edition came from The Forum for Planning Action, The University of British Columbia Centre for Human Settlements, The University of British Columbia Task Force on Healthy and Sustainable Communities, Friends of the Earth, and from the National Round Table on the Environment and the Economy, which published and distributed the first edition.

An earlier version of Chapter 3 first appeared in *Local Environment* 1(2) 1996, and a chapter based on an earlier version of material in Chapter 1 appeared in J.T.Pierce and A. Dale, Editors, *Communities, Development, and Sustainability across Canada* (Vancouver: UBC Press, 1999), pp. 190-207.

Last but by no means least, I am beholden to Susan Day, my friend, confidant, advisor and partner, for carrying much of my load during this long and demanding process, and for sustaining our dreams; to my stepson Sean Rigby, and to my children Miranda Roseland and Aaron Roseland, who represent the future we are trying to make sustainable. Miranda and Aaron came into this world since the last edition; their arrival has made my life circumstances surrounding the production of this edition markedly slower but infinitely sweeter.

PART 1

SUSTAINABLE COMMUNITIES, SUSTAINABLE PLANET

CHAPTER 1

The Context for Sustainable Communities

A quiet transformation is taking place in communities all over North America and around the world. Thousands of citizens and their governments are embracing a new way of thinking and acting about their future.

Motivations for involvement vary, but they include a desire to improve the quality of community life, protect the environment, and participate in decisions that affect us; concern about poverty and other social conditions, whether in far away countries or in our own towns; longing for a sense of satisfaction that money can't buy; and pride in the legacy left for our children.

These motivations are all coming together now in a movement toward sustainable communities. As the following chapters demonstrate, this synergistic approach will enable our communities to be cleaner, healthier, and less expensive; to have greater accessibility and cohesion; and to be more self-reliant in energy, food, and economic security than they are now. Sustainable communities are not merely about "sustaining" the quality of our lives — they are about *improving* it.

This chapter explores the context for sustainable communities. Acting locally is more significant when we think globally, so that is where we begin our discussion of "sustainable development." We then examine the concept of "community capital" as a way to "do development differently," as well as to begin building a framework for sustainable community development.

THINKING GLOBALLY

Many people around the world are starting to consider that the population problem in the South is less significant a problem than over-consumption and wasted resources in the North.

The average person in a developed country uses 9 times as much fossil fuel and 20 times as much aluminum as his or her counterpart in developing countries. In terms of waste, the average person produces 4 times as much household refuse, 11 times more carbon dioxide, 26 times more chloroflourocarbons, and 75 times more hazardous wastes. Average Americans use 43 times as much gasoline as average Indians,

45 times as much copper, and 34 times as much aluminum (ICPQL, 1996). North Americans have double the "ecological footprint" of Europeans, and seven times the average footprint of Asians and Africans (WWF et al., 2004).

Many in both northern and southern countries now argue that gross population figures must be corrected by adding figures reflecting per-capita resource consumption. By these calculations, the US population is in the tens of billions, and is viewed as the biggest contributor to the global population problem (Henderson, 1996).

Bringing the Third World up to North American living standards would require a five- to 10-fold increase in world industrial output (WCED, 1987), yet the contingent combination of depleted resource stocks (e.g., fossil fuels, fisheries, forests) with degraded life-support systems (e.g., ozone depletion, global warming, acid rain) demonstrates the impossibility of the entire world consuming and polluting at the rate of North Americans.

SUSTAINABLE DEVELOPMENT

In December 1983, in response to a United Nations General Assembly resolution, the U.N. Secretary-General appointed physician Gro Harlem Brundtland of Norway as Chairman of an independent World Commission on Environment and Development. In April 1987, the Commission released its report, *Our Common Future*. The report showed that the poorest fifth of the world's population has less than 2 percent of the world's economic product while the richest fifth has 75 percent; the 26 percent of the world's population living in developed countries consumes 80 percent to 86 percent of nonrenewable resources and 34 percent to 53 percent of food products (WCED, 1987). At the core of the report is the principle of sustainable development. Embracing sustainable development as an underlying principle gave political credibility to a concept many others had worked on over the previous decade. The Commission defined sustainable development as meeting "the needs of the present without compromising the ability of future generations to meet their own needs."

The term sustainable development has been criticized as ambiguous and open to a wide range of interpretations, many of which are contradictory. Confusion has resulted from using the terms sustainable development, "sustainable growth," and "sustainable use" interchangeably, as if their meanings were the same. They are not. Sustainable growth is a contradiction in terms: nothing physical can grow indefinitely. Sustainable use is applicable only to renewable resources: it means using them at rates within their capacity for renewal (IUCN, 1991).

Many people use the term sustainable development to simply mean either "environmental protection" or else sustained economic growth (presumably to pay for, among other things, environmental protection). Even the Brundtland Commission accepted the need for a five- to 10-fold increase in world industrial output as essential for sustainable development.

The very concept of environmental protection is based on the separation of humanity from nature. As a society, we point to a few things we think of as nature — some trees here, a pond there — draw a box around them, then try to "protect" what's within the box. Meanwhile, we ignore the fact that human activity *outside* that box — housing, economic development, transportation, and so on — has a far greater impact on the environment than do our "environmental" policies.

Environmental protection is like foam padding — it offers some protection from a fall. We congratulate ourselves if we double our spending to double the thickness of the foam, because we assume thicker foam means more protection. However, *we only get more protection if we fall the same distance*. Meanwhile, *unsustainable* development constantly increases the distance we're likely to fall. Sustainable development must therefore be more than merely "protecting" the environment: it requires economic and social change to *improve human well-being while reducing the need for environmental protection*.

Social equity demands that we balance the needs of the biosphere with the needs of the vast majority of the human population, the world's poor. Within the developed nations, this in turn means that we must balance the needs of the biosphere with the needs of our own poor. But in doing so we can no longer rely on our 200-year tradition of material growth as the primary instrument of social policy.

Like other political objectives of its kind (e.g., justice, democracy), we all agree with the ideal of sustainable development and disagree over what it entails. Nevertheless, sustainable development has a core meaning which remains, however it is interpreted. The three elements of sustainable development are (Jacobs, 1993):

• *Environmental considerations must be entrenched in economic policy-making.* Environmental and economic objectives must be placed within a common framework in which a variety of parallel objectives can be recognized.

• *Sustainable development incorporates an inescapable commitment to social equity.* This requires not simply the creation of wealth and the conservation of resources, but their fair distribution both between and within countries, including at least some measure of redistribution between North and South. Sustainability also requires the fair distribution of environmental benefits and costs between generations.

• "Development" *does not simply mean "growth,"* as represented by faulty measures of economic performance such as increases in gross national product (GNP). Development implies qualitative as well as quantitative improvement.

In sum, sustainable development must be a *different kind of development*. It must be *a pro-active strategy to develop sustainability*.

COMMUNITY CAPITAL

There are myriad ways to understand and conceptualize community. In terms of sustainable community development, however, we are discovering that it is useful to think of community in terms of assets, or *capital*. All forms of capital are created by spending time and effort in transformation and transaction activities (Ostrom, 1993).

In the last few years there have been several efforts to describe sustainable development in terms of three or four types of capital (e.g., Goodland, 2002, Rainey et al., 2003). For example, Canada's National Round Table on the Environment and the

Economy, which published the original edition of this book in 1992, is using a capital model based on four types of capital (NRTEE, 2003).

Recent explorations by the SFU Centre for Sustainable Community Development (e.g., Roseland, 1999; 2000) and others (e.g., Hancock, 2001) are attempting to create a notion of *community capital* as a foundation for sustainable community development.

Our perspective on community capital includes *natural, physical, economic, human, social, and cultural forms of capital*.[1]

Natural Capital

Global resource depletion and pollution are forcing recognition that existing patterns of development and resource use are not sustainable. Even conservative neoclassical economists are recognizing that the sustainable component of development requires that human activities today do not deplete what can be termed "natural capital" or "environmental capital." Although the idea of natural capital originated nearly a century ago, only recently has the term gained prominence (primarily among ecological economists, themselves a relatively new breed), to further our understanding of sustainable development (e.g., Jansson et al., 1994; Wackernagel and Rees, 1996, Goodland, 2002). Natural capital refers to any stock of natural assets that yields a flow of valuable goods and services into the future. For example, a forest, a fish stock, or an aquifer can provide a harvest or flow that is potentially sustainable year after year. The forest or fish stock is natural capital and the sustainable harvest is "natural income."

The total stock of environmental assets which comprise this natural capital may be divided usefully into three categories:
- non-renewable resources, such as minerals and fossil fuels;
- the finite capacity of natural systems to produce "renewable resources" such as food crops, forestry products, and water supplies — which are renewable only if the natural systems from which they are drawn are not overexploited; and
- the capacity of natural systems to absorb our emissions and pollutants without side effects, which imply heavy costs passed onto future generations (such as chemicals that deplete the atmosphere's ozone layer, and greenhouse gases which may cause serious climatic imbalances).

Natural capital also provides such critical ecological services as waste assimilation, erosion and flood control, and protection from ultraviolet radiation (the ozone layer is a form of natural capital). These life support systems are counted as natural income. Since the flow of services from ecosystems often requires that they function as intact systems, the structure and diversity of the system may be an important component of natural capital (Wackernagel and Rees, 1996, Goodland, 2002).

Although natural capital is a relatively new way of framing choices for social policy and action, it has helped considerably to refine the sustainability debate. For example, there is no doubt that the stock of non-renewable resources is finite, nor is there any doubt that eco-systems (individually and collectively within the biosphere) have limits in their capacity to absorb pollutants. There is also agreement that some environmental assets, such as areas of outstanding natural beauty, are irreplaceable.

According to Mitlin and Satterthwaite (1991):

> The debate centers on which environmental assets are irreplaceable and the extent to which current (and projected) future levels of resource use degrade the capital stock of environmental assets for future generations, the extent to which one resource can be substituted for another (for instance, a synthetic substance replacing a natural one) and the extent to which pollutants derived from human activities are damaging the biosphere.

Strong or Weak Sustainability?

Some analysts (e.g., Pearce et al., 1989) argue that "future generations should be compensated for reductions in the endowments of resources brought about by the actions of present generations"; they suggest that each generation should leave the next a stock of assets at least as great as that which they inherited themselves. There are two possible ways to interpret this: "weak sustainability," which aggregates all types of assets, and "strong sustainability," which differentiates between assets that are "natural" and those that are not. Strong sustainability argues that whatever the level of human-made assets, an adequate stock of environmental (or natural) assets alone is critical in securing sustainability (Daly, 1989; Rees, 1992).

Weak sustainability reflects the neoclassical economic assumption that non-natural assets can substitute for natural assets; therefore it is acceptable to use up natural assets so long as the profits they generate provide an equivalent endowment to the next generation. Yet in some cases, natural and non-natural assets are clearly not substitutable. For example, a sawmill cannot be substituted for a forest since the sawmill (non-natural capital) needs the forest (natural capital) in order to function (Daly, 1989). Weak sustainability also assumes that other forms of capital (e.g., manufactured, financial, or human capital) can be converted back into natural capital. This interpretation does not take into account irreversible processes such as the extinction of species or the destruction of ecosystems.

All this suggests that weak sustainability is grossly insufficient; natural capital stock should only be destroyed if the benefits of doing so are very large or if the social costs of conservation are unacceptably large (Pearce et al., 1990). Yet this begs the key question: *are we capable of knowing the full costs and benefits of destroying or conserving natural capital stock?*

Ecological economists can put a price on resources such as timber and fisheries; but the value of ecological process resources such as carbon absorption or photosynthesis cannot easily be quantified and monetized (Rees, 1991). The very concept of economic "trade-offs" depends upon being able to put a *price* on the items traded (see Pricing the Planet). Resources that cannot be quantified or monetized also cannot be priced. It may be theoretically possible to trade-off some value of a fishery for some value of a timber harvest, but it may not be possible to realistically price the value of the ozone shield.

The economic benefits of destroying natural capital stock or the social costs of conservation may *seem* large, but only as a function of our inability to adequately assess such costs and benefits. If the potential benefits of conservation approach infinity, the costs are irrelevant (Rees, 1991). This suggests that it is time for a different kind of framework for planning and decision-making, guided by the understanding that *natural capital stock should not be destroyed.*

In terms of the life-support functions of natural capital, destruction of any single significant natural asset can be likened to destruction of any single bodily organ or system. The destruction of the ozone layer may have the same consequences, in planetary terms, as destruction of the immune system has for the human body; global warming may be analogous to a high fever.

We do not ask those who suffer from heart disease to trade normal brain functioning for a healthier heart. Such choices are the stuff of literature's great tragedies; they only become more tragic if we insist upon this approach to deciding complex societal choices.

Like a thermometer registering a fever, the accumulating trends of ecological decline (e.g., decrease in stratospheric ozone, increase in greenhouse gases, extinction of species, loss of biodiversity, etc.) are the indicators of our condition.

The "ecological bottom line" is that we must learn to live on the "interest" generated by our remaining stocks of living natural capital, and not deplete those stocks. In short, we must *minimize our consumption of essential natural capital.*

This applies particularly in developed countries, where one-quarter of the world's people consume three-quarters of the world's resources (ICPQL, 1996; WCED, 1987). For North Americans to contribute to global sustainability will require major shifts in lifestyles of the affluent. A wide variety of approaches are called for, including reducing atmospheric emissions and water pollution, waste reduction and recycling, and greening our cities. The most important adaptation for minimizing consumption of natural capital is a reduction of our present levels of materials and energy consumption. This will require a more globally conscious kind of local development than we are accustomed to.

Minimizing our consumption of essential natural capital means living within ecological limits, conserving and enhancing natural resources, sustainable resource management (soil, air, water, energy, agriculture, etc.), cleaner production, and minimizing waste (solid, liquid, air pollution, etc.).

Minimizing consumption of natural capital has profound implications for urban form, for the material basis of urban life, and for community social relationships in the 21st century. *If the basic science is correct, we have no choice but to shift to more sustainable patterns of resource use and development.* The longer we wait, the greater the

---

Pricing the Planet

A team of 13 ecologists, economists and geographers, in a report in the journal *Nature,* estimated the present global value of 17 ecosystem "services" at US$16 trillion to $54 trillion a year, with a likely figure of at least $33 trillion. That figure is based on the cash value of such things as water, air, forests, animals, dirt, coral reefs, grasslands, and other aspects of the natural world. Most of this lies outside formal markets and is therefore not reflected in market prices, the customary gauge of economic value. Ecosystem services are services essential to the human economy, including climate regulation, water supply, soil formation, pollination, food production, raw materials, genetic resources, recreation and culture.

To come up with the $33 trillion figure, the team, headed by University of Maryland ecological economist Robert Costanza, found published estimates of the economic value of natural ecosystems. After finding credible estimates of how much each of 17 ecosystems is worth, they multiplied that value by the total areas of each type of feature on earth.

The purpose of the study was to put a price tag on what people would have to pay to replace — if that were possible — the ecosystem services of the natural environment. In comparison, the gross national product of the world, which is all the goods and services produced by people each year, is about $18 trillion (Stevens, 1997).

risk of having to impose rigid regulations in times of crisis. The sooner we make these shifts, the more options we will have to create mechanisms of adjustment that are socially acceptable and economically feasible.

Despite the interest in "natural capitalism" (Hawken et al., 1999), putting a price tag on everything in nature will not solve all of our planetary woes. Economic growth and industrialization as presently practiced are accompanied almost invariably with increasing energy demand and growing ecological waste, even when the intensity of energy use is falling. This means that technological improvements can be expected to slow down the rate of ecological damage only marginally, so long as the scale of production is increasing rapidly. Ultimately, social issues — including the nature and purpose of economic development — must be addressed (Foster, 1997).

Physical, Economical and Human Capital

Physical capital is the stock of material resources such as equipment, buildings, machinery and other infrastructure that can be used to produce a flow of future income. The origin of physical capital is the process of spending time and other resources constructing tools, plants, facilities and other material resources that can, in turn, be used in producing other products (Ostrom, 1993). Physical capital is sometimes referred to as *produced capital* (NRTEE 2003), *manufactured capital* (Goodland 2002) or *public capital* (Rainey et al., 2003).

Improving physical capital includes focusing on community assets such as public facilities (e.g., hospitals and schools); water and sanitation; efficient transportation; safe, quality housing; adequate infrastructure and telecommunications.

Economic capital refers to the ways we allocate resources and make decisions about our material lives. Economic capital should be maintained in order for people to live off the interest, or income. Goodland (2002) argues that economic and manufactured capital can be substituted: "There is much capitalization of manufactured capital, such as too many fishing boats and sawmills chasing declining fish stocks and forests."

Strengthening economic capital means focusing on: making more with less — maximizing use of existing resources (e.g., using waste as a resource); making the money-go-round — circulating dollars within a community; making things ourselves — replacing imports; making something new — creating a new product (Nozick, 1992); trading fairly with others; and developing community financial institutions.

Human capital is the "knowledge, skills, competencies and other attributes embodied in individuals that facilitate the creation of personal, social and economic well-being" (OECD, 2001). Human capital is formed consciously through training and education and unconsciously through experience (Ostrom, 1993).

Health, education, skills, knowledge, leadership and access to services constitute human capital. Human capital needs continual maintenance by investments throughout one's lifetime (Goodland, 2002).

Increasing human capital requires a focus on areas such as health, education, nutrition, literacy, and family and community cohesion. Basic determinants of health such as peace and safety, food, shelter, education, income and employment are necessary prerequisites (Hancock, 2001).

Social and Cultural Capital

Social capital is "the relationships, networks and norms that facilitate collective action" (OECD, 2001), or the shared knowledge, understandings, and patterns of interactions that a group of people bring to any productive activity (Coleman, 1988, Putnam, 1993). Social capital refers to the organizations, structures and social relations which people build up themselves, independently of the state or large corporations. It contributes to stronger community fabric, and, often as a by-product of other activities, builds bonds of information, trust, and inter-personal solidarity (Jacobs, 1961; Coleman, 1990; Woolcock, 2001).

Social capital includes community cohesion, connectedness, reciprocity, tolerance, compassion, patience, forbearance, fellowship, love, commonly accepted standards of honesty, discipline and ethics, and commonly shared rules, laws, and information. When social capital is undercapitalized, the result is high levels of violence and mistrust. Western-style capitalism can weaken social capital to the extent it promotes competition and individualism over cooperation and community (Goodland, 2002).

Though largely neglected in discussions of public policy, Putnam (1993) argues that social capital substantially enhances returns to investments in physical and human capital. However, unlike conventional capital, social capital is a public good, i.e., it is not the private property of those who benefit from it. Thus, like other public goods, from clean air to safe streets, social capital tends to be under-provided by private agents. The ties, norms and trust that constitute social capital are most often created as a byproduct of other social activities and then transferred from one social setting to another.

Social capital constitutes the "glue" that holds our communities together. It has both an informal aspect related to social networks and a more formal aspect related to our social development programs. High levels of what have been termed "social cohesion" and "civicness" are rooted in social networks and in participation in society, including the governance processes through which decisions are made. In addition to these informal forms of social capital, there are also the more formal forms of social capital that result from society's investment in social development that ensures people have equitable access to such basic determinants of health as peace and safety, food, shelter, education, income and employment (Hancock, 2001). The shared cognitive aspects of social capital help account for two unusual characteristics that differ from physical capital. First, social capital does not wear out upon being used more and more; and second, if unused, social capital deteriorates at a relatively rapid rate (Ostrom, 1993).

Social capital differs from other forms of capital in several significant ways. It is not limited by material scarcity, meaning that its creative capacity is limited only by imagination. Consequently, it suggests a route toward sustainability, by replacing the fun-

---

Champagne on a Beer Budget

Kerala, a state of 29 million people in southern India, has a per capita income estimated by various surveys to be between US$298 and $350 per year, about one-seventieth the US average. Yet data for life expectancy, literacy, and birth rates for Kerala are comparable to those for the US "One-seventieth the income means one-seventieth the damage to the planet. So, on balance, if Kerala and the United States manage to achieve the same physical quality of life, Kerala is the vastly more successful society" (McKibben, 1996).

---

damentally illogical model of unlimited growth within a finite world with one of unlimited complexity, not bound by the availability of material resources.

However, social capital also has limitations which other forms of capital do not. It cannot be created instantly, and the very fact of trying to consciously create it or direct it can create resistance. People resist being instrumentalized for even the best of reasons. Social capital takes time to develop, and is inherently non-transferable (Flora and Flora, 1993). It is also fragile and subject to erosion not only by direct assault but more importantly, by neglect, if there are many or strong competitors for investment of emotional significance or time.

The modern concept of social capital is described as the *relations between* individuals and groups. It can take several forms, some of which are mutually recognized bonds, channels of information, and norms and sanctions.

In this sense, social capital is related to the concept of social ecology, as developed in the works of Murray Bookchin. Social ecology is the study of both human and natural ecosystems, and in particular, of the social relations that affect the relation of society as a whole with nature. Social ecology goes beyond environmentalism, insisting that the issue at hand for humanity is not simply protecting nature but rather creating an ecological society in harmony with nature. The primary social unit of an ecological society is the sustainable community, a human-scale settlement based on ecological balance, community self-reliance, and participatory democracy (Bookchin, 1987).

Multiplying Social Capital

Beyond understanding the basic nature of social capital, we need to know where to locate and how to *multiply social capital* for sustainable community development.

Social networks can be divided into those with and without closure (Coleman, 1988). A network with closure is one where most of the individuals within it know each other, and the relationship of each to the others. In contrast, a network without closure is one where each individual's circle of acquaintances overlaps only partially or not at all with those of the others, and the degree of overlap is generally unknown.

Formally organized groups are the necessary recourse of societies without closure. Organized groups have established procedures for adherence and keep membership lists, follow recognized procedures to conduct their affairs, and often administer budgets and own property. Examples are churches, ethnic associations, unions, trade associations, sports associations, theater societies, or environmental groups. However, a formal organization may also be a public representation of a more primary closure society. Churches, especially ethnically-rooted ones, tend to fall into this category. Organizations which have survived an intense struggle in a hostile social environment, such as some unions and environmental groups, can also take on something of this character of closure.

Informal groups can be regular customers of a shop, users of a park, sports fans, music fans, mothers of children who play together, or groups of street youth who mutually protect each other. Members of such groups may not necessarily know each other, or even that they constitute a group, yet they can be a useful resource for each other, and an immense reservoir of energy and imagination if it can be accessed and organized.

Multiplying and using social capital is not without its problems. By its very nature, social capital can tend to mirror existing power structures. Marginalized people are sometimes marginalized exactly because they are unable to access social capital, as is often the case with the mentally ill or other people with poor social skills.

Even in a society with closure, social capital may be divided among different factions who regard each other as rivals or threats. While there are possible tools to deal with this, their success is uncertain, and the difficulties are worse in situations like larger North American cities, where there are many groups competing with others without closure, who may not even be able to communicate because of language or cultural barriers or both. This is not to claim that we should give up on prospects for sustainable community development in urban centers, but rather that we should not deceive ourselves about the challenge involved.

Community "civicness" is key to maximizing the potential of communities as agents of sustainable development (Selman and Parker, 1997). Civicness in a community will lubricate social life, enhance productivity and facilitate action; in practice, it will then become a proxy for successful policy implementation (Putnam, 1993). It is also an important component of sense of place, which is critical for community sustainability.

Along with ecological carrying capacity, we also need an increase in the "social caring capacity" of our communities (UBC Task Force on Healthy and Sustainable Communities, 1994). Social caring capacity, reflected by networks of social capital, is a prerequisite for sustainable development. Evidence from the Indian state of Kerela (see Champagne on a Beer Budget) suggests that quality of life can increase while industrial production decreases; i.e., social capital can substitute for manufactured capital. Furthermore, whereas natural capital diminishes with exploitation, social capital accumulates with regular use (Selman and Parker, 1997).

Multiplying social capital requires attention to effective and representative local governance, strong organizations, capacity-building, participatory planning, access to information, and collaboration and partnerships.

Cultural capital is the product of shared experience through traditions, customs, values, heritage, identity, and history. Although sometimes subsumed under the heading of social capital, I have become convinced as I have worked with communities in different parts of the world that cultural capital deserves its own category.

Cultural capital is particularly important in aboriginal communities and in other communities with a long history. In mainstream western society, particularly in North America, it is too often under-valued.

Enhancing cultural capital implies attention to traditions and values, heritage and place, the arts, diversity, and social history.

Strengthening Community Capital for Sustainable Community Development

Minimizing the consumption of essential natural capital means living within ecological limits, conserving and enhancing natural resources, sustainable resource management (soil, air, water, energy, agriculture, etc.), cleaner production, and minimizing waste (solid, liquid, air pollution, etc.).

Improving physical capital includes focusing on community assets such as public facilities (e.g., hospitals and schools), water and sanitation, efficient transportation, safe, quality housing, adequate infrastructure, and telecommunications.

Strengthening economic capital means focusing on: making more with less — maximizing use of existing resources (eg. using waste as a resource); making the money-go-round — circulating dollars within a community; making things ourselves — replacing imports; making something new — creating a new product; trading fairly with others; and developing community financial institutions.

Increasing human capital requires a focus on areas such as health, education, nutrition, literacy, and family and community cohesion. Basic determinants of health such as peace and safety, food, shelter, education, income and employment are necessary prerequisites.

Multiplying social capital requires attention to effective and representative local governance, strong organizations, capacity-building, participatory planning, access to information, and collaboration and partnerships.

Enhancing cultural capital implies attention to traditions and values, heritage and place, the arts, diversity and social history.

Strengthening these six forms of community capital is the foundation for sustainable community development.

The Foundation for Sustainable Community Development

Strengthening these six forms of community capital is the foundation for Sustainable Community Development. The key to understanding this approach to development is recognizing that it is based largely on appreciation of community *assets* (as well as realistic acknowledgement of challenges or, in conventional terms, deficits).

For example, a transportation system that is oriented to walking, cycling and public transportation rather than the private automobile contributes to natural capital by saving energy and reducing emissions. It contributes to human capital by reducing health-damaging air pollution and motor vehicle accidents, and by increasing the amount of exercise people get. It may contribute to social capital by increasing the social networking required for car sharing, car pooling and other more social means of getting around, in addition to the social interaction that may occur in the use of public transport. Finally, it contributes to economic capital by reducing congestion and by reducing the costs of transportation if people do not need to own a car or perhaps are only part owners in a car-sharing or car-pooling system. This in turn increases disposable income, which may be spent on more health-enhancing products and services (Hancock, 2001).

DOING DEVELOPMENT DIFFERENTLY

Several key arguments inform this book. First, the term sustainable development acquires tangible meaning when understood in terms of natural capital and natural income. The bottom line for sustainability is that we must learn to live on our natural income rather than deplete our natural capital. Economic growth with an ecological deficit is anti-economic and makes us poorer rather than richer in the long-term (Daly and Cobb, 1989). Sustainability therefore requires that we minimize our consumption of essential natural capital.

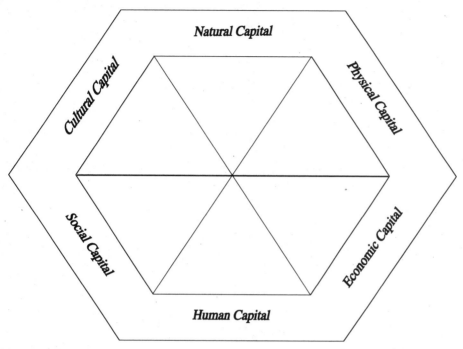

Figure 1: Community Capital is the foundation for sustainable community development. Each triangle represents the ways we can strengthen that form of capital.

Second, community capital and social equity demand that North Americans, who are among the world's most inefficient and wasteful consumers of materials and energy (ICPQL, 1996; WCED, 1987), find ways of living more lightly on the planet. At a minimum, we will have to increase the efficiency of our resource and energy use. More likely, we will also have to reduce our present (not to speak of projected) levels of materials and energy consumption.

Third, reducing our materials and energy consumption need not diminish and, in fact, would likely enhance our quality of life and the public domain — in other words, it could strengthen our community capital. It is important to distinguish here between "quality of life" and "standard of living" (Jacobs, 1993). Standard of living generally refers to disposable income for things we purchase individually, whereas quality of life can be considered as the sum of all things which people purchase collectively (e.g., the health care system, public education, policing), or those things which are not purchased at all (e.g., air quality). Standard of living refers solely to the private domain, whereas quality of life refers to the public domain, the realm of community capital.

Fourth, the critical resource for strengthening community capital is not money — rather, the critical resources are trust, imagination, courage, commitment, the relations between individuals and groups, and time, the literal currency of life. Many of the issues that people relate to most intimately — family, neighborhood, community, decompression from work, recreation, culture, etc. — depend on these resources at least as much as money. This is not to say that economic security isn't important — it is — but focusing solely on money to provide security is using 19th century thinking to address 21st century challenges.

Taken together, the direction to which these arguments point is clear. We must explicitly aim to nurture and strengthen community capital in order to improve our economic and social well-being. Government and corporate decisions should be reviewed for their effects on all forms of community capital. Programs and policies need to be effected at every level to ensure that community capital is properly considered.

In a nutshell, we need to *do development differently.*

---

[1]The term "community capital" more conventionally refers to economic or financial capital. For example, in the US, National Community Capital is a network of more than 150 private-sector community development financial institutions (CDFIs) that provides financing, training, consulting, and advocacy for CDFIs. Active in all 50 states, the National Community Capital network invests in small businesses, quality affortable housing, and vital community services that benefit economically disadvantaged people and communities. National Community Capital is committed to leading the community development finance system to scale through capital formation, policy and capacity development. Details at http://www.communitycapital.org/

REFERENCES

Bookchin, M. 1987. *The Rise of Urbanization and the Decline of Citizenship.* San Francisco: Sierra Club.

Boothroyd, P. 1991. "Distribution Principles for Compassionate Sustainable Development." In *Perspectives on Sustainable Development in Water Management: Towards Agreement in the Fraser Basin,* ed. A.H.J. Dorcey. Vancouver: Westwater Research Centre.

Bridger, J. C., & Luloff, A. E. 2001. "Building the sustainable community: Is social capital the answer?" *Sociological Inquiry,* 71(4): 458-472.

Canadian Conservation Commission. 1915. In *Towards a Liveable Metropolis.* Toronto: Metropolitan Plan Review Report. No. 13, May 1991.

Coleman, J.S. 1988. "Social Capital in the Creation of Human Capital." *American Journal of Sociology* 94 (supplement): S95-S120.

Coleman, J.S. 1990. *Foundations of Social Theory.* Cambridge, Mass.: Harvard University Press.

Daly, H.E. 1989. "Sustainable Development: From Concept and Theory Towards Operational Principles." In *Population and Development Review.* Hoover Institution Conference.

Daly, H.E., and J.B. Cobb, Jr. 1989. *For the Common Good: Redirecting the Economy Toward Community, the Environment, and a Sustainable Future.* Boston: Beacon Press.

Flora, C.B., and J.L. Flora. 1993. "Entrepreneurial Social Infrastructure: A Necessary Ingredient." In *Annals of the American Academy of Political and Social Science* 529 (September): 48-58.

Foster, J.B. 1997. "Natural Capitalism?" *Dollars and Sense* 211, May/June: 9.

Goodland, R. "Sustainability: Human, Social, Economic and Environmental," *Encyclopedia of Global Environmental Change*. John Wiley & Sons Ltd., 2002.

Hancock, T. "People, Partnerships and human Progress: Building Community Capital," *Health Promotion International* 16 (3), Sep 2001: 275-280.

Hawken, P., Lovins, A. and Lovins, L. H. 1999. *Natural Capitalism: Creating the Next Industrial Revolution*. Little, Brown and Co., Boston, MA.

Henderson, H. 1996. *Building a Win-Win World: Life Beyond Global Economic Warfare*. San Francisco: Berrett-Koehler Publishers.

Independent Commission on Population and Quality of Life (ICPQL). 1996. *Caring for the Future*. New York: Oxford University Press.

International Council for Local Environmental Initiatives (ICLEI), International Development Research Centre (IRDC), and United Nations Environment Program. 1996. *The Local Agenda 21 Planning Guide*. Toronto: ICLEI and Ottawa: IDRC.

Jacobs, J. 1961. *The Death and Life of Great American Cities*. New York: Random House.

Jacobs, M. 1993. *The Green Economy: Environment, Sustainable Development, and the Politics of the Future*. Vancouver: University of British Columbia Press.

Jansson, A-M., M. Hammer, C. Folke, and R. Costanza, eds. 1994. *Investing in Natural Capital: The Ecological Economics Approach to Sustainability*. Washington, DC: Island Press.

McKibben, B. 1996. "The Enigma of Kerala: One State in India is Proving Development Experts Wrong." *Utne Reader* 74, March/April: 102-12.

Mitlin, D., and D. Satterthwaite. 1991. Sustainable Development and Cities. Prepared for How Common Is Our Future? A Global NGO Forum, Habitat International Coalition, Mexico City, 4-7 March.

National Round Table on the Environment and the Economy (NRTEE). 2003, *Environment and Sustainable Development Indicators for Canada*, Ottawa: NRTEE.

OECD 2001. *The Well-Being of Nations: The Role of Human and Social Capital Organization for Cooperation and Development* (OECD).

Ostrom, E. 1993. Social Capital and Development Projects. Prepared for Social Capital and Economic Development, American Academy of Arts and Sciences, Cambridge, Mass, 30-31 July.

Pearce, D.W., E. Barbier, and A. Markandya. 1989. *Blueprint for a Green Economy*. London: Earthscan Publications.

Pearce, D.W., E. Barbier, and A. Markandya. 1990. *Sustainable Development: Economics and Environment in the Third World*. Brookfield, Vt.: Gower Publishing.

Porrit, J. 1989. "Seeing Green: How We Can Create A More Satisfying Society." *Utne Reader* 36, November/December: 70-77.

President's Council on Sustainable Development. 1996. *Sustainable America: A New Consensus for Prosperity, Opportunity, and a Healthy Environment for the Future*. Washington, DC: US Government Printing.

Putnam, R., R. Leonardi, and R. Nanetti. 1993. *Making Democracy Work: Civic Traditions in Modern Italy*. Princeton, NJ: Princeton University Press.

Putnam, R.D. 1995. "Bowling Alone: America's Declining Social Capital." *Journal of Democracy* 6:1, January: 65-78.

Rainey, D. V., Robinson, K. L., Allen, I., & Christy, R. D. 2003. "Essential forms of capital for sustainable community development." *American Journal of Agricultural Economics*, 85(3): 708-715.

Rees, W.E. 1991. "Economics, Ecology, and the Limits of Conventional Analysis." *Journal of the Air and Waste Management Association* 41, October:1323-27.

Rees, W.E. 1992. "Understanding Sustainable Development: Natural Capital and the New World Order." Vancouver: UBC School of Community and Regional Planning.

Roseland, M. 1999. "Natural Capital and Social Capital: Implications for Sustainable Community Development," in J.T.Pierce and A. Dale, Editors, *Communities, Development, and Sustainability across Canada*. Vancouver: UBC Press: 190-207.

Roseland, M. 2000. "Sustainable Community Development: Integrating Environmental, Economic, and Social Objectives," *Progress in Planning*, Volume 54 (2), October : 73-132.

Selman, P., and J. Parker, 1997. "Citizenship, Civicness and Social Capital in Local Agenda 21." *Local Environment* 2 (2): 171-84.

Stevens, W.K. 1997. "The Value of Nature." *New York Times*. Reprinted in *Vancouver Sun*, 24 May 1997: G9.

University of British Columbia (UBC) Task Force on Healthy and Sustainable Communities. 1994. "Tools for Sustainability: Iteration and Implementation." In *The Ecological Public Health: From Vision to Practice*, eds. C. Chu and R. Simpson. Toronto: University of Toronto Centre for Health Promotion; Australia: Institute for Applied Environmental Research at Griffith University.

Wackernagel, M., and W. Rees. 1996. *Our Ecological Footprint: Reducing Human Impact on the Earth*. Gabriola Island, BC: New Society Publishers.

Woolcock, Michael. 2001. "The Place of Social Capital in Understanding Social and Economic Outcomes." *ISUMA: Canadian Journal of Policy Research*, Vol. 2, No. 1: 11-17.

World Commission on Environment and Development (WCED). 1987. *Our Common Future*. New York: Oxford University Press.

World Conservation Union (IUCN), United Nations Environment Program (UNEP), and World Wide Fund for Nature (WWF). 1991. *Caring for the Earth: A Strategy for Sustainable Living*. Gland, Switzerland: IUCN, UNEP, WWF.

World Wildlife Fund et al. 2004. *Living Planet Report 2004*. Gland, Switzerland: World Wildlife Fund, United Nations Environment Program, and Global Footprint Network.

TOWARD SUSTAINABLE COMMUNITIES

What is a sustainable community? The concept does not describe just one type of neighborhood, town, city or region. Activities that the environment can sustain and that citizens want and can afford may be quite different from community to community. Rather than being a fixed thing, a sustainable community is continually adjusting to meet the social and economic needs of its residents while preserving the environment's ability to support it (Bridger and Luloff, 2001). Here's how some Minnesota citizens defined sustainable community:

> [A sustainable community is] a community that uses its resources to meet current needs while ensuring that adequate resources are available for future generations. A sustainable community seeks a better quality of life for all its residents while maintaining nature's ability to function over time by minimizing waste, preventing pollution, promoting efficiency and developing local resources to revitalize the local economy. Decision-making in a sustainable community stems from a rich civic life and shared information among community members. A sustainable community resembles a living system in which human, natural and economic elements are interdependent and draw strength from each other (Minnesota SEDEPTF, 1995).

This chapter examines sustainability at the community level. It begins with a look at communities in developed and developing parts of the world, proceeds to investigate some of the reasons why our North American communities are presently unsustainable, explores some characteristics and images of more sustainable communities, and concludes with the role of citizens and their governments in moving us toward sustainable communities.

SUSTAINABLE COMMUNITIES NORTH AND SOUTH

For the first time in history, nearly half of the world's people now live in urban areas — areas characterized by human structures and activities. The way our communities develop will largely determine our success or failure in overcoming environmental challenges and achieving sustainable development. Cities and towns provide enormous, untapped opportunities to solve environmental challenges; they must and can pioneer new approaches to sustainable development and community management. Local governments must also assume the responsibility and marshal the resources to address the sustainability problems facing their communities (ICLEI, 2002).

CHAPTER 2

No one fully understands how, or even if, sustainable development can be achieved; however, there is a growing consensus that it must be accomplished at the local level if it is ever to be achieved on a global basis (ICLEI et al., 1996).

The communities of the developing (southern) world face distinctly different challenges than those faced by the communities of the developed (northern) world. From the perspective of sustainable development, the basic problem with northern cities is that they are unsustainable, whereas the basic problem with southern cities is that they are underdeveloped. Most northern city dwellers are adequately housed and fed, but they meet their needs by consuming at rates the planet cannot afford and polluting at rates the planet cannot tolerate. Many southern city dwellers cannot meet their basic needs for food, clean water, clean air, fuel, transport and an environment free of disease-causing agents. While this dichotomy is not absolute — i.e., there is poverty in most northern cities, and many southern cities live beyond their means in terms of consumption of natural resources such as firewood and water — it helps illuminate the essential challenge of urban sustainability both North and South: meeting basic needs without depleting or degrading natural capital (Devuyst, 2001, Lithgow, *et al.,* 2005).

The cities of the industrial world, with their inadequate urban policies and technology, set the standard to which city managers in low-income countries aspire — low density single family dwellings, cars, expressways, waste creation, air conditioning and profligate water use (Newman and Kenworthy, 1999). The role of the cities of the industrial world deserves much more scrutiny in the context of human settlements and the environmental crisis, precisely because their impact on the world's changing ecosystems is so enormous.

Approaches to accounting for the environment in urban economic development illustrate the differences between traditional environmental economics and a more ecological approach. Traditional environmental economics perceives environmental problems in terms of a deteriorating local environment, e.g., land-fills approaching capacity from the growing waste stream. Solutions are cast in terms of finding efficient trade-offs between economic growth and environmental quality and finding policy instruments that will internalize the costs of pollution to those firms causing the problems. In contrast, the ecological ("strong sustainability") approach reveals new facets of the problem that are invisible to conventional economic policy models. Here attention is on the total relationship between the human population of the urban region, prevailing levels of ecologically significant consumption, and the sustainability of the resource base (Rees, 1992).

THE UNSUSTAINABLE COMMUNITY

It is becoming apparent that almost every issue of sustainable development which emerges at the local level will be replicated, in one form or another, at the provincial, national and international levels (Connell, 1991).

Most North American cities were built using technologies that assumed abundant and cheap energy and land would be available forever. Communities therefore grew inefficiently, and became dependent on lengthy distribution systems. Cheap energy influenced the construction of our spacious homes and buildings, fostered our addiction to the automobile, and increased the separation of our workplaces from our homes. As described by Calthorpe (1989):

> The current round of suburban growth is generating a crisis of many dimensions: mounting traffic congestion, increasingly unaffordable housing, receding open space, and stressful social patterns. The truth is, we are using planning strategies

that are [now over fifty] years old and no longer relevant to today's culture. Our household makeup has changed dramatically, the work place and work force have been transformed, real wealth has shrunk, and serious environmental concerns have surfaced. But we are still building World War II suburbs as if families were large and had only one breadwinner, as if jobs were all downtown, as if land and energy were endless, and as if another lane on the freeway would end congestion.

Urban sprawl is one legacy of abundant fossil fuel and our perceived right to unrestricted use of the private car whatever the social costs and externalities. Other local and regional consequences of sprawl, such as congestion, air pollution, jobs-housing location "imbalance," and longer commuting times are now commonly recognized. Yet until recently, few researchers acknowledged that the land use pattern of North American cities also has serious *global* ecological ramifications.

For example, residents of most Canadian cities annually produce about 20 tons of carbon dioxide per capita, placing Canada among the top three or four nations in terms of per capita contribution to potential climate change. In contrast, citizens of Amsterdam produce only 10 tons of carbon dioxide per capita per year. Sprawl, exclusionary zoning, and low density account for much of this difference. If North American cities modeled future development on cities like Amsterdam, future carbon dioxide emissions here would be far less than current gloomy projections now indicate (Beatley, 2000; Newman and Kenworthy, 1999).

One way to consider the impact of a community on natural resources and eco-systems is to consider its "ecological footprint": the land area and the natural capital on which it draws to sustain its population and production structure (Wackernagel and Rees, 1996). Cities and towns demand a high input of resources — water, fossil fuels, land, and all the goods and materials that their populations and enterprises require. The more populous the city and the richer its inhabitants, the larger its ecological footprint is likely to be in terms of its demand on resources and, in general, the larger the area from which these are drawn.

Although some of our cities may appear to be sustainable, analysis of the ecological footprint of industrial cities shows that they appropriate carrying capacity not only from their own rural and resource regions, but also from distant elsewhere — in other words, they "import" sustainability. The flip side of importing sustainability is exporting ecological degradation, or unsustainability, since the production or extraction of natural resources in distant places often causes serious problems of environmental degradation there. Most North American cities (as well as those in Europe, Japan, Australia, and other developed parts of the world) can only have forests, parks, and nature reserves nearby because such land is not being used to meet the demand for food and other natural resources which are instead imported.

The average North American's footprint has grown to measure 4-5 hectares (about 10-12 acres), somewhat more than three city blocks, while the amount of ecologically productive land available has decreased this century from over 5 hectares to less than 1.5 hectares per person in 1994. Ecological footprint analysis shows that the residents of the Lower Fraser Valley (which includes the City of Vancouver, BC), with 1.8 million

During the period that environmentalism became a force in North American public life, our cities and communities have sprawled without consideration for resource efficiency. Infrastructure has been constructed — housing, roadways and sewage systems, for instance — which encourages disregardful resource consumption. Water sources have been taxed or polluted. Built environments have been designed which alter microclimates and promote photochemical smog formation. Environmental services, such as public transit systems, have been left without public support. Our settlements have not only become less and less habitable for humans and most other species. They now stand as the geographic point sources of most regional and global environmental problems, and threaten even the most distant wild areas saved by environmental advocates (Brugmann, 1992).

inhabitants and a population density of 4.5 people per hectare, depend on an area 19 times larger than that contained within its boundaries for food, forestry products, carbon dioxide assimilation, and energy. The country of Holland, with 15 million people, or 4.4 per hectare, requires about 15 times the available land within their own country for food, forest products, and energy use, even though Dutch people consume less on average than North Americans (Wackernagel and Rees, 1996).

Ecological footprint analysis confirms our need to minimize consumption of essential natural capital. If everyone lived like today's North Americans, it would take at least two additional planet Earths to produce the resources, absorb the wastes, and otherwise maintain life-support. Humanity's ecological footprint in 2001 was 2.5 times larger than in 1961, and we are already exceeding Earth's biological carrying capacity by 20 percent. The average footprint per capita on a global basis is 2.2 hectares. North American footprints are double European footprints, and seven times that of the average Asian or African footprint (WWF et al., 2004).

THE SUSTAINABLE COMMUNITY

The postwar pattern of Western urban development is not only ecologically unconscionable but economically inefficient and socially inequitable. In contrast, sustainable development implies that the use of energy and materials be consistent with production by such natural capital processes as photosynthesis and waste assimilation (Rees 1990a,b). To some authors this implies increasing community and regional self-reliance to reduce dependency on imports (California Office of Appropriate Technology 1981; Morris 1982; RAIN, 1981). The benefits would be reduced energy budgets, reduced material consumption, and a smaller, more compact urban pattern interspersed with productive areas to collect energy, grow crops, and recycle wastes (Van der Ryn and Calthorpe, 1986; Sheltair Group, 1998; CitiesPlus, 2003).

Movement toward sustainable communities requires a new kind of ecosystem thinking about human settlements. As described by Brugmann and Hersh (1991):

> In this century, the city has been imagined by sociologists, planners, and engineers as a bazaar, a seat of political chaos, an infernal machine, a circuit, and, more hopefully, as a community, the human creation "par excellence." These different ways of thinking about cities, their social forces, their market behaviours, their reliance on materials and processes from the natural world, both shape and constrain the programmes and policies that local governments put forward to serve the needs of urban people.
>
> The city can also be imagined as an ecosystem. Such a concept provides a tool to understand the complex relations between human activities and the environment, and how communities can organise their activities to both meet human needs and benefit the environment....
>
> Like a natural system such as a pond or forest, an urban ecosystem transforms energy (human labour, capital, fossil fuels) and materials (timber, iron, sand and gravel, information, etc.) into products that are consumed or exported, and into by-products. In natural systems by-products are recycled. We have designed and man-

aged our cities so that these by-products often go unused as wastes. The impact of human activity on the environment can be highlighted by charting the dynamics of the system — the movement of materials and people, the flows of energy and capital, the locations where energy is stored or expended, the rates at which wastes are generated and recycled. By looking at the city as a whole, by analyzing the pathways along which energy and pollution move, we can begin to see how human activities create and direct pollution into local, regional, and global ecosystems. We can also see how these activities can be reorganised and reintegrated with natural processes to increase the efficiency of resource use, the recycling of "wastes" as valuable materials, and the conservation of energy.

Australian researchers Peter Newman and Jeff Kenworthy (1999) note that the most unsustainable form of settlement yet developed — the low density suburb — has been a relatively recent phenomenon, motivated by a strong anti-urban Anglo-Saxon sentiment and facilitated by the automobile. Social organization for ecological sustainability will need to reverse this settlement pattern. Their analysis of settlement patterns and sustainability suggests that sustainable settlements require making cities more urban and making the countryside more rural.

Making cities more urban can be accomplished by "re-urbanizing" city centers and sub-centers; re-orienting transport infrastructure away from the automobile; removing subsidies on the automobile; and providing a more public-oriented urban culture, assisted by attractive urban design (townscapes, streetscapes, malls and squares) and by "traffic calming" measures to facilitate bicycle and pedestrian use of residential areas and major roads. Making the countryside more rural can be accomplished by means such as protecting and encouraging sustainable agriculture and forestry in rural areas and moving towards bioregionalism (e.g., air- and watershed management) as the basis of local government boundaries and responsibilities.

The ideal urban form for a particular locale will depend to some extent on the nature of the energy supply options: for example, higher densities make most efficient use of district heating and public transport networks, while lower densities may make solar energy more viable. The location, gross density and form of new development should therefore be determined in conjunction with programs for energy supply and conservation technologies (Owens, 1990; CitiesPlus, 2003). This principle is illustrated by a San Jose, California study that compared development pressures with or without a "greenbelt" to constrain development. Without it, 13,000 exurban homes would be developed which, compared to an equivalent number of units downtown and along the transit corridor, would require at least an additional 320,000 kilometers (200,000 miles) of auto commuting plus an additional 11 million plus liters (three million gallons) of water *every day*, as well as 40 percent more energy for heating and cooling (Yesney, 1990; City of San José, 2001).

This is not only an "urban" phenomenon. Rural large-lot development, often viewed as an environmentally friendly form of development and supported in plans and bylaws, should properly be classified as rural sprawl. Impacts and costs such as loss of wildlife habitat, resource consumption and storm water contamination associated with urban, suburban and rural sprawl are not equal and can be viewed as a con-

Sustainable urban development is ultimately a cultural statement about ourselves, how we want to live, and our ability to manage our needs, desires, and dreams in ways that are effective and caring. . . . Ultimately the city is the expression of the only ecosystem that we have helped to create; it is the unique contribution of our species, and the creation against which we are most likely to be judged (Jacobs, 1992).

On Natural and Built Environments

We must recognize that the distinction between environment as commonly understood and the built environment is artificial and that the urban [arena] and everything that goes into it is as much part of the solution as it is a contributing factor to ecological difficulties. The tangible recognition that the mass of humanity will be located in living environments designated as urban says that environmental politics must pay as much if not more attention to the qualities of those built environments as it now typically does to a fictitiously separated and imagined 'natural' environment.... A crucial preliminary is to find an adequate language in which to discuss possible futures in a rapidly urbanizing world, a language that actively recognizes that urbanization is both a constituent of, as well as constituted by, the ways such possibilities might potentially be grasped (Harvey, 1996).

tinuum, increasing as lot size increases. Rural sprawl may well be the most damaging and costly form of sprawl (Buchan, 2004).

What this demonstrates is that *the pattern of growth is more important than the amount of growth* in determining the level and efficiency of resource use and traffic congestion. They also show that a critical sustainability objective for our communities is more efficient use of urban space. This objective, as we will see throughout this book, is very compatible with the community capital objectives discussed in Chapter 1, in particular *minimizing consumption of natural capital*, and *multiplying social capital*.

Images of Sustainable Communities

Yaro et al. (1988) developed practical planning standards which rural New England towns can adopt to protect their distinctive character, while at the same time accommodate economic growth. Illustrating actual sites in western Massachusetts, their drawings show each site before development, after conventional development, and after what the authors call "creative development" (Figure 2). In both development schemes, the same number of units have been added. While many aspects differ between the two development approaches, the most critical is that the conventional approach dramatically alters the land-use pattern (e.g., agricultural lands are lost to suburban sprawl),

Reprinted with permission from the Center for Rural Massachusetts/ University of Massachusetts at Amherst, *Dealing With Change in the Connecticut River Valley: A Design Manual for Conservation and Development* by Yaro et al.

Figure 2a: Before Development **Figure 2b: After Conventional Development** **Figure 2c: After Creative Development**

Before development, after conventional development, and after "creative development."
In both development schemes, the same number of units have been added.

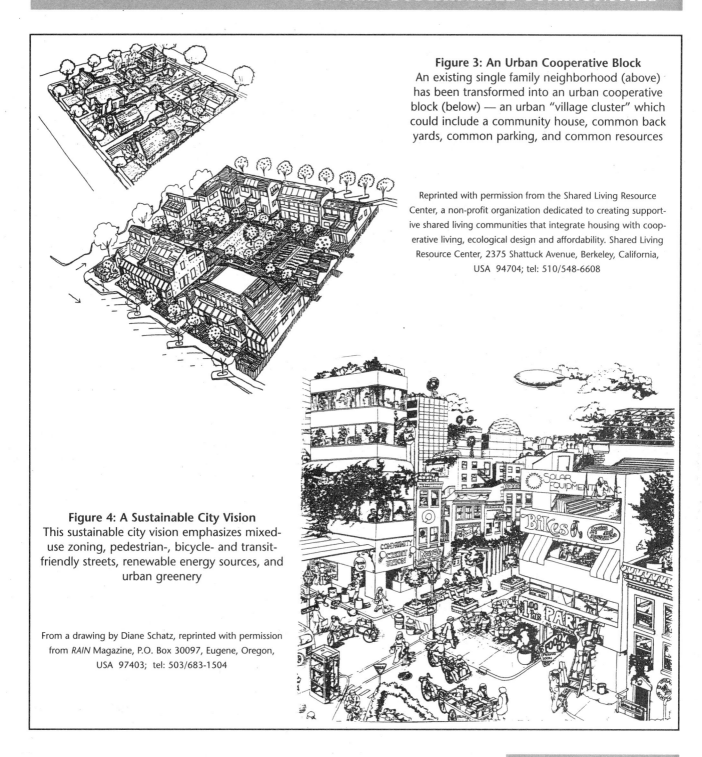

Figure 3: An Urban Cooperative Block
An existing single family neighborhood (above) has been transformed into an urban cooperative block (below) — an urban "village cluster" which could include a community house, common back yards, common parking, and common resources

Reprinted with permission from the Shared Living Resource Center, a non-profit organization dedicated to creating supportive shared living communities that integrate housing with cooperative living, ecological design and affordability. Shared Living Resource Center, 2375 Shattuck Avenue, Berkeley, California, USA 94704; tel: 510/548-6608

Figure 4: A Sustainable City Vision
This sustainable city vision emphasizes mixed-use zoning, pedestrian-, bicycle- and transit-friendly streets, renewable energy sources, and urban greenery

From a drawing by Diane Schatz, reprinted with permission from *RAIN* Magazine, P.O. Box 30097, Eugene, Oregon, USA 97403; tel: 503/683-1504

 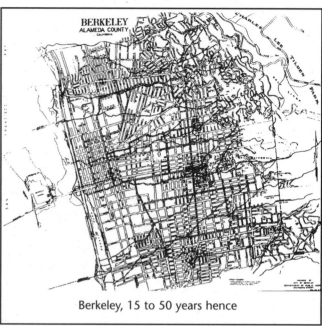

| Berkeley and its Centers | Berkeley, 15 to 50 years hence |

Figure 5: A Nodal Vision of Urban Development

"The underlying concept behind drawing these circles [in Berkeley and its Centers] is simply that distance requires energy and time to traverse. The greater the distance people have to travel, the higher the use of resources and the greater the production of pollution and waste of time. Therefore, we should build relatively compact centers. These areas will then work well with any public transit connecting them to other relatively high-use areas. Within and between the spots of higher activity, people can find it easy and pleasant to walk and bicycle.

while the creative approach absorbs growth without destroying future options (e.g., agricultural "capital" remains intact).

Norwood (1990) illustrates a similar concept, but within the setting of a typical suburban block (see Figure 3). Variations on this theme are increasingly popular in new private-market developments. In this case, an existing single-family neighborhood, characterized by under-utilized backyards, garages, attics, basements, and bedrooms, has been transformed into what the author calls an "urban cooperative block." The urban cooperative block concept could be organized around one or more small or home businesses; it could be designed to "recycle" obsolete corporate/industrial parks, shopping centers, and office complexes; or, as shown here, it could be the center of a "village cluster" typical of the popular Danish cohousing communities, with a community house, common backyards, common parking, and common resources. Many forms of ownership are possible, ranging from a condominium corporation to a non-profit corporation with resident control, a limited equity cooperative, a community land trust, or a mutual housing association. Potential economic advantages include

Berkeley, 25 to 90 years hence

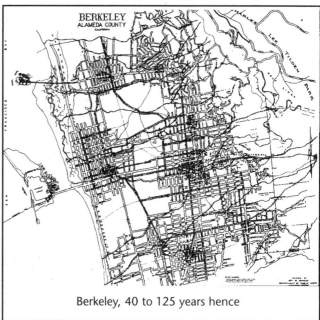
Berkeley, 40 to 125 years hence

This pattern of 'spots' of development is based on the size of the human body and the speed of walking. It contrasts sharply with 'strip' (one-dimensional or linear development) and 'sprawl' (two-dimensional or flat development) created by and for things that weigh 10-40 times as much and travel up to 50 times as fast: automobiles" (Register, 1987).

Reprinted with permission from Register, *Ecocity Berkeley: Building Cities for a Healthy Future.*

lowering housing costs through creating additional units and/or bedrooms, renting rooms and units, and allowing cottage industries or home businesses. By improving affordability, this model has the potential of serving a diversified and intergenerational cross-section of the population.

Figure 4 illustrates a similar concept, but this time the setting is in a downtown core. Many ideas for urban sustainability are illustrated in this drawing, such as mixed-use zoning; streets devoted to walking, cycling, and public transport; heavy reliance on renewable energy sources; rooftop gardens and greenery; and separate "waste" containers for compost and trash. Note the integration of work and home, which reduces the need for travel. As described earlier, a San Jose, California study compared the impacts of 13,000 units of this kind of development downtown and along the transit corridor to an equivalent number of exurban homes. It found that the kind of development pictured here saved at least 320,000 kilometers (200,000 miles) of auto commuting plus an additional 11 million plus liters (three million gallons) of water every day, and required 40 percent less energy for heating and cooling (Yesney, 1990).

Figure 5 brings the discussion to the level of the urban region, using the City of Berkeley, California as an example. Although these maps may at first appear to show the *history* of Berkeley, they actually demonstrate a sustainable *future* development pattern for this urban region. The first map in this set shows Berkeley and its town and neighborhood "centers." These centers were selected as a compromise between the "ideal" centers — according to the natural features of the landscape such as ridge lines and steep slopes — and the existing centers. Over time, urban development is concentrated near these centers while surrounded by non-urban lands. Once again, the key feature is the *pattern* of urban growth.

These drawings demonstrate a "nodal" rather than a "centralized" vision — a network of smaller, compact communities surrounded by non-urban land. As the city grows, and its centers become increasingly compact, the surrounding land can be reclaimed — as open space, forests, agricultural land, and wildlife habitat — to simultaneously benefit people and the environment.

MOBILIZING CITIZENS AND THEIR GOVERNMENTS

There is no (and perhaps should not be any) single accepted definition of sustainable communities. Communities must be involved in defining sustainability from a local perspective. The dilemma is how to encourage democracy (e.g., participatory local processes) within a framework of sustainability. As we have seen, elements of this framework include minimizing consumption of essential natural capital and improving physical capital, which in turn require the more efficient use of urban space. This sustainability framework also includes strengthening economic capital, increasing human capital, multiplying social capital, and enhancing cultural capital. However, an additional element is necessary to coordinate, balance and catalyse the others.

There are legitimate causes for concern about the dislocations, economic costs, and potential inconveniences associated with sustainability measures and their distribution across society. Both the gain and the pain of adjustment should be shared fairly by community members. Participation in the decision process by affected groups "can help make the attendant redistribution of costs and benefits fairer and more widely understood. Democratic mobilization is essential to the achievement of such policies in the face of the opposition [by vested interests they] inevitably engender" (Paehlke and Torgerson, 1990).

Environmental organizations and activists, especially in the United States and Canada, have tended to focus narrowly on specific campaigns of one kind or another, and may find it difficult to see how their work fits into the larger social, political and economic context. Yet the current popularity of the term sustainable development requires those concerned with environmental protection to cooperate with others in meshing environmental critiques, goals and strategies with those of peace, social justice, equality and economy, etc. (Gibson, 1991; PCSD, 1996).

In general, sustainable development strategies should favor bottom-up over top-down approaches; redistribution over "trickle-down;" self-reliance over dependency; a local rather than a regional, national, or international focus; and small-scale projects

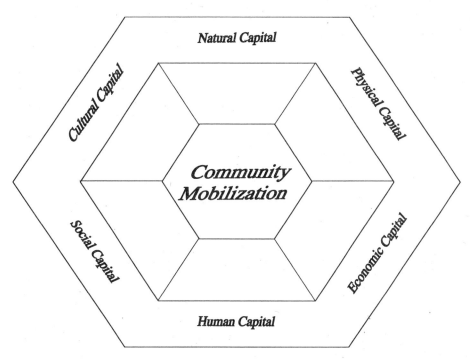

Figure 6: A Framework for Sustainable Community Development. Sustainable development requires mobilizing citizens and their governments to strengthen all forms of community capital. Community mobilization is necessary to coordinate, balance and catalyse community capital.

rather than grand-scale or megaprojects. As well, they should be designed with extensive public participation; seek to improve society and the environment as well as the economy; and result in increased equity, equality and empowerment (Brohman, 1996).

Democracy is an inherent part of the sustainable development process. Sustainable development must be participatory development. Real visions for change rarely come from government or from the marketplace, but from civil society (Newman and Kenworthy, 1999). For people to prosper anywhere they must participate as competent citizens in the decisions and processes that affect their lives (Gran, 1987). Sustainable development is thus about the quantity and quality of empowerment and participation of people. Sustainable development therefore requires community mobilization, i.e., mobilizing citizens and their governments toward sustainable communities.

In summary, applying the concept of sustainable development to North American communities requires mobilizing citizens and their governments to strengthen all forms of community capital. Elements of this framework include minimizing consumption of essential natural capital and improving physical capital, which in turn require the more efficient use of urban space. This sustainability framework also includes strengthening economic capital, increasing human capital, multiplying social capital, and enhancing cultural capital. Community mobilization is necessary to coordinate, balance and catalyse community capital (Figure 6). The significance of these criteria for the future of our communities and our society is elaborated in the following chapters.

REFERENCES

Alcamo, J.M. 1990. Compact City Design as a Strategy to Cut Dangerous Air Pollution. Presented to First International Ecocity Conference, Berkeley, California, March 29-April 1.

Beatley, T. 2000. *Green Urbanism: Learning from European Cities*. Washington,DC: Island Press.

Bridger, J. C. & Luloff, A. E. 2001. "Building the sustainable community: Is social capital the answer?" *Sociological Inquiry*, 71(4): 458-472.

Brohman, J. 1996. *Popular Development: Rethinking the Theory and Practice of Development*. Oxford: Blackwell Publishers.

Brugmann, J. 1992. "Preface." In M. Roseland, *Toward Sustainable Communities: A Resource Book for Municipal and Local Governments*. Ottawa: National Round Table on the Environment and the Economy.

Brugmann, J. and R. Hersh. 1991. Cities as Ecosystems: Opportunities for Local Government. Draft. Toronto: ICLEI.

Buchan, R. "The Costs and Impacts of Rural Sprawl: Not All Sprawl Is Equal" *Plan Canada* 44(3), 2004: 38-40.

California Office of Appropriate Technology (CalOAT). 1981. *Working Together: Community Self-Reliance in California*. Sacramento: California Office of Appropriate Technology.

Calthorpe, P. 1989. "Introduction: A Reverse Definition." In *The Pedestrian Pocket Book: A New Suburban Design Strategy*, ed. D. Kelbaugh. New York: Princeton Architectural Press.

CitiesPlus. "A Sustainable Urban System: The Long-term Plan for Greater Vancouver," The Sheltair Group Inc. et al. Vancouver: The Sheltair Group, 2003. www.citiesplus.ca.

City of San José, California, 2001. "Smart Growth," *Inside San José*, Fall/Winter: 6-7.

Connell, G.E. 1991. Letter to the Prime Minister. In *A Report to Canadians*. Ottawa: National Round Table on the Environment and the Economy(NRTEE).

Devuyst, D., et al. 2001. *How Green Is the City? Sustainability Assessment and the Management of Urban Environments*. NY: Oxford University Press.

Gibson, R. 1991. "Should Environmentalists Pursue 'Sustainable Development'?" *Probe Post* 13(4) Winter: 22-25.

Gran, G. 1987. *An Annotated Guide to Global Development: Capacity Building for Effective Social Change*. Pittsburgh: University of Pittsburgh Economic and Social Development Program.

Harvey, D. 1996. "Cities or Urbanization." *City Magazine*. London, UK. 1:2.

International Council for Local Environmental Initiatives (ICLEI), International Development Research Centre (IDRC), and United Nations Environment Program. 1996. *The Local Agenda 21 Planning Guide*. Toronto: ICLEI and Ottawa: IDRC.

International Council for Local Environmental Initiatives (ICLEI). 2002. *Accelerating sustainable development: Local action moves the world*. New York: United Nations Economic and Social Council.

Jacobs, P. 1992. "Sustainable Urban Development." In *Architecture in the Year 2000: Conference Proceedings*. Royal Architectural Institute of Canada.

Lithgow, M., M. Bloomfield, and M. Roseland, *Green Cities: A Guide for Sustainable Community Development* (Victoria, BC: Harmony Foundation of Canada, 2005).

Minnesota Sustainable Economic Development and Environmental Protection Task Force (SEDEPTF). 1995. *Common Ground: Achieving Sustainable Communities in Minnesota.* St. Paul: Minnesota Planning.

Morris, D. 1982. *Self-Reliant Cities: Energy and the Transformation of Urban America.* San Francisco: Sierra Club Books.

Morris, D. 1990. "The Ecological City as a Self-Reliant City." In *Green Cities: Ecologically Sound Approaches to Urban Space*, ed. D. Gordon. Montreal: Black Rose Books: 21-35.

Newman, P. 1990. "Social Organization for Ecological Sustainability: Toward a More Sustainable Settlement Pattern." In *Social Structures for Sustainability*, ed. P. Cook. Fundamental Questions Paper No. 11. Canberra: Centre for Resource and Environmental Studies, Australian National University.

Newman, P. and J. Kenworthy. 1999. *Sustainability and Cities: Overcoming Automobile Dependence.* Washington, DC: Island Press.

Norwood, K. 1990. "The Urban Cooperative Block." *Permaculture Activist* VI(4) November.

Owens, S.E. 1990. "Land Use Planning for Energy Efficiency." In *Energy, Land, and Public Policy,* ed. J.B. Cullingworth. New Brunswick, NJ: Transaction Publishers. Pp. 53-98.

Paehlke, R. and D. Torgerson, eds. 1990. *Managing Leviathan: Environmental Politics and the Administrative State.* Peterborough: Broad View Press.

President's Council on Sustainable Development (PCSD). 1996. *Sustainable America: A New Consensus for Prosperity, Opportunity, and a Healthy Environment for the Future.* Washington, DC: US Government Printing.

RAIN editors. 1981. *Knowing Home: Studies for a Possible Portland.* Portland: *RAIN.*

Rees, W.E. 1990a. "Sustainable Development and the Biosphere: Concepts and Principles." In *Teilhard Studies.* No. 22 (Chambersburg, PA: Anima Books for the American Teilhard Association.

Rees, W.E. 1990b. "The Ecology of Sustainable Development." *The Ecologist* 20(1):18-23.

Rees, W.E. 1992. Ecological Footprints and Appropriated Carrying Capacity: What Urban Economics Leaves Out. Presented to Globe '92, Vancouver, BC, 18 March.

Register, R. 1987. *Ecocity Berkeley: Building Cities for a Healthy Future.* Berkeley, Calif.: North Atlantic Books.

The Sheltair Group Inc., in association with M. Roseland and others. 1998. "Visions, Tools and Targets: Environmentally Sustainable Development Guidelines for Southeast False Creek," commissioned by Central Area Planning, City of Vancouver, April.

Van der Ryn, S., and P. Calthorpe. 1986. *Sustainable Communities: A New Design Synthesis for Cities, Suburbs, and Towns.* San Francisco: Sierra Club Books.

Wackernagel, M., and W.Rees. 1996. *Our Ecological Footprint: Reducing Human Impact on the Earth.* Gabriola Island, BC: New Society Publishers.

White, R. and J. Whitney. 1990. Human Settlements and Sustainable Development: An Overview. Prepared for Colloquium on Human Settlements and Sustainable Development, University of Toronto Centre for Urban And Community Studies, Toronto, 21-23 June.

World Wildlife Fund et al. 2004. *Living Planet Report 2004*. Gland, Switzerland: World Wildlife Fund, United Nations Environment Program, and Global Footprint Network.

Yaro, R.D. et al. 1988. *Dealing With Change in the Connecticut River Valley: A Design Manual for Conservation and Development*. Amherst, Mass.: Center for Rural Massachusetts, University of Massachusetts at Amherst.

Yesney, M. 1990. "The Sustainable City: A Revolution in Urban Evolution." *Western City* LXVI:3, March: 4-44.

MAKING COMMUNITY POLICY

There are many ways to mobilize citizens and their governments toward sustainable communities, but there are also many barriers and obstacles that hamper our progress in this direction. We cannot realistically expect most people to choose sustainable options if they appear to be more difficult or expensive than unsustainable choices. The question arises, then, how can we change the systems around us, "level the playing field," and provide ample opportunities for individuals to make behavioral choices that improve their communities?

In recent years there has been increasing interest in the use of "economic instruments" in environmental policy. These tools influence the behavior of economic agents by providing financial incentives to environmentally improved behavior, or disincentives to damaging behavior. Such instruments — taxes, charges, subsidies, tradable permits, deposit-refund schemes, performance bonds and so on — have been particularly favored within the discipline of environmental economics, where they originated. As the influence of environmental economics has grown, so too has the discussion intensified over the introduction of economic instruments into fields such as pollution control, biodiversity conservation and energy consumption (Roseland and Jacobs, 1995; Pearce and Barbier, 2000; Mulder and Van den Bergh, 2001; Olerup, 2002; Di Leva, 2002).

Economic instruments should not be seen in isolation. When introduced they are inevitably part of a structure and process of community management which in turn reflect wider objectives — environmental, economic, social and ethical — in society.

For communities to move effectively toward sustainability, citizens and their governments should understand the range of policy instruments available to them and the wider context of how community policy is made. This chapter explores the use of policy instruments in sustainable community planning and development, and reviews the different types of instruments that are available to community decision-makers.

POLICY ISSUES FOR LOCAL GOVERNMENTS

Although the precise characteristics of sustainable communities may be debated, characteristic objectives of local activity towards sustainable development can be applied virtually anywhere. Sustainable community development requires action to create viable local economies that are just, peaceful, resilient and eco-efficient. In order for these objectives to be achieved, a political culture of community involve-

Table 1: Policy Instruments

Categories	Instruments
Regulations	1. Laws
	2. Licenses, Permits, and Standards
	3. Tradable Permits
	4. Quid Pro Quos
Voluntary Instruments	1. Information
	2. Volunteers, Volunteer Associations, and NGOs
	3. Technical Assistance
Expenditure	1. Expenditure and Contracting
	2. Monitoring
	3. Investment and Procurement
	4. Enterprise
	5. Public/Private Partnerships
Financial Incentives	1. Pricing
	2. Taxes and Charges
	3. Subsidies and Tax Incentives
	4. Grants and Loans
	5. Rebates, Rewards, and surety Bonds
	6. Vouchers

ment, stakeholder participation and consensus-building must be created and maintained (Otto-Zimmermann, 2002). With all of these objectives, local governments can be identified as playing an important role, as will be evident in the following chapters. (Unless otherwise noted, most examples referred to in this chapter are detailed elsewhere in the book.) Areas of local government involvement include ecologically efficient use of resources and their waste residues; energy efficient transportation and land use patterns; reducing social and economic polarization; and the integration of marginalized people into efforts towards sustainable community development.

Given these general concerns for local governments, some broad policy goals might include the following: reducing per capita car use; reducing per capita water consumption; increasing the percentage of local land contained in parks; and improving cycling and pedestrian infrastructure, etc. Policy instruments can be employed to achieve these specific policy objectives.

POLICY INSTRUMENTS

Two target populations for policy instruments can be identified: the general public and individual firms or industries. The use of instruments to influence the behavior of the public can be called *demand management* (see chapters on energy, water, transportation, and community economic development). One of the most important requirements for sustainability is a reduction and equitable distribution of per capita consumption of resources as communities grow (Wackernagel and Rees, 1996; Rees, 2002). Since supply of resources can only be augmented to a certain point, this inherently requires that *demand* for resources be managed. Instruments that try to influence the behavior of firms and industries are not usually considered to be demand management, but they serve the same purpose-to reduce the consumption of natural resources. In considering particular instruments, it is important to note their target populations.

In table 1, the instruments are divided into broad categories according to Jacobs (1993), although many instruments could actually fall into more than one category. The various policy instruments can be slotted into four categories. The first is traditional regulations such as permits and licenses that have a legal basis. A second category is voluntary mechanisms or actions taken that generally do not require expenditure. The third is direct government expenditure such as money spent on improved infrastructure. Lastly, there are financial incentives such as taxes, subsidies, tradable permits, and rewards. Financial incentives assume that the manipulation of the costs of certain activities will result in individual behaviour changes, and do not usually require as much enforcement as regulations.

Regulations

Regulations are the most pervasive policy instruments. They include laws; licenses, permits, and standards; tradable permits; and quid pro quos. Requirements for catalytic converters in cars or insulation in homes are both typical regulations. Detailed regulations such as a prohibition on the use of barbecue lighter fuels make up Southern California's Air Quality Management Plan; it has an astounding 5,500 pages of regulations designed to reduce smog levels.

Laws

The traditional way that governments discourage certain behavior is by making specific activities illegal. Enforcement of laws can be a problem, but they are still useful. For example, government can manage the demand for a certain product by restricting the amount that any individual can consume. Desirable behavior can also be achieved by getting rid of outdated or inefficient regulations (deregulation), although deregulation *for the sake of deregulation* is hard to justify. Governments can use building code laws, rent control laws, and zoning laws to encourage particular kinds of community development.

A simple law can have significant effects. Cheap parking rates in urban areas are known to encourage automobile use. A simple law setting a minimum price for parking may be a substantial incentive for employees to use transit.

In another vein, many jurisdictions have implemented "Take Back" laws that place the financial or physical responsibility on industry for end-of-life management of their products and packaging (Lombardi & Goldstein, 2001).

Licenses, Permits, and Standards

These are also regulatory instruments. Standards such as municipal effluent discharge standards may be based on a desirable ambient water quality level (performance standards) or industries may simply be required to use certain technologies (technology standards). Best-available-technology standards can be used for industrial effluent and emissions. Conservation plumbing standards in Oakland have saved the Oakland Housing Authority $189,000 in water costs (and 36 million gallons of water) by requiring all new developments to install low-flow (6 litres or 1.6 gallons) toilets (Ogorzalek, 2003).

There must of course be a penalty associated with non-compliance if legal standards are to be effective. For example, a Ride Share Ordinance in Montgomery County, Maryland, penalizes employers that do not achieve a particular increase in transit use among employees. The result was a 31.7 percent increase in carpools and a 59.6 percent increase in transit use in just one year.

Santa Monica is one of many cities that has set recycling space standards for new buildings. Residential buildings with 10 units must allocate 9 square meters (100 square feet) to recycling, and additional area for additional units. The standard is similar for commercial buildings.

As part of Boulder, Colorado's growth management strategy, development permits are issued based on standards designed to recognize the financial and ecological limits to growth in the area. For example, new housing development permits are allocated according to a formula of 25 percent market housing, 55 percent affordable housing (determined by a number of criteria) and 20 percent permanently affordable housing maintained through deed restrictions on resale.

Tradable Permits

Although monitoring is still required when tradable permits are used, the total allowable resource use or emission outputs can easily be set as the sum of all permits, creating an explicit limit. Emitters may comply with their permits by emitting just as much pollution as they have allowances for, by purchasing excess allowances from other firms, or reducing pollution more than is required in order to sell allowances to others. Since the costs faced to comply with a permit limit varies among different firms and may not be the same as the costs faced to control emissions, flexibility in pollution control is integrated with a command approach (Farrell et al., 1999). Tradable permits are a useful instrument only if they can be easily enforced and if initial allocation is not too difficult.

Quid Pro Quos

Governments may require firms to do something in exchange for the right to build or produce a product. In Boston, for example, developers pay a linkage fee for development that goes towards job training or affordable housing (Boston Redevelopment Authority, 2003). The use of property is also convenient — governments may actually give land to developers in exchange for a particular type of development.

Voluntary Instruments

Voluntary mechanisms can be defined as actions taken by firms, individuals or governments that generally do not require regulations or financial incentives. Volunteer associations and non-governmental organizations (NGOs) can be organized by firms or individuals. Some organizations use volunteers to clean up residential neighborhood garbage or carry out other activities that benefit communities. Government agencies can provide information and technical assistance to firms and individuals to promote certain behavior. Though classified as voluntary instruments, these may involve some expenditure as well. Government pleas to conserve water in times of drought are a useful alternative to shutting down water supply.

Information

Expenditure on educating the public is a valuable tool-if people know that their behavior is socially or environmentally harmful, they may change it. The Power Smart program in British Columbia has resulted in voluntary reductions in energy use in the province. This type of education is a valuable form of demand management. Community policy development should be based on clear objectives, acceptable policy instruments, and public support for initiatives, which can be best determined through a participatory process involving all sectors of the community (Lafferty, 2001). Education can be achieved indirectly as well through financial support for NGOs.

Without expenditure, individual politicians can educate people with public statements that can influence public behavior. By publicly condemning certain behaviors, people may feel obligated to stop or change them. Choice programs can also be an integral part of education. For example, if a community wishes to sustain its organic produce industry, it may initiate a program that clearly labels all produce as either organic or not. Accompanied by a public education program on the community benefits of buying organic, consumers will be well informed about the choices they are making.

Volunteers, Volunteer Associations, and NGOs

The use of volunteers is an efficient way to work towards community objectives. Not only can government choose the activities that it wants to organize, it can also help foster a healthy sense of community. Government need not get directly involved. It may instead promote volunteer associations or fund NGOs or private firms that can then organize activities. Small-scale voluntary recycling organizations are a common example.

Technical Assistance

Governments can not only provide financial resources, but also expertise for NGOs and firms. The City of Santa Monica sends brochures to small businesses which describe specific waste reduction measures in detail. Eco-counsellors are common in Europe, and provide detailed information and advice to individuals or businesses on a range of environmental issues.

Expenditure

Expenditure consists of any use of public money such as contracting, monitoring, investment, procurement, enterprise, and public-private partnerships. The Danish City of Copenhagen successfully used some regulatory and expenditure measures to reduce automobile use. In the 1960s, people wanted isolated homes and their own cars, desiring to imitate the American way of life. The city planners decided to reduce automobile use by reducing urban sprawl. Copenhagen set out to make the downtown core more attractive. It reduced parking by three percent each year, rebuilt city housing, and made the streets pedestrian-friendly and more hospitable by providing outdoor seating, etc. The result has been decreased traffic, a tripling of recreational and social activity in the major streets, and a decline in the market for isolated homes far from the downtown core (Newman, 1993b; Beatley, 2000).

Expenditure and Contracting

Government can directly work towards specific community objectives by spending money on specific activities, or by offering contracts that serve those purposes. Of course expenditure requires money (see Leithe and Joseph, 1991 for a review of financing alternatives for local governments). Furthermore, traditional engineering approaches often encourage expansion of infrastructure and supply augmentation, rather than alternatives such as demand management.

Still, investment in improved technologies, such as better garbage or sewage treatment systems, can be a valuable form of expenditure. A good example of an innovative public-private partnership investment is Guelph, Ontario's Wet-Dry recycling program that uses an anaerobic digester to convert wet waste (compostable material) to biogas used for electricity production (Smith et al., 2000). Small-scale energy-efficient sewage treatment plants such as those built in Providence, Rhode Island, and in Harwich, Massachusetts are also innovative. The technology is available for small-scale, self-contained sewage treatment plants that use sunlight, bacteria, plants, and fish to change sewage into clean water. Any technology that encourages the recycling of resources should be seriously considered by communities that attempt to plan for sustainability.

Although expenditure has been traditionally used as a solution to many policy problems, it is not necessarily effective on its own. While some increases in transit use have been observed in the US, the $2.5-billion a year spent by the federal government since 1979 has not been as effective as hoped; although the systems are in place, people have not been given any real incentive to try transit (Plous, 1994). As long as public subsidies for roads and parking keep driving costs low, it is simply too easy to continue driving. It is apparent that federal expenditure on transit would be much more effective if it were accompanied by increased costs on automobile use.

Monitoring

A valuable form of expenditure is on the monitoring of infrastructure to ensure efficient operation. In 2003 alone, New York's Leak Detection Unit saved an additional 225 million litres (60 million gallons) of water per day (NYCDEP, 2003). Leaks cannot be detected easily anywhere that water is not metered, simply because it is not possible to measure the volume of water arriving at a site.

Investment and Procurement

Governments can invest money in firms whose behavior is desirable in order to ensure their survival. They can also buy products from the firms that they choose, and thereby favor particular firms or industries. The municipality of Kolding, Denmark's initiative amongst private and public kitchens to purchase organic food has raised the profile of more sustainable food systems. The "Buy It Green" — Network (BIG-Net) provides a forum for municipalities in Europe to share their green purchasing knowhow and expertise (ICLEI, 2002a).

Enterprise

When the market fails to provide desirable outcomes, governments can create their own businesses. These may be, but are not limited to, situations in which natural monopolies exist. Governments may also create private businesses that are non-profit. Community Development Corporations are private corporations with a responsibility to meet the needs of all members of the community. Residents join for a fee and can then vote on activities to be undertaken. Community Development Credit Unions can

Creating Markets for Recycled Materials

London Remade is a partnership between businesses, London boroughs, regional government, waste management companies and NGOs to develop and promote new markets and industries based on the reprocessing and reuse of London's recycled materials. By 2004, London Remade will have invested £13 million in reprocessing capacity to divert 250,000 tons from landfills back into the manufacturing sector (London Remade, 2004).

help a community by serving low- and moderate-income individuals that may not get financial services from banks. Their goal is to empower all citizens in the community. Public enterprises may also be set up that support community agriculture or utilize forestry as a source of revenue.

Public/Private Partnerships

Governments can enter partnerships with particular firms that either have resources that are valuable to the government or have enough employees to do useful community labor. For example, Adopt-a-Park programs have evolved in Seattle and other US cities, in which private companies take responsibility for the maintenance of public parks (Osborne and Gaebler, 1993).

Joint developments between private firms and transit authorities in Toronto have resulted in efficient use of land around transit stations (Newman and Kenworthy, 1999). High density development around stations has encouraged reduced automobile use and commuting times.

Financial Incentives

Financial incentives are an attractive alternative to traditional regulatory instruments. They do not generally require expenditure on enforcement because they create a constrained market environment in which firms behave as they normally would. Examples include pricing, taxes, charges, subsidies, tax incentives, grants, loans, rebates, rewards, surety bonds and vouchers. A water conservation program in Santa Monica, California offered rebates to cover installation of low-flow toilets and shower heads. At the same time, a conservation incentive fee (a tax) was collected from households that did not participate in the program (as part of their water bills), and this money was used to partly finance the conservation program. Per capita consumption of water for indoor use has dropped from 303 to189 liters (80 to 50 gallons) per day.

Pricing

Goods that have traditionally been provided for free can be priced as a method of demand management. For example, water metering can significantly reduce consumption. The City of Vernon, BC saw its average water consumption decrease by 15% and its peak demand by 29 percent when water metering was installed (City of Kamloops, 2001). The federal government in Canada reduced the number of employees driving to work by 23 percent after increasing parking rates. Although some equity problems emerge when pricing is used, there is a growing realization that natural-resource constraints are leaving few alternatives (Newman, 1993a).

Corporate Environmental Responsibility

The Coalition for Environmentally Responsible Economies (CERES) is a broad coalition of environmental organizations and socially responsible investment groups formed to promote environmental responsibility among businesses and local governments. In September 1989, CERES set forth the Valdez Principles as broad standards for evaluating corporate activities that directly or indirectly affect the biosphere. The principles were adopted in the hope of working with companies to create a voluntary mechanism of self-governance, and to help investors make informed decisions. The Valdez Principles call for elimination or minimization of pollution, sustainable use of natural resources, reduction and safe disposal of waste, energy conservation, environmental risk reduction, marketing of safe products and services, damage compensation, hazard disclosure, selection of environmental directors and managers, and annual environmental audits.

Several governments and over 70 major corporations have signed the Valdez Principles or use environmental investment guidelines based on them. For example, corporate signatories include American Airlines, Coca Cola, Ben & Jerry's, Nike, The Body Shop, Interface and VanCity Savings.

CERES provides information and assistance in relation to the Valdez Principles, corporate shareholder campaigns, and community efforts to encourage local governments to adopt environmental investment policies.

In 1985, the City of Freiburg, Germany (with a population of 191,000), lowered the cost of season-pass fares for transit by more than a third to give people an incentive to switch from cars to transit. The result was a 23 percent increase in the use of transit in the first year and transit ridership has more than doubled since then (Beatley, 2000). More than 30 other German communities have adopted the same program based on the success in Freiburg.

Congestion charges and road pricing is one step towards accounting for the full cost of automobile use. The Central London congestion charging scheme has reduced car congestion by 30 percent, with public transit accommodating displaced car users (Transport for London, 2004).

Taxes and Charges

Taxes and charges can be used to discourage certain behavior, while providing revenue for the government. Impact fees are taxes on activities that have undesirable social or environmental impacts. Real estate taxes can be used to discourage urban sprawl. The information needed by agencies in order to administer appropriate taxes or charges may be substantial, but the use of an imperfect charge is surely more valuable than no charge at all.

Sweden has been successful in implementing green taxes on such things as sulphur, nitrogen oxide and carbon, which has resulted in significant reductions in pollution. The carbon tax has resulted in a major shift to the use of biofuels in municipal district heating systems (Beatley, 2000). An alternative to taxing an undesirable output is taxing an undesirable input. Taxes on the use of natural resources are a method of encouraging firms to try to minimize resource use in production processes. It makes sense to tax more the undesirable things (e.g., natural resource use, pollution) and to tax less the desirable things (income, labor) (Rees 1995a, 1995b; Hoerner and Bosquet, 2001).

Subsidies and Tax Incentives

Many of the available policy instruments could be labelled generally as subsidies. It is important to identify many of these instruments as subsidies explicitly, and justify them as such. Economists may argue that subsidies create inefficiencies in markets, but this is not necessarily the case. Social and environmental externalities are not taken into account by conventional market economics, and financial mechanisms used to encourage desirable or environmentally-friendly behavior are actually attempts to make the market more efficient in these ways.

In an effort to promote downtown revitalization and the intensification of residential land use, the City of Saskatoon provides property tax abatements, phased in over five years for new developments in the downtown core. The program has resulted in two new projects with a total of 104 rental units being constructed in the first three years (Tomalty, 2003).

Seattle uses both reduced tipping fees and tax incentives to encourage commercial recycling. Companies are not charged a tipping fee when they deliver a load of recyclables to the city transfer station and the city excludes recyclables from the additional tax on waste collection.

Grants and Loans

Direct financial awards to researchers or firms are a useful way to encourage the development of particular industries and technologies. Seed money for firms to start up is a common form of financial grants. In the Netherlands, a successful green fund has been developed as a major source of private funding for ecological projects and investments. Private banks operate the fund, but the investments are certified and guaranteed by the government, and interest on investments is tax-free. In the program, the banks are required to invest at least 70 percent of these funds into certified green projects. As a result of these funds, projects such as district heating, organic farming, ecological landscape and nature restoration projects, and sustainable building projects have been supported (Beatley, 2000).

Rebates, Rewards, and Surety Bonds

Another type of financial incentive, rewards can be made to firms that are most successful at behaving in a particular way. For example, firms that build the most energy-efficient housing complex in a municipality in a given year can be rewarded financially for their achievement. Similar to rewards, surety bonds are deposits of money made by a firm before an activity is undertaken. If the activity (e.g., successful pollution reduction) is successful, the deposit can be refunded; otherwise it is spent by the government agency for the same purpose.

The German City of Saarbrücken (with a population of 128,000) rewards citizens who use solar energy by allowing them to sell excess power back to the municipal utility. The city buys back solar power at a price of about US$0.15 cents per kilowatt hour.

Vouchers

Consumer behavior can be influenced drastically by providing vouchers that effectively make a particular product cheaper. Vouchers for public transit passes would likely encourage people to try switching from cars to public transit. BC Hydro delivers coupons for the purchase of energy efficient compact fluorescent light bulbs to all of their customers. It is recognized that people perceive discounts off of regular prices as more of a benefit than an equivalent reduction in the regular price and they also increase purchase satisfaction (Darke, 2003). This psychological tendency can be used by policy-makers to encourage certain behavior.

CONSTRAINTS ON IMPLEMENTATION

As noted previously, many policy instruments could fall into more than one category. In some cases there might be an overlap between regulations and financial incentives; it is also possible to have elements of two or more categories (e.g., expenditures and voluntary instruments) in the same policy measures. The critical challenge, however, is not in sorting the instruments by category, but rather in determining those situations and circumstances in which it is appropriate to employ particular instruments.

An additional challenge is determining the efficacy of various instruments over longer time frames than are yet known for most of the examples discussed here. Organizations such as ICLEI — Local Governments for Sustainability (formerly the International Council for Local Environmental Initiatives), as well as various local government associations in several countries, can serve a valuable role in monitoring and evaluating progress over time.

Although it is beyond the scope of this chapter to examine whether or not each of the instruments could be utilized in specific circumstances at the local level, some general observations can be made. In many situations, some of the instruments perhaps may be used best only at a federal or state/provincial level, while others may be used best by local governments. In cases where jurisdictional limitations prevent local governments from taking essential actions, state/provincial governments can be lobbied to use their jurisdictional power to carry out initiatives that will benefit multiple communities.

The principle of subsidiarity requires that policy decisions should be made at the most local level possible, while balancing the recognition that local areas are parts of larger systems and do not exist in isolation (Devuyst, 2001). The success that local governments have had in sustainable development can be attributed to the efficiency, accountability and flexibility of policies developed at the level of government closest to the people (ICLEI, 2002b). They are able to create unique policies that address their unique environmental, economic, social, historical and cultural circumstances.

Local governments in recent years have been particularly innovative in initiating sustainability policies (ICLEI et al., 1996; Roseland 1996, 1997; Parkinson and Roseland, 2002; ICLEI, 2002c). In the US, although there is some power at the local level to take actions to pursue local objectives, some local planning initiatives have been viewed by the courts as inconsistent with state policies (Stone and Freilich, 1991). Local governments in Canada can also expect to be constrained by jurisdiction. Some analysts argue that the division of powers in Canada does not delegate enough power to communities, and prevents them from looking after their own affairs (McAllister, 2004). Still, an instrument that is not feasible in one set of circumstances may work in another, so local policy-makers should consider all alternatives.

A system of government that does not give adequate legal power to local governments, and does not allow local governments considerable flexibility in the use of funds, cannot be expected to achieve all community objectives (Osborne and Gaebler, 1993). Central governments must give local governments permission to take measures towards sustainable community planning, even though that requires giving them power to address broader issues. At the same time, when issues that should be addressed at national and international levels are not addressed, local governments may be able to take action individually. For example, San Francisco is one of over 150 local governments in the US that have made commitments to achieve CO_2 reductions beyond the reduction goals of the Kyoto protocol, despite the fact that the Kyoto protocol has not been ratified by the federal government (San Francisco Department of the Environment, 2004).

It is interesting to speculate on the efficacy of economic instruments vis-a-vis other kinds of policy instruments in promoting sustainable community development (for example, in comparison with some of the social policies described in Chapter 11: Housing and Community Development). However, given the general reluctance (and perhaps inability) of governments at all levels today to consider non-economic and, particularly, non-market policy instruments, it is wise as well as timely for citizens to improve their understanding of economic policy instruments for sustainable communities.

Advantages of Subsidiarity

Compared to centralized institutions, decentralized institutions are more flexible, more effective, more innovative and generate higher morale, more commitment, and greater productivity. In their influential Reinventing Government, *Osborne and Gaebler (1993) explain the principle of subsidiarity with this rule of thumb: "Unless there is an important reason to do otherwise, responsibility for addressing problems should lie with the lowest level of government possible. The closer a government is to its citizens, the more they trust it. The closer it is, the more accountable its officials tend to be."*

REFERENCES

Beatley, T. 2000. *Green urbanism: Learning from European cities.* Washington, DC: Island Press.

Boston Redevelopment Authority. 2003. *The Boston economy — 2003.* Boston: City of Boston. Retrieved from www.ci.boston.ma.us/bra/PDF/Publications//Rpt589.pdf

City of Kamloops. 2001. *Water use efficiency committee: Final report.* Retrieved from www.city.kamloops.bc.ca/water/

Darke, P. R. 2003. Fairness and discounts: The subjective value of a bargain. *Journal of Consumer Psychology,* 13(3): 328-338.

Devuyst, D. 2001. Introduction to sustainability assessment at the local level. In D. Devuyst (Ed.), *How green is the city? Sustainability assessment and the management of urban environments*: 1-36. New York: Columbia University Press.

Di leva, C. E. 2002. The conservation of nature and natural resources through legal and market-based instruments. *Review of European Community and International Environmental Law,* 11(1): 84-95.

Farrell, A., Carter, R., & Raufer, R. 1999. The NOx budget: Market-based control of tropospheric ozone in the Northeastern United States. *Resource and Energy Economics,* 21(2): 103-124.

Hoerner, J. A., & Bosquet, B. 2001. *Environmental tax reform: The European experience.* Washington, DC: Center for a Sustainable Economy. Retrieved from www.rprogress.org/programs/sustainableeconomy/eurosurvey.pdf

International Council for Local Environmental Initiatives (ICLEI), International Development Research Centre (IDRC), and United Nations Environment Program. 1996. *The Local Agenda 21 Planning Guide.* Toronto: ICLEI and Ottawa: IDRC.

International Council for Local Environmental Initiatives (ICLEI). 2002a. *Eco-procurement: The path to a greener marketplace.* Retrieved from www.iclei.org/procurement/relief/RELIEF_results.pdf

International Council for Local Environmental Initiatives (ICLEI). 2002b. *Accelerating sustainable development: Local action moves the world.* New York: United Nations Economic and Social Council.

International Council for Local Environmental Initiatives (ICLEI). 2002c. *Local governments' response to Agenda 21: Summary report of local agenda 21 survey with regional focus.* Toronto: ICLEI.

Jacobs, M. 1993. *The Green Economy: Environment, Sustainable Development, and the Politics of the Future.* Vancouver, BC: UBC Press.

Lafferty, W. M. 2001. Local agenda 21: The pursuit of sustainable development in subnational domains. In D. Devuyst (Ed.), *How green is the city? Sustainability assessment and the management of the urban environment.* (pp. 63-84). New York: Columbia University Press.

Leithe, J. L., and J. C. Joseph. 1991. "Financing Alternatives." *In Balanced Growth: A Planning Guide for Local Government*, ed. J.M. Degrove. Washington, DC: International City Management Association.

Lombardi, E., & Goldstein, J. 2001. Beyond recycling...zero waster or darn near. *BioCycle,* 42: 75-76.

London Remade. 2004. *The mayor of London's green procurement code.* Retrieved from www.londonremade.com/download_files/GreenProcurementCode.pdf

McAllister, M.L. 2004. *Governing Ourselves? The Politics of Canadian Communities.* Vancouver, BC: UBC Press.

Mulder, P., & Van den Bergh, J. C. J. M. 2001. Evolutionary economic theories of sustainable development. *Growth and Change*, 32(1): 110-134.

New York City Department of Environmental Protection (NYCDEP). 2003. *New York City 2003 drinking water supply and quality report.* Retrieved from www.ci.nyc.ny.us/html/dep/pdf/wsstat03.pdf

Newman, P. 1993a. "Sustainable Development and Urban Planning: Principles and Applications in an Australian Context." *Sustainable Development* 1(1): 25-40.

Newman, P. 1993b. Towards an Urban Bruntland. Prepared for London into the Next Century: An Agenda for the Responsible City, London, Ontario, 27-29 October.

Newman, P., & Kenworthy, J. R. 1999. *Sustainability and cities: Overcoming automobile dependence.* Washington, DC: Island Press.

Ogorzalek, T. 2003. Water smarts. *Journal of Housing & Community Development, 60*(4): 24-29.

Olerup, B. 2002. Mitigating global warming: Traditional versus alternative approaches in a planning versus a market context. *Energy Policy, 30*(8), 709-716.

Osborne, D., and T. Gaebler. 1993. *Reinventing Government.* New York: Plume.

Otto-Zimmermann, K. (2002). Local action 21: Motto-mandate-movement in the post-Johannesburg decade. *Local Environment*, 7(4): 465-469.

Parkinson, S., & Roseland, M. 2002. Leaders of the pack: An analysis of the Canadian 'sustainable communities' 2000 municipal competition. *Local Environment*, 7(4): 411-429.

Pearce, D. W., & Barbier, E. 2000. *Blueprint for a sustainable economy.* London: Earthscan.

Plous, K.F. 1994. "Off the Road, Vehicles." *American Planning Association* 60(9): 8-12.

Rees, W.E. 1995a. "More Jobs, Less Damage: A Framework for Sustainability, Growth and Employment." *Alternatives* 21(4): 24-30.

Rees, W.E. 1995b. "Taxing Combustion and Rehabilitating Forests: Achieving Sustainability, Growth and Employment through Energy Policy." *Alternatives* 21(4): 31-35.

Rees, W. E. 2002. An ecological economics perspective on sustainability and prospects for ending poverty. *Population and Environment, 24*(1): 15-46.

Roseland, M. 1996. "Economic Instruments for Sustainable Communities." *Local Environment* 1(2): 197-210.

Roseland, M. 1997. *Eco-City Dimensions: Healthy Communities, Healthy Planet.* Gabriola Island, BC: New Society Publishers.

Roseland, M., and M. Jacobs. 1995. *Sustainable Development, Economic Instruments, and the Sustainable Management of Aquatic Resources and Ecosystems: A New Framework for Water Management in the Fraser River Basin.* Burnaby, BC: School of Resource and Environmental Management, Simon Fraser University.

San Francisco Department of the Environment. 2004. *Climate action plan for San Francisco.* Retrieved from www.temp.sfgov.org/sfenvironment/aboutus/energy/cap.pdf

Stone, K.E., and R.H. Freilich. 1991. *Balanced Growth: A Planning Guide for Local Government*, J.M. Degrove, ed. Washington DC: International City Management Association.

Tomalty, R. 2003. *Residential intensification case studies: Municipal initiatives.* Ottawa: Canada Mortgage and Housing Corporation.

Transport for London. 2004. *C-Charge Annual Report.* Retrieved from www.tfl.gov.uk/tfl/press-releases/2004/april/press-1009.shtml

Wackernagel, M., and W.E. Rees. 1996. *Our Ecological Footprint: Reducing Human Impact on the Earth.* Gabriola Island, BC: New Society Publishers.

SUSTAINABLE COMMUNITY BUILDING BLOCKS

*T*he framework introduced in Part 1 proposes that applying the concept of sustainable development to North American communities requires mobilizing citizens and their governments to strengthen all forms of community capital. Community mobilization is necessary to coordinate, balance and catalyse community capital. This section of the book, Part 2, is a set of sustainable community "building blocks." Each chapter provides an overview explaining the topic and its relevance to sustainable communities, followed by a set of "Tools and Initiatives," and "Resources." These building blocks are a set of planning tools, practical initiatives, and associated resources that have helped citizens and their governments move toward sustainable communities. While not every tool will "fit" every community, many of them will fit quite well.

Since the powers of municipal and local governments vary considerably, proponents of sustainable community initiatives must research their issues and fashion an approach that works within the specific legal framework of their jurisdiction. For example, a creative municipal solid waste management bylaw will have to fit the specific municipal situation, as well as the legislative framework of the province or state.

CHAPTER 4

GREENING THE CITY

Greening the city refers to strategies and techniques that protect and restore ecology within urban communities. It means a fruit tree-lined street, a creek meandering through an urban neighborhood, geraniums and basil adorning a window box, wildflowers blossoming amid rows of houses, and tomato plants growing in a community garden. It means combining urbanism and nature to create healthy, civilizing, and enriching places to live (Hough, 1995).

Greening the city is a manifestation of bioregionalism (Berg et al., 1989). The central idea of bioregionalism is place. Bioregionalism comes from *bio*, the Greek word for life, as in "biology" and "biography," and *regio*, Latin for territory to be ruled. Together they mean "a life-territory, a place defined by its life forms, its topography and its biota, rather than by human dictates; a region governed by nature, not legislature" (Sale, 1985).

A bioregion is about the right size for human-scale organization: it is a natural framework for economic and political decentralization and self-determination. The primary social unit of a bioregional society is a human-scale, sustainable settlement based on ecological balance, community self-reliance, and participatory democracy (Bookchin, 1987). Bioregional practice is oriented toward resistance against the continuing destruction of natural systems, such as forests and rivers; and toward the renewal of natural systems based on a thorough knowledge of how natural systems work and the development of techniques appropriate to specific sites.

Many urban areas lack green space, especially in lower income neighborhoods. However, simply creating more "green" — flowers, grass and trees — does not necessarily lead to a more sustainable environment. In fact, conventional greening can be wholly unsustainable in its design. Although playing fields, parks and sod strips along boulevards add aesthetic or recreational value, they demand costly amounts of water, fertilizer, herbicides and maintenance, and contribute little in terms of wildlife habitat and food self-sufficiency.

Urban ecology strives to create, preserve and restore green and open spaces *sustainably*. It uses climate- and region-appropriate plants, xeriscaping to minimize the need for fertilizer and water, and uses land for multiple functions such as food production, wildlife habitat, recreation *and* beautification. Urban ecology provides many environmental benefits: it reduces the urban heat island effect, minimizes our use of pesticides, conserves energy, cleans urban air, and absorbs carbon dioxide from the atmosphere.

Urban ecology offers much more than environmental benefits. It offers an opportunity to foster a greater understanding of and connection with nature. Conventional urban design and city living causes alienation between humans and the natural world. Many urbanites think food comes from supermarkets, water comes from faucets, and wastes are simply taken "away." Environmental awareness and activism often focuses on issues outside the city. We support endangered species campaigns or oil spill cleanups, while neglecting the ecological health of our urban spaces. Yet cities and towns are where most of us live. Getting involved in community gardens, planting trees, or participating in stream stewardship projects can improve our health, protect our ecosystem, foster local-self reliance, build community, and even provide some of our food needs. Who doesn't enjoy a fresh, home-grown tomato?

RETHINKING URBAN GREEN SPACE

Urban Parks and Open Space

Creating sustainable green spaces can begin with parks, as they offer a host of ways to reduce the environmental impact of cities. The restoration and preservation of open spaces is another target for sustainable green initiatives, as is the desire to incorporate greening into private outdoor spaces. Many urban neighborhoods need more green space, period. Other communities are struggling to overcome the "parks as ornaments, something to look at but not use" problem. Conventional parks are designed and managed by parks departments or professionals who often lack experience in ecological landscaping. They may also fail to appreciate the range of community needs and wants. When space is a premium in urban areas, diversity is key. Naturalized parks are multifunctional, offering a wide range of opportunities for recreation, education, naturalist activities, wildlife habitat, community gardens, and indigenous species planting.

For example, the Queen's Park Xeriscape garden in Toronto, Ontario, developed by the Ontario Ministry of Natural Resources, features 140 drought-resistant plants that are well suited to the regional climate. Local residents, university students, and faculty conduct projects and experiments in the garden. Plants and clippings are available for sale, and the ecological design reduces maintenance, operating, and water costs of the garden by about 70 percent (Chaplin, 1994). Studies in dryer regions, such the Mojave Desert, have demonstrated that xeriscaping reduces water use by up to 80 percent, and results in a 30 percent decrease in maintenance costs and labor (Sovocool and Rosales, 2001). From 1999 through 2003, about 7,500 property owners in Southern Nevada converted more than 1.7 million square meters (18.3 million square feet) of grass to xeriscape, resulting in more than 5.3 billion liters (1.4 billion gallons) of long-term, annual water savings (SNWA, 2004). Planners, local governments and developers are getting the message — sustainability in urban green space is not only possible, but profitable, too.

Our best crop is concrete. Our diesel buses chug along emitting black clouds like mechanical squids. And our rivers turn into toilet bowls every time heavy rains cause our sewage system to overflow. No wonder, come weekends, any New Yorker with a really disposable income heads for the Hamptons of Long Island or the north woods (Nixon, 1991).

A naturalized back yard

Integrated pest management is a non-chemical alternative for pest control. There is no one fix-all, so the key is to think holistically and use many techniques together. Some strategies include: planting pest resistant species, encouraging beneficial critters like toads and ladybugs, and planting marigolds, garlic, onion, and pansies, which all naturally deter insects.

Citizens and non-government organizations in some communities are also taking initiatives to develop, maintain, and use local open spaces such as vacant lots, traffic islands, rooftops, and abandoned industrial lands to address the unique recreational and ecological needs of their neighborhoods. These open spaces, created by community members, reflect local values because their own sweat and labor are the impetus for implementation.

Greening Private Spaces: In My Backyard Please

Backyards, corporate parks, and private gardens share many of the same opportunities for urban ecology as parks and public spaces. Local governments can foster change by implementing bylaws and regulations restricting use of turf and pesticides on private property, or encouraging change by offering education and incentives. Voluntary programs, such as British Columbia's Naturescape BC, provide pointers on inexpensive ways to increase wildlife habitat at home (and yes, there is wildlife in cities!). Pamphlets explain how to get squirrels, birds, and butterflies to frequent balconies and backyards.

In addition to government and private homeowner initiatives, a growing number of enlightened developers and landscape architects are going green. Recognizing a growing market for environmentally responsible real estate, some developers are incorporating trails and nature preserves, and protecting existing vegetation in residential housing projects. In an urban redevelopment project on Chicago's eastside, one developer converted dreary alleys into courtyards with gardens, park benches and places for people to gather. Companies are also joining in by revolutionizing the concept of corporate office parks. AT&T converted the manicured lawns at two of their corporate campuses in Illinois into prairie wildflowers, saving about $75,000 in maintenance, fertilizer and irrigation costs, and UPS protected creeks and woodlands at their headquarters building in Atlanta, Georgia (Rocky Mountain Institute, 1998). Boeing incorporated jogging trails and restored a wetland in Renton, Washington, and Patagonia planted fruit trees at their headquarters in Nevada.

Golf courses are another private land use in and around our cities, and they're notoriously unsustainable. Conventional golf courses carve fairways out of forests and deserts; guzzle massive amounts of water for irrigating miles of Kentucky blue grass, fertilizers, and pesticides; and require endless labor in raking each sand trap to perfection. "What was once accepted as a benign form of open space is under attack for its impacts on water quality, wildlife habitat, and land use," explains Paul Parker of the Center for Resource Management. However, a number of golf courses are going green. Audubon International and other agencies now have programs to assist golf-course designers and maintenance staff create ecologically responsible golf courses. Boardwalks at Squaw Creek Golf Course in Squaw Valley, California have carried golfers over marsh and meadow areas since its opening in 1992. Design firm Robert Trent Jones Jr. restored acres of native grasses and enhanced natural filtration ponds that feed Squaw Creek. Audubon certified Squaw Creek as a "cooperative sanctuary" and, apart from using small amounts of nitrogen, the golf course is maintained organically to protect the aquifer it sits upon.

Benefits of Functional Green Space

Decrease Energy Costs: The US National Renewable Energy Laboratory, Department of Energy reports that properly positioned trees provide shade, wind-breaks, and evapo-transpiration (lowering ambient temperatures), and save about 20 percent to 25 percent of average annual residential energy costs, compared with the costs for the same house in an unsheltered area.

Reduce Urban Heat Island Effect: Urban areas are significantly hotter than surrounding rural areas. The difference in temperature ranges from as little as 1.1° to 4.4°C (2°F to 8°F) in St. Louis Missouri, to 5.6°C (10°F) in New York City, to as much as 10°C (18°F) in Mexico City. The heat island effect occurs as urban surfaces, such as concrete, asphalt,

A rooftoop lawn

and brick absorb the sun's heat and radiate it out, causing increased urban temperatures. Highrises create an "urban canyon," also reducing heat loss to the atmosphere. In contrast, plants absorb and metabolize solar energy, helping to moderate hot temperatures. As well as discomfort, urban heat islands cost money. About 3 percent to 8 percent of air conditioning use in the US is for compensating for the heat island effect. Scientists at the Lawrence Berkeley Laboratory estimate the country's total electricity costs for offsetting the effects of summer heat islands at more than $1 billion per year. And the problem appears to be growing: a study of Houston, Texas revealed an increase of almost 1°C (1.8°F) in the urban heat island effect between 1999 and 2001 (MacPherson and Rowntree, 1994; Streutker, 2003).

Decrease Water Use: Indigenous species or native plants are adapted to local climates so they require less irrigation than non-native species. Xeriscaping gardening practices use native plants and drought-tolerant species which require less water and chemicals. The term is derived from the Greek word for dry, *xeros*.

Increase Absorption of Pollutants: Plants act as a "sink" for pollutants, absorbing carbon dioxide and other deleterious substances. A Douglas-fir is capable of removing 18 kilograms (39.6 pounds) of sulfur dioxide from the atmosphere a year without harm to itself (Haughton and Hunter, 1994).

Increase Urban Wildlife Habitat: Urbanization has radically altered both natural and wildlife communities. Urban land use has fragmented forests and other ecosystems, and created isolated islands of habitat. Ideally, critical habitat is identified before development, and urban activities can accommodate or integrate areas for birds and animals. Maintaining vegetation diversity helps provide for breeding, cover, and food sources.

Improve Drainage: Often close to 50 percent of urban areas are paved over. High percentages of impervious surfaces regularly lead to storm water run-off problems.

Properly planted land absorbs the rain that falls on it, eliminating excessive run-off that otherwise requires expensive storm sewers that often overflow and flood. (See also Chapter 5: Water and Sewage).

Act as Indicators of Ecological Health: The vigor and robustness of native animals and plants indicate how clean the air and water are, and can help us assess the health and life-supporting capacity of the entire ecosystem.

Increase Community Space and Aesthetics: Aside from all of the ecological benefits identified above, there are many social and psychological benefits associated with thoughtful urban ecology. Green spaces can provide places to play, meditate, gather, rest, and rejuvenate.

Create More Livable Cities and Connect with Nature: Green space in cities can enhance our connection with ecological processes. "These strong ties between people and trees cannot be explained by increased property values, reductions in air pollutants, and moderation in temperature" (Dwyer, Schroeder, and Gobster 1994). Getting involved brings you closer to the natural environment and strengthens communities by creating opportunities to know your neighbors. Plant a tree! Restore a stream!

Save Money: Sustainable landscaping and gardening saves money. Simply by planting trees and using alternative ground cover to sod, citizens and their municipalities can enjoy lower water, energy, and maintenance costs.

TOOLS AND INITIATIVES

Policy and Regulatory

Bioregionalism considers people to be part of a place, as dependent on nature as native plants and animals (Aberley 1993, 1994).

Municipal governments play an integral role in the sustainable management of green space, and citizens can influence their local officials to act. Efforts can take the form of government policy, bylaws, or regulations, and/or be driven by NGOs, citizens, or private initiatives. Governments can conduct Environmentally Sensitve Area (ESA) studies and inventories to determine which areas are in greatest need for protection and/or reclamation, and use official community plans and development permits to dictate substantial leave strips, setbacks, and protection of green space and watercourses. Conservation commissions and environmental advisory boards can partner with local organizations and other municipal governments to initiate local greening initiatives. The list is long once the political will is in place.

ESA Strategy: In 1994, Burnaby, British Columbia City Council adopted an initial ESA strategy that continues to serve as the comprehensive policy framework for environmental sustainability within the city. The ESA applies environmentally sensitive planning and management principles to protect public green lands. The city also engages in annual State of the Environment Reporting, has enacted a watercourse protection bylaw, and partners with local NGOs and other levels of government on a variety of initiatives, from streamkeeping to land management plans (City of Burnaby, 2004).

Natural Planting Ordinance: In a critical aquifer district in the town of Southampton on Long Island, New York, a natural planting ordinance requires that at least 80 percent of each lot remain in its natural state, and no more than 15 percent of any lot can be planted in fertilized lawns or plants. These restrictions still leave landowners with ample landscaping choices; sites are left in woodland vegetation or planted in meadow grasses, perennial wildflowers, ivy, or other dense plantings that need little or no fertilizing (Lowe, 1991).

Green Roofs: In Germany, 43 percent of cities offer financial incentives for roof greening, and green roofs are often required by conditions attached to construction permits in order to meet the federal requirements for mitigating the ecological impact of building construction. Flat green roofs save energy and increase residents' comfort by limiting the temperature spread, and reduce heating and air conditioning requirements. Green roofs have 60 percent less runoff than gravel or asphalt tiles, reducing the costs of drainage systems and, in sufficient numbers, improving the urban micro-climate. North America is considered to be at least ten years behind Europe in investing in green roof infrastructure (English Nature, 2003; Peck and Kuhn, 2001).

Xeriscape Bylaw: In 1991, Florida passed the first state xeriscape bylaw in the US requiring that xeriscaping be applied to all newly developed and existing public properties over a period of five years. In 2000, the South Florida Water Management District (SFWMD) passed a "Xeriscape Incentive Rule" which provides technical assistance to local governments that submit draft xeriscape ordinances. All local governments that operate water supply systems throughout the state have adopted water conservation ordinances, and even citizens are affected. Anyone who buys automatic lawn sprinklers must also install a rain sensor to ensure the system shuts off when it begins to rain

Land Trusts and Conservation Trusts

These are effective tools for preserving land, and are typically funded by government, citizens or NGOs. Land is put into trust protecting it from development for an agreed purpose — typically for parks, preserves, or community gardening. Trusts employ a variety of strategies: obtain title to land; obtain conservation covenants; buy land, place a covenant and resell; or buy land and develop it in a limited way to pay for preserved area; encourage private philanthropists to buy and preserve land; and/or help individuals or governments manage land. (See also Chapter 11: Housing and Community Development.)

Education and Promotion Programs

Water Efficient Landscaping: There are numerous examples of communities promoting water-efficient landscaping. A study comparing conventional and water-efficient landscapes in Northern California found savings of 54 percent for water, 25 percent for labor, 61 percent for fertilizer, 44 percent for fuel, and 22 percent for herbicides (Rocky

---

Land Trust Success Stories

• Over 1000 local US land trusts protect over 4 million acres. National US organizations protect an additional seven million acres.

• From 1988-92, San Francisco Bay Area land trusts acquired 80,000 acres — 56 percent of the new open space in the region.

• About 25 percent of Maryland's Protection Open Space programs involve land trusts.

• In Vermont, land trusts and affordable housing groups have leveraged $60 million in state government grants to produce $235 million in conservation and affordable housing projects.

• Recognizing that greenways are part of the transportation system in sustainable cities of the future, the Netherlands devotes 10 percent of gas taxes for greenways and related initiatives.

• In over 30 states, taxpayers can simply check a box if they want to send their tax refund to a habitat acquisition fund (Sandborn, 1997).

A community garden in East Vancouver

Community food security is a condition in which all community residents obtain a safe, culturally acceptable, nutritionally adequate diet through a sustainable food system that maximizes community self-reliance and social justice. Mike Hamm and Anne Bellows (CFSC, 2004).

Mountain Institute, 1998). Homes and businesses receive rebates for installing water-efficient landscaping in Mesa, Arizona. These properties use 30 percent to 50 percent less water than similar sites with turf-intensive landscapes (City of Mesa, 2003).

Cool Communities: American Forests implemented the Cool Communities program from 1991-1996 in an effort to educate and mobilize communities to promote the use of trees as energy conservation tools. At the end of the program, a survey of Miami residents showed that 97 percent of respondents were aware of the money-saving energy benefits of trees. In a 2001 study, American Forests found that tree cover in the metro Atlanta area saved residents approximately $2.8 million annually in reduced energy costs, and similar trends have been found throughout the country. American Forests has also developed "CITYgreen" software, a desktop GIS program that calculates the value of trees to urban environments (American Forests, n.d.).

Trees for Tucson: This Tucson, Arizona program is affiliated with the American Forests' Global ReLeaf Program. It provides information to homeowners, neighborhood groups, and schools on low-water plants and trees appropriate to the local environment. In its first decade of operation (1993-2003), the program provided community members with over 30,000 trees. According to the organizer's calculations, each tree will save more than $20 in air conditioning costs by providing shading and evapotranspiration, saving a total of $236.5 million in the next 40 years. Officials also estimate that planting 500,000 trees will save the city $600,000 in storm drainage management in 40 years. Programs include Trees for Shade and Trees for School (Centre of Excellence, 1996; MacPherson, 1994; TCBI, 2004).

Volunteer / NGO Urban Greening Projects

Turn a Lot Around: This Chicago Resource Center focuses on vacant lots as the centerpieces of community renewal efforts. Volunteer work includes the clearing of debris, garden creation, and building playgrounds. One project, City Farm, is an urban sustainable organic farm between two neighborhoods that sells produce to restaurants and residents (CRC, 2004).

Green Guerrillas: This organization began in 1973 with a group of neighbors on the lower east side of Manhattan in New York City. Tired of the destruction of their community, they cleaned and greened a vacant lot in an area known as Bum's Row. Today that lot has meandering paths, a grape arbor, a pond, and all kinds of flowers, fruits, and vegetables; and the metasequoia tree they planted is now 12.2 meters (40 feet) tall. Anything that will grow in an urban environment is there — it even has a bee hive. That the garden is in an area known for its urban blight is significant. The group now helps over 300 community organizations green lots throughout New York City (Green Guerrillas, 2004; Keller, 1990).

Greening the Great River Park: Since 1995 in St. Paul Minnesota, over 12,000 volunteers have planted 35,000 native trees and shrubs, and more than 16,500 prairie grasses and wildflowers in the Mississippi, Minnesota and St. Croix river valleys. The initial work focused on a mostly privately-owned 4.8-kilometer (3-mile) industrial stretch of the Mississippi River. A volunteer design team including a landscape architect, a community representative, and an ecologist drafted a plan for each parcel of land and reviewed it with the owner. The success of the initial project led to the creation of the nonprofit organization, Great River Greening, in 1999. The state's Environment and Natural Resources Trust Fund and charitable donations fund the program (GRG, 2004).

La Société de verdissement du Montreal metropolitain (Greening Society of Metropolitan Montreal): This program recaptures the diversity of the original hardwood forests in the greater Montreal, Quebec region. The society grows and provides native trees and shrubs which they make available to individuals, community groups, schools, and businesses to plant around Montreal. The goal is to plant two million trees by 2010. They also distribute information on care and planting of trees and shrubs.

Urban agriculture can be beautiful as well as nourishing

URBAN AGRICULTURE

Most urbanites pay little attention to where food comes from, or how much waste and environmental damage is associated with its production and transportation. On average in the US, food in a supermarket travels about 2,000 kilometers (1,300 miles) between its point of production and its point of consumption. "The principle of proximity is simple: food should be consumed as close to the point and condition of production as possible" (Kneen, 1993). Agribusiness pumps chemicals onto fields and farmworkers. Processing, packaging and shipping wastes energy and materials, and freshness, nutritional value, and good taste are often lost somewhere along the way.

A just and sustainable food system protects the land which produces the food; supports the local economy through local production; empowers communities through self-reliance, and gives them increased food system security; enhances community well-being through increased health, decreased illnesses; increases sense of community; and increases environmental health because of reduced transportation of food. Local food systems are inherently tied not only to the health of individuals, but to the short and long-term economic, social, and environmental health of communities. Where food systems become unjust and unsustainable due to state/provincial, national, and international forces, it is communities that bear the burden (Kneen et al., 1997).

Urban agriculture can address many of these problems. It can take the form of community gardens, locally-supported farms on the fringe of cities, or backyard plots, greenhouses, and balconies full of beans and herbs. Small-scale food growing efforts are often organically-managed, and permaculture techniques can reduce the need for labor and materials.

A community garden in East Vancouver

Communities are growing food in every location imaginable — in parks, vacant lots, abandoned industrial lands, rooftops, and on vertical surfaces — but they often face challenges. Health bylaws prevent farmers' markets within city limits; other bylaws restrict park use for growing food; codes and covenants favor lawns and parking lots; and real estate development competes for land tenure. But the benefits outweigh the challenges, as people reconnect with one of nature's most basic processes, save money on food bills, and enjoy greater local self-reliance.

There are many other environmental and social benefits of urban agriculture. Local farms and gardens can use the city's organic wastes for compost, helping to reduce burden on local landfills (organic wastes account for about 30 percent of household waste), and home-grown food reduces packaging waste and energy consumption. Edible planting and permaculture also exposes the public to environmentally sound alternatives to conventional urban landscaping, and it expands opportunities for people to have access to personal green space.

Perhaps the greatest benefit of urban agriculture is the provision of affordable food supplies for lower-income people. North America is touted as having one of the most abundant food systems in the world, yet close to a million people (including 328,000 children) visit over 550 food banks across Canada monthly (CAFB, 2004). The number of US residents participating in federal food stamp programs per month rose to 24 million in 2004, representing nearly 8 percent percent of the population (FRAC, 2004). Urban food production can help feed the poor. On the east side of Vancouver, locals share the fruits of their labor with homeless people, and low-income residents rely on the seasonal bounty of the Strathcona community garden for much of their food supply.

TOOLS AND INITIATIVES

Community Gardens

City of Seattle's P-Patch Program: In conjunction with the nonprofit P-patch Advisory Council, this program provides community garden space for residents of 35 Seattle neighborhoods. More than 1,900 plots serve over 4,600 urban gardeners on 12 acres of land. Special programs serve refugees, low-income, disabled and youth gardeners, and the Lettuce Link project delivers 8-10 tons of fresh produce to food banks every year. All gardening is organic; no insecticides or herbicides are permitted. Since its inception, 53 community gardens have been started throughout Seattle, and a community-supported agriculture (see below) program has also been initiated (Seattle, 2004).

Gardening Angels: In Detroit, Michigan, the Gardening Angels aim to use the power of planting to heal a city ravaged by declining industry, depopulation, and nar-

Community gardens provide a means for gardening and growing together with friends and neighbors. Gardens range in size, location, and participation; they can be small, local neighborhood gardens in vacant lots or parks, communal rooftop gardens, or municipally maintained allotment gardens (Guberman, 1995).

cotics wars. About 60 local people have planted over 200 gardens on derelict sites throughout Detroit. They've managed to drive off drug gang and crack house activity, encourage youth participation and entrepreneurship, and partner with a diverse group of folks including residents, churchgoers, inmates from a nearby prison, drug and alcohol rehabilitation patients, the Hunger Action Coalition, and City Council. The gardens feed the homeless, and tentative steps are being made to market their fruit and vegetables. Many people in the city see the gardens as a metaphor for recovery as well as a practical means to it (Urban Ecologist, 1996; Boggs, 1998).

Community Supported Agriculture

Many urban dwellers across North America are benefiting from community supported agriculture, a means of feeding people that allows both growers and consumers to share responsibilities for growing food. Typically, local farmers on the urban fringe grow food for a pre-determined group of

The Living Wall Garden Project in Vancouver, BC

consumers (guaranteed market), with whom they enter into an agreement (usually money in exchange for produce) before a season begins. By keeping money in the community, this form of agriculture secures the livelihood of local family farmers, supports the local economy, fosters greater self-reliance for food supplies, and helps people remain connected with the food they consume.

Prairie Crossing: In a new residential community outside Chicago, Illinois, the developers of Prairie Crossing clustered much of the housing development to preserve agricultural lands. Realizing that farmers on the urban fringe are often struggling to survive, the developers are organizing community supported agriculture to encourage new residents to support local farmers.

Food Policy Organizations

Food policy organizations are community, city, or regional groups that aim to improve the security of the local food system. They are essentially vehicles for food activists to undertake projects and programs that move toward sustainable food policy. Such organizations initiate, support, and connect community projects and programs with policy-making. They are holistic, dealing with both the causes and effects of hunger, and work for short and long-term change on issues of food production, processing, distribution and access, public education and research, waste reduction, and policy. Examples may include hospital and institutional buy-local policies, community shared agriculture, farmers' markets, school breakfast and hot lunch campaigns, community kitchens, breastfeeding support programs, and community gardens.

Food Policy Action Coalition and Food Share: The number of organizations addressing food policy, urban agriculture and food security issues has increased significantly in recent years. Groups range in structure from informal volunteer groups such as Peterborough's Food Policy Action Coalition, to more established nonprofit

New York City has 2.6 million street trees, and 700-800 community gardens, from pocket parks to small farms such as one in the South Bronx that produces 8,000 pounds of fruit and vegetables a year. (Nixon, 1991).

organizations such as Toronto's Food Share, an organization with an executive director, 10 paid staff, a volunteer board, and upwards of 500 volunteers (Kneen et al., 1997). Municipal governments have begun to recognize local food security as a priority through the creation of positions and agencies such as Vancouver's Food Policy Coordinator and Food Policy Task Force (Vancouver, 2004).

Training and Mentoring to Learn Gardening Skills

Living Wall Garden Project: This Vancouver, BC project aims to create, beautify, mentor, educate, promote self-sufficiency, celebrate possibility, and improve the city for its future inhabitants. At-risk youth research and practice vertical gardening techniques, and volunteer community mentors, such as master gardeners, landscape architects, and youth counsellors help with site design, construction, and youth training. The longer-term goals are to establish a youth-owned vertical gardening cooperative, and encourage similar urban agricultural projects throughout the inner-city.

From the Ground Up: This organization started in Washington, DC in 1992 as a food security project for low-income groups. It provided welfare-to-work apprenticeships until 1996 when the project evolved into a community-supported agriculture operation for low-income and other investors. Their goal is to provide nutritious, fresh produce to all income levels in the community. Half of the farm's harvest is targeted for low-income, and the other half is used to create a stable funding base for the program. Vegetables are grown on a farm 3 miles from the DC line using environmentally sensitive practices, where people from all socioeconomic backgrounds gather together to harvest the crops. Volunteers are used in the vegetable production and are educated about the connections between agriculture and social justice (WHY, 2004). Low-income residents involved in the program learn business skills, and inner-city youth are taught about nutritional, environmental and food security issues. In 1996, the group's 3-hectare (8-acre) farm on the outskirts of the city produced over 50,000 kilograms (110,000 pounds) of fresh vegetables (Nelson, 1996).

InSightOut's Youth Employment and Education Project: Another Vancouver, BC project organized a small group of young adults to work with a herbalist to plant medicinal herbs on the roof of the cancer treatment center at Vancouver General Hospital. What better place for plants to bring their healing powers?

URBAN AQUATIC SYSTEMS

Urban aquatic areas — streams, ponds, beaches and marshes — are often filled-in, neglected or manipulated beyond recognition. Protection and restoration of streams and other aquatic systems revitalize neighborhoods and commercial areas, and give us a place to find the child again (who loved to play by them). Healthy aquatic systems are full of life and offer communities a place for art, science, and a celebration of nature. Conceiving restoration projects in this way can infuse community activism with a creative and inspirational dimension that has profound implications for grassroots efforts to revitalize our cities.

Stream corridors, creeks, and marshes are vehicles for education about local history and ecology, and places for rest, recreation, and neighborhood beautification. Preservation and restoration projects in urban areas also have numerous ecological benefits. They can increase biodiversity, provide habitat for fish and wildlife, restore native vegetation, act as a natural filtration system for greywater, and accommodate storm water run-off.

Creek "daylighting" is another restoration strategy. It involves returning creek beds to the surface from their current underground, culverted state. This is an expensive endeavor in terms of up-front costs, but the benefits are many. Stream corridors represent one of the most varied ecosystems, and streams are effective in storing and absorbing storm water run-off over their vegetated and riparian surfaces.

TOOLS AND INITIATIVES

Developer- and City-run Stream Restoration and Preservation Projects

Watercourse Protection Bylaw: Communities that have raised and restored their creeks include San Luis Obispo and Berkeley, California (Steere 1990). Burnaby, BC passed a resolution in 1972 that its streams must be preserved and conserved, and passed a watercourse protection bylaw in 1988. Housing developments must incorporate existing streams into their landscaping, and individual homeowners are not allowed to build right down to the bank (setbacks are required).

Creek Daylighting Project: El Cerrito, California recently undertook a creek daylighting project and restored a strip of long-culverted creek as part of a city-wide storm drain renovation program. The Urban Creeks Council suggested that the Waterways Restoration Institute become involved. This nonprofit agency uses hands-on educators to work with local governments and citizens to develop alternatives to traditional flood control. They created gentle meanders, pools and riffles to diversify flow, increase water quality, and halt erosion. Banks were stabilized with native plant species (Urban Ecologist 1997). The Urban Creek Council also has restoration projects ongoing in Oakland, Martinez, San Pablo, Berkeley, Richmond and Albany (UCCC, 2004).

Watershed Restoration: The Wheaton Branch restoration is the first phase of a larger, ongoing watershed restoration of Sligo Creek by an interdisciplinary team composed of staff from public agencies, including the Maryland National Capital Park and Planning Commission. Located in a highly urbanized area, 55 percent of Wheaton Branch's watershed is covered by impervious surfaces. The project is addressing everything from controlling run-off at the headwaters of the stream to bank stabilizing and fish restocking (Thompson, 1996; Montgomery County, 2004).

Stream Stewardship Programs

Once stream restoration projects are complete, there are many more activities to be done. Volunteer community groups can organize clean-up and education programs, or partner with local governments and others to obtain funding for monitoring programs. Citizens can lobby for stricter ordinances protecting riparian zones (through Official Community Plan policies, zoning and environmental protection bylaws, development permit areas, comprehensive development and density bonusing, conservation covenants, ESA studies, and the list goes on.) These measures involve individuals interested in moving from private to participatory citizenship, taking responsibility for the local ecosystem in our urban areas (see Chapter 5: Water and Sewage for examples of initiatives).

River Stewardship: The Virginia River Conservation Society in St. John's, Newfoundland has worked to return the river to its original condition and encourage river stewardship. With foundation funding, members cleaned up the river banks and restored sensitive fish habitat in areas where urban development had damaged the river's ecology. In one eroded area they made a lattice-work of logs, covered them with soil and peat, and planted native plants to stabilize the ground.

RESOURCES

Center for Watershed Protection publishes a quarterly journal, *Watershed Protection Techniques*. The summer 1995 issue focused specifically on urban stream restoration. The Center also offers a bibliography of useful sources and courses on a range of topics, such as the design of best-management practices. Website: www.cwp.org

Centre for Studies in Food Security at Ryerson University in Toronto, Canada, is an information clearinghouse and research centre on local and global food security issues. Website: www.ryerson.ca/foodsecurity/index.html

City Farmer is touted as "Canada's Office of Urban Agriculture." The group's web site offers information on almost every aspect of urban agriculture, and maintains a large list of links to other relevant sites. Website: www.cityfarmer.org/

Community Food Security Coalition (CFSC) is a nonprofit North American organization dedicated to building strong, sustainable, local and regional food systems that ensure access to affordable, nutritious, and culturally appropriate food for all people at all times. CFSC has over 250 member organizations and operates training and outreach programs throughout North America. Website: www.foodsecurity.org/

Department of Fisheries and Oceans and the BC government created a stewardship series of documents to provide tools and information for citizens, planners, and municipal governments to protect local streams and fish habitat. The series includes *Stream Stewardship: A Guide for Planners and Developers* and *The Streamkeepers Handbook: A Citizens Guide to Stream Stewardship*. Website: www.dfo-mpo.gc.ca

Green City Project is a volunteer network linking over 425 San Francisco Bay Area environmental groups. The network provides a point of entry for residents, schools, companies, and other organizations to become active with these groups. Website: www.sustainable-city.org/orgs/gcp.htm

Green Roofs for Healthy Cities North America Inc. is a non-profit industry association consisting of public and private organizations and individuals whose mission is to develop a market for green roof infrastructure products and services in cities across North America. Website: www.greenroofs.org/

REFERENCES

Aberley, D. 1993. *Boundaries of Home: Mapping for Local Empowerment.* Gabriola Island, BC: New Society Publishers.

— — — , ed. 1994. *Futures By Design: The Practice of Ecological Planning* Gabriola Island, BC: New Society Publishers.

American Forests. n.d. *Trees and Energy Conservation.* From www.americanforests.org/graytogreen/energy/

Berg, P., et al. 1989. *A Green City Program for San Francisco Bay Area Cities and Towns* San Francisco: Planet Drum Books.

Boggs, G. 1998. "Living for Change: An Autobiography." Minneapolis, Minnesota: University of Minnesota Press

Bookchin, M. 1987. *The Rise of Urbanization and the Decline of Citizenship.* San Francisco: Sierra Club.

Canadian Association of Food Banks (CAFB). 2004. "Hungercount 2004". Retrieved from http://foodbank.duoweb.ca/documents/HC04.pdf

Centre of Excellence for Sustainable Development. 1997. "Cooling Our Cities." Retrieved from www.eren.doe.gov/cities_counties/coolcit.html

Chaplin, S. 1994. *Water Efficient Landscaping: A Guide for Utilities and Community Planners.* Water Efficiency Implementation Report No. 6. Denver, Colo.: Rocky Mountain Institute.

Chicago Resource Center (CRC). 2004. *City Farm.* Retrieved from www.resourcecenterchicago.org/70thfarm.html

City of Burnaby. 2004. *Official Community Plan.* (PDF file) Available from www.city.burnaby.bc.ca/cityhall/departments_planning/plnnng_plans_offclc.html

City of Mesa. 2003. *Water development fee rebate.* Retrieved from www.cityofmesa.org/utilities/conservation/landscape_rebate.asp

City of Seattle, Department of Neighborhoods. 2004. "P-Patch Community Gardens." Retrieved from www.seattle.gov/neighborhoods/ppatch/

City of Vancouver. 2004. Retrieved from www.city.vancouver.bc.ca

Community Food Security Coalition (CFSC). 2004. *Recommended Resources for more information about Community Food Security (CFS) issues.* (PDF file) Retrieved from www.foodsecurity.org/CFS_resource_list.pdf

Dwyer, J., H. Schroeder, and P. Gobster. 1994. "The Deep Significance of Urban Trees and Forests." In *The Ecological City: Preserving and Restoring Urban Biodiversity,* R. Platt, R. Rowntree, and P. Muick, eds. Amherst: University of Massachusetts Press.

English Nature. 2003. *Green Roofs: their existing status and potential for conserving biodiversity in urban areas; Research Report 498.* (PDF file). Available from www.english-nature.org.uk/pubs/publication/PDF/498.pdf

Food Research and Action Centre (FRAC). 2004. "Food Stamp Program Participation Data". Retrieved from www.frac.org/html/federal_food_programs/programs/fspparticipation.html

Great River Greening (GRG). 2004. *Our History.* Retrieved from www.greatrivergreening.org/history.asp

Green Guerillas. 2004. *What we do.* Retrieved from www.greenguerillas.org/info.asp

Guberman, C. 1995. "Sowing the Seed of Sustainability: Planning for Food Self-Reliance." In *Change of Plans: Towards a Non-Sexist Sustainable City*, M. Eichler, ed. Toronto: Garamond Press.

Haughton, G., and C. Hunter. 1994. *Sustainable Cities*. Regional Policy and Development Series 7. London: Jessica Kingley Publishers.

Hough, M. 1995. *Cities and Natural Processes*. New York: Routledge.

Keller, T. 1990. "The Greening of the Big Apple." In *Green Cities: Ecologically Sound Approaches to Urban Space*. Montreal: Black Rose Books.

Kent A. Sovocool, Kent A. and Janet L. Rosales. 2001. *A five-year investigation into the potential water and monetary savings of residential xeriscape in the Mojave Desert*. (PDF file) Retrieved from Southern Nevada Water Authority www.snwa.com/assets/pdf/xeri_study.pdf

Kneen, B. 1993. *From Land to Mouth: Understanding the Food System*. Toronto: NC Press Limited.

Kneen, B., C. McDougall, and C. Kneen. 1997. *A Baseline for Food Policy in British Columbia*. Vancouver: Farm Folk/City Folk Society.

Lowe, M.D. 1991. "Shaping Cities: The Environmental and Human Dimensions." Worldwatch Paper 105. Washington, DC: Worldwatch Institute.

MacPherson, G., and R. Rowntree. 1994. "Energy Efficient Landscapes." In *Urban Forest Landscapes: Integrating Multidisciplinary Perspectives*, G. Bradley, ed. Seattle: University of Washington Press.

Montgomery County, Department of Environmental Protection. 2004. Retrieved from www.montgomerycountymd.gov/deptmpl.asp?url=/content/dep/csps/watersheds/csps/html/sligo.asp

Nelson, T. 1996. "Closing the Nutrient Loop." *WorldWatch* 9(6): 10-17.

Nixon, W. 1991. "The Greening of the Big Apple: If It Can Happen Here, It Can Happen Anywhere." *E- The Environmental Magazine* II:5.

Peck, S. and Kuhn, M. 2001. Design Guidelines for Green Roofs. Canadian Mortgage and Housing Corporation (CMHC). Retrieved from www.cmhc-schl.gc.ca/en/imquaf/himu/himu_002.cfm

Rocky Mountain Institute. 1998. *Green Development: Integrating Ecology & Real Estate*. New York: John Wiley and Sons Publishers.

Sale, K. 1985. *Dwellers in the Land: The Bioregional Vision*. Gabriola Island: New Society Publishers.

Sandborn, C. 1997. *The Green Zone Priorities for Tomorrow Conference Workbook*. Burnaby, BC: Greater Vancouver Regional District.

Southern Nevada Water Authority (SNWA) 2004. "Zeriscape Study". Retrieved from www.snwa.com/html/ws_xeri_study.html

Steere, J. 1990. "Creeks Alive!" In *Report of the First International Ecological City Conference*. Berkeley, Calif.: Urban Ecology.

Streutker, David R. 2003. *Satellite-measured growth of the urban heat island of Houston, Texas* (PDF file) Retrieved from www.isu.edu/~stredavi/uhi_growth_web.pdf

Thompson, J.W. 1996. "Down by the Creekside." *Landscape Architecture* 86(10): 82-93.

Tucson Clean and Beautiful, Inc. (TCBI). 2004. *Trees for Tucson*. Retrieved from www.ci.tucson.az.us/tcb/tcbtothp.htm

Urban Creeks Council of California. 2004. Retrieved from www.urbancreeks.org/

Urban Ecologist. 1996. 3.

Urban Ecologist. 1997. 1

World Hunger Year (WHY). 2004. Retrieved from www.worldhungeryear.org/comm_conn/ display_ria.asp?ria_ndx=95

CHAPTER 5

WATER AND SEWAGE

Norh America is abundant in lakes and rivers yet, in many regions, water resources are in critical supply. Even the moist Pacific Northwest has begun to feel the pinch as drier seasons and urban growth overwhelm infrastructure and water supplies. Despite some conservation initiatives, especially in California and other arid regions, Canada and the US consume more water per capita than any other countries in the world.

Citizens also bear the burden of exorbitant costs for expansion of infrastructure for dam and reservoir construction, and chlorination plants. Costs for operating, maintaining and expanding sewage treatment facilities continue to compete for our tax dollars, while water pollution and the rapid rate of water extraction is causing damage to fish stocks as well as other environmental degradation. Water consumption and treatment also influences energy demand, as energy is required to pump and process water supplies and wastewater. Even more energy, such as natural gas and electricity, is used to provide domestic hot water and heated water for commercial and industrial needs.

Some communities are addressing these problems by seeking solutions that satisfy people's needs while reducing or minimizing environmental and financial costs associated with supply and sewage treatment infrastructure expansion. Demand-side management, alternative sewage treatment, wastewater reclamation and integrated resource planning are some of the most significant and successful strategies used currently for sustainable stewardship of this critical resource.

SUPPLY AND DEMAND

We waste our water because we think it's cheap, but is it? In most places in North America, a portion of our water supply and sewage treatment costs are paid through general tax revenue or property taxes. Apart from industrial customers, most users pay a flat rate rather than pay per volume, so we don't realize the actual cost of our consumptive patterns. These low costs and hidden subsidies have a significant impact on the amount of water we use, and several studies indicate that increasing the cost of water and enforcing user pay (per volume) rates on customers will encourage conservation (NRTEE, 1996; Pinkham & Davis, 2002).

True cost pricing may be the simplest solution, but faced with population growth and soaring demand, many cities are seeking physical and financial ways to expand water supply. Yet, by encouraging and even demanding more *efficient* use of existing resources, communities can satisfy their needs while *saving* money and conserving existing water supplies.

From simple faucet aerators and low-flush toilets to sonar leak detection units and computerized water modeling for decision-making, there are a host of low- and high-tech solutions for reducing waste and improving water-efficiency. The challenge is to reduce our consumption without compromising our comfort, and it can be done if communities use water-efficient products and devices, and adopt strategies or techniques that foster water conservation. Some of these approaches can be employed by individual homeowners, tenants, building owners or occupants; others can be implemented by builders or developers; and others require participation of local or regional governments, water service departments or public works departments.

Financial benefits include direct savings from lower water usage, and reduced sewage costs resulting from less wasted water. Additionally, the city and its taxpayers avoid

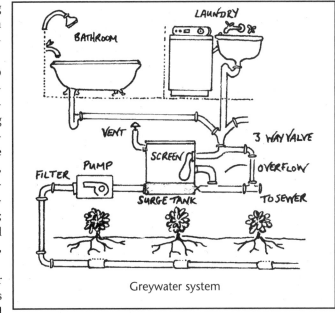

Greywater system

the cost of treatment and supply for each gallon, liter or cubic foot of water conserved. While consumers may not realize it when they leave a tap dripping, or a lawn sprinkler running, efficient use of water may also help avoid the huge capital cost of constructing reservoirs and expanding treatment plants. These demand side management strategies make sense from an environmental and financial perspective, yet municipal governments may need to introduce incentives or policies for water conservation, and restrictions or penalties encouraging water conservation initiatives. (See Chapter 7: Energy Efficiency and Renewables for more discussion of demand side management.)

TOOLS AND INITIATIVES

There are many ways to achieve water efficiency in communities. Perhaps the most common solutions are voluntary and mandatory curtailment programs, requesting or requiring customers to water their gardens only at certain times or on certain days. These programs work best if accompanied with education and promotional programs, helping customers understand the financial savings and environmental benefits, as well as local supply issues associated with water consumption. Incentive programs and education about efficient hardware and techniques can also promote customer participation in water conservation programs, as can bylaws and ordinances requiring efficient plumbing and irrigation products and techniques.

Audit Programs
Often, the first step to water conservation is awareness of the opportunities for savings. Many local governments, water utilities, water service companies, and even volunteer organizations offer water audits to residents and/or businesses.

Home Audits and Upgrades: The City of Everett, Washington, provides water audits for residents and businesses as well as providing free "conservation kits" consisting of high-efficiency showerheads, faucet aerators, hose nozzles and moisture testers (Everett Public Works n.d.).

Rebates and Replacement Programs

Toilet and Showerhead Incentive Program: From 1994 to 1997, the Department of Environmental Protection in New York City conducted a Toilet Rebate Program that provided a financial incentive to property owners to replace old toilets and showerheads with new low-consumption models. By the time the program ended, 1.34 million toilets had been replaced. DEP estimates that 189 to 302 million liters (50 to 80 million gallons) of water a day are saved as a result of this program, with an average water savings of 29.3 percent per building (NYCDCP, 2002).

Low-Flow Toilets Distributed Free: In 1995 the Mothers of East Los Angeles-Santa Isabel started a program to buy ultra-low flow toilets (ULFTs) at bulk discounts, distribute them free to low-income residents, and collect rebates of $100 per toilet from the local water district in California. The rebate money paid for the toilets and nine salaries for local employees to distribute efficient toilets, lights, and showerheads, assist with their implementation, and conduct follow-up inspections. The program has grown to include four community organizations that provide free ULFTs to any customer of the Los Angeles Department of Water and Power. Homeowners and renters save from $30 to $120 in water and energy bills per year (Roseland & Jacobs, 1995; Mono Lake Committee, 2004).

Rebates for Water-Efficient Landscaping: Homes and businesses receive rebates for installing water-efficient landscaping in Mesa, Arizona. These properties use 30 percent to 50 percent less water than similar sites with turf-intensive landscapes (City of Mesa, 2003).

Grants, Loans, and Tax Credits

Connection Fee Discount and "Cash for Grass": Residents of Glendale, Arizona, can receive a $100 cash rebate for installing or converting more than half of their landscapable area to non-grass vegetation. The Glendale Water Conservation Office conducts an inspection of the converted lawn to ensure compliance with rebate requirements and then issues a rebate check to the homeowner. Similarly, the City of El Paso, Texas has a Turf Rebate program that provides $1 per square foot of grass converted (USEPAOW, 2002b; EPWU, 2004).

Grants from Water Wholesalers: The Metropolitan Water District of Southern California's 'Innovative Conservation Program' provides grants to test and develop new water conserving technologies. Other programs, such the City Makeover Program established in 2003, provide grants for water conservation projects and offer rebates to residents and businesses to encourage water efficiency. Since 1988, MWD has funded more than 1.6 million ultra-low-flow toilets, creating savings in excess of 68 billion liters (18 billion gallons) per year. Businesses can receive rebates for installing cooling towers, water-pressurized brooms, and re-circulating systems (MWDSC, 2004).

Education and Demonstration Programs

All over North America, cities such as Denver, Palo Alto, Tucson, Vancouver, and New York City have education and information programs providing literature on water-efficient products and appliances, and water-efficient landscaping. (See also Chapter 4: Greening the City for more water-efficient gardening initiatives.)

Public Education: Colorado Springs Utilities sponsors a public Xeriscape Demonstration Garden and the "Xeriscape Beautiful" garden contest. They also offer courses on water and energy conservation, online "Efficiency Profile" tools and financing for home efficiency improvements (Colorado Springs Utilities, 2003).

Toilet Demonstration Program: The Massachusetts Water Resources Authority implemented a municipal toilet demonstration program installing a thousand 6 liter- (1.6 gallon-) per-flush toilets in municipal buildings in 28 communities. The goal was to familiarize the public with ultra-low-flow toilets, and to monitor the water savings and toilet performance. The Authority also sponsors workshops, trade show presentations, and provides printed information to educate plumbers, building facilities engineers, and maintenance personnel to increase acceptance of water-conserving products and devices.

Leak Detection and Repair Programs

Community Services and Environmental Education Program: New York City's Department of Environmental Protection offers a Residential Water Survey Program, providing free leak inspections and reports, as well as showerheads and aerators to residential customers. By 2002, more than 350,000 housing units had been surveyed by the program. The City has also set up a hot line for reporting leaks and water wastage, and has established a set of Water Use Restrictions with penalties of up to US$1,000 for non-compliance (NYCDCP, 2002; NYCDEP, 2002).

Leak Detection Program: Boston and New York conduct Leak Detection Programs. Thousands of leaks have been discovered in the cities' water mains and in 2003 alone repairs by New York's Leak Detection Unit saved an additional 225 million liters (60 million gallons) of water per day. Additional benefits are protecting the sewer lines from leakage infiltration and associated increases in wastewater flows (NYCDEP, 2003).

Rate Restructuring, Metering Programs, and User Fees

Surcharge: In the late 1990s, Los Angeles began requiring irrigators of large turf areas (i.e., in excess of 1.2 hectares or 3 acres) to reduce their outdoor water use by 10 percent compared to water consumption rates in 1986. Those who did not comply were charged a surcharge which increased by 10 percent monthly to a maximum of 100 percent. Most people have complied.

Ten-Year Program to Install Meters: Starting in 1988, this program focused on all buildings in New York City. By 2002 meters had been installed in 94 percent of the City, and those properties that have refused to meter have been assessed with a 100 percent

A naturalized fountain

surcharge on their annual flat-rate water/sewer bill (NYCDCP, 2002).

Increasing Block Rates: The city of Flagstaff, Arizona has used its rate structure as a conservation tool. It has a three tiered inclining block structure for single family homes that increases costs for high water users. Similar programs in Tuscon, Arizona, resulted in a 94.7-liter (25-gallon) per-capita per-day reduction in water use (13 percent) (Pinkham & Davis, 2002).

Sliding-Scale Hookup Fee Program: In Sacramento, CA, sewer hook-up fees are based on location, reflecting the distance-dependent costs associated with sewer service and encouraging development in central locations. In 2004 the cost for hooking up a house in a new neighbourhood was US$5,255 whereas in existing urban areas the cost was only US$2,314. Other sliding-scale programs in US states charge fees for hook-up proportional to the anticipated water use, resulting in rebates for installing water-efficient fixtures and applicances (USEPA, 2004).

Permits, Bylaws, and Ordinances

Many communities have established standards for water-efficient building products, fixtures, and water offset requirements for new development. In some places, city policies dictate efficient landscaping and irrigation practices.

Developers Required to Replace Old Toilets: In existing buildings in San Luis Obispo, Santa Barbara and Santa Monica, California, developers must replace old toilets with low-flow models to offset the water that will be required by new buildings.

Water-Wasting Ordinance: Clark County, Las Vegas Valley (Nevada) Water District adopted a water wasting ordinance that makes it illegal to allow water to flow into a gutter or storm drain for more than 20 consecutive minutes. On the first day of the ordinance, the city reported 310 water wasters.

Model Water-Efficient Landscape Ordinance: In 1992, the California Department of Water Resources adopted a Model Water-Efficient Landscape Ordinance. Development projects use a water budget approach to designing, installing, maintaining and evaluating the water efficiency of landscaping. Cities and counties may adopt this state model or develop an ordinance based on this model.

Land-Use Planning for Water Conservation

Comprehensive Plan: The County of Santa Barbara established a policy within its Comprehensive Plan that requires development applicants to demonstrate an adequate supply of services. and resources, including water. If any improvements or expansions are needed in order to cope with increased demand, the developer must finance those improvements. This encourages developers to look beyond their own subdivisions to realize the impact of growth on water supplies, and to seek ways to minimize new demand. The county also assesses potential environmental impacts, such as groundwater recharge rates, of proposed developments.

Regulatory and Incentive Programs

Audits, Restructured Rates, Rationing, and Education: In 1994, Albuquerque New Mexico adopted a comprehensive Water Resources Management Strategy, which

included plans to reclaim wastewater and shallow groundwater for irrigation and other non-potable uses, as well as
implementing an aggressive water conservation program
funded by increased water rates. Program elements included a summer water rate surcharge, rebates for efficient toilet
and washer upgrades, free water audits, and a Xeriscape
incentive program. They also required high-volume users to
implement water conservation programs and adopted an
ordinance restricting outdoor water use. By the end of 2001,
per-capita water use had dropped to 775 liters (205 gallons)
per day from 945 liters (250 gallons) per day in 1995, and
peak water use had declined 14 percent from 1990 levels
(USEPAOW, 2002a).

WATER QUALITY AND SEWAGE TREATMENT

The quality of water affects the quality of the life it touches.
Both groundwater and surface water systems have deterio-
rated in quality in many urban areas. Water pollution in combination with a too rapid
rate of water extraction can cause serious harm to hydrological systems. Wastewater
treatment is a particular concern in many communities, and conventional wastewater
treatment technologies are major environmental polluters on at least three fronts:

- they produce an often-toxic byproduct called sludge which is difficult to dispose of;
- they use hazardous compounds in the treatment process that end up in the
  environment; and
- without massive federal subsidies, most communities cannot afford to build
  and operate advanced wastewater treatment facilities.

In many North American cities, storm water and sewage are combined and sent to
wastewater treatment facilities. Often during heavy rains, such systems overflow, sending raw sewage directly into rivers and streams. Efficient use of water can also improve
water quality by helping reduce loads on sewage treatment plants. Treatment plants
and septic tanks work better with reduced flows because detention time can be
increased if plants aren't overburdened. Efficiency can further benefit water quality by
avoiding a draw on water supplies, which can cause seepage of saltwater or soil contaminants from agricultural pesticides or fertilizers, landfills, toxic-waste sites, or
sewage lines.

Water quality is also affected by pollution from agriculture, industry, households,
automobiles, and sedimentation from cleared land. Reducing pollution and preventing degradation to the quality of our water is the most sustainable way to preserve this
precious resource, which requires changes in our patterns of land use, auto dependency, and economic activities. While there are many efforts in this direction, this section
will primarily discuss "end of the pipe" strategies for wastewater treatment.

Water Quality and Land Use

"While it is commonly recognized that specific activities such as sewage treatment or paper processing can be notorious water polluters, it is less widely understood that whole categories of land use are also inherent threats to water quality. For example, car-dominated urban areas contaminate stormwater runoff with salt, oil, and toxic fluids from roads and parking lots. Suburbs allow large amounts of chemical fertilizers and pesticides to runoff golf courses and large lawns. Construction sites from which trees and other natural vegetation are stripped add large amounts of eroded soil to runoff. Often, stormwater from cities and suburbs — together with agricultural runoff containing chemicals and animal wastes — constitute a greater hazard to water quality than factories and other specific sources do" (Lowe, 1991).

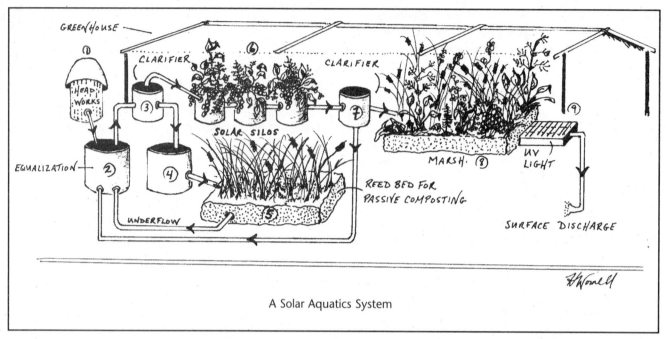

A Solar Aquatics System

Sewage treatment plants themselves are major contributors to water pollution, as many cities only have primary treatment (settling tanks that remove two-thirds of suspended solids and one-third of the biological oxygen demand) of waste, so contaminants are discharged in local waterways causing degradation of aquatic systems and fish. Other urban areas provide secondary treatment, removing most of the biological oxygen demand and suspended solids. However, very few plants conduct tertiary treatment to purify wastewater before discharge. The high monetary cost of treatment precludes these efforts, yet the true cost of degradation to the ecosystem and deteriorating water quality and fish stocks may be greater to communities. Sustainable water management aims to treat effluent at its pollution source, thus the polluter is responsible for avoiding or eliminating water contamination. The goal is also to treat wastewater so that it is as high or higher quality than water coming into urban water systems.

Many strategies are available for reducing wastewater and improving water quality through reclamation and reuse of treated wastewater (instead of discharging it to waterways). In California alone, over 600 million cubic meters (500,000 acre-feet) of water is reused each year for irrigation, industrial cooling and processing, and groundwater recharge (CSWRCB, 2003). In some cases, treated wastewater is applied directly to the land with treatment standards less stringent than those required for drinking water. The nutrient-rich wastewater can be used as fertilizer and applied to forests, agricultural crops, parks, or golf courses. Water is filtered as it is stored in the vegetated soils and woodlands, and percolates through the ground to recharge water tables. Another strategy for minimizing demand for potable water supplies is to use seawater for industrial processes, such as cooling.

Use of aquatic plants, marshes or wetlands is an effective, yet little known way of processing wastewater. Marshland is effective at absorbing nitrates and phosphates, and sedimentation and filtration also help to purify water. Some developers and communities are using existing marshes, or constructing artificial wetlands or solar aquatic systems (SAS) for wastewater treatment.

SAS is a biologically integrated technology that treats sludge, sewage, and industrial process wastewater to high quality specifications at low cost. It uses plants and micro-organisms in greenhouses to filter and consume contaminants. SAS mimic wetlands in processing waste, but are typically more compact so more waste can be processed in a smaller area. The water is purified and could be reused, but in North America, fear of system failure precludes reuse of SAS-treated water, so the clean water is typically discharged or used for irrigation.

Inside the solar aquatic waste treatment facility in Providence, Rhode Island

In addition to providing ecologically responsible ways of processing sewage without toxic chemicals, wetlands and SAS can serve as recreational amenities, bird sanctuaries and tourist attractions. Other ecological water management strategies can also be integrated into urban design and landscaping. Pavement and other impermeable surfaces increase run-off in urban areas. In some communities, instead of using culverts or underground storm drains, run-off is managed through permeable surface drainage and overland flow in creeks and swales (vegetated surface channels for runoff). Water quality is improved as percolation through soil and vegetation helps to purify water before it reaches rivers and reservoirs, and it can also help reduce erosion and sedimentation. Another economical way of controlling and purifying run-off is through retention ponds and lakes. Pollutants from rain, paved surfaces, and rooftops settle out, and flow is modified, helping to avoid "shock loads" during periods of wet weather (Hough, 1995).

TOOLS AND INITIATIVES

Water monitoring programs

Hot Spots Remediation Project: The Baynes Sound Hot Spots Remediation Project (1996-1998) involved dozens of local volunteers conducting stormwater monitoring programs of drains around Comox and Courtenay on Vancouver Island, British Columbia. Concern over water pollution impacting both residents and local shellfish promoted the cooperative initiative between community mem-

The Solar Aquatic System™, or SAS, mimics the natural water purification processes of freshwater wetlands

bers and government ministries. In Courtenay, the test discovered that excessively high fecal counts were caused by ten household lines that had mistakenly been connected to storm drains.

Education and Information Programs

Stewardship Initiative: The Baynes Sound Stewardship Initiative began with provincial and local government agencies, but grew to include more than 60 volunteers from the community who help clean up water contamination in the local watershed. Volunteers distribute information on septic system care, and educate citizens about what should enter storm drains. One local group, Citizens for Action on Recycling and the Environment, organized "septic socials." Local residents attended summer barbecues hosted by neighbors that mixed a party atmosphere with informal talk about septic system management. Says group member Dick Drake, "If we called it a workshop, we'd lose 90 percent of the audience. The socials have become so popular, sometimes we have trouble getting people to go home."

Nature Interpretive Centre: The Toronto Board of Education established the Nature Interpretive Centre at the Boyne Conservation Area in Ontario. A small SAS in the building functions both as a treatment system for the center's wastewater and a learning tool for students.

Pollutant Reduction: By reducing the amount of pollutants needing treatment, the small town of Alekulla, Sweden was able to avoid expansion of their near capacity sewage treatment plant. In spring 1989, each resident was given free samples of low phosphate cleansers and detergents, and the local shop began selling those same products. As a result, the phosphate levels in the domestic wastewater was reduced by more than 50 percent.

Bylaws, Ordinances and Performance Standards

Wastewater Bylaw: Standards for maximum acidity levels and concentration of certain toxic substances discharged into the treatment system are set by the Greater Vancouver Sewerage and Drainage District (GVS&DD). The Sewer Use Bylaw requires any operation that discharges more than 300 cubic meters (10,500 cubic feet) within a 30-day period to have a permit specifying allowable concentration levels of various substances (GVS&DD, 2000).

Industrial and Commercial Standards: Standards for industrial and commercial polluters have been set by a program in Stockholm, Sweden since the 1960s. The standards have forced many industries to introduce new technologies for treating pollutants at source. For example, the graphics industry and photo processing must separate and treat all fixing solutions and other chemical solutions instead of discharging into sewage system, and dentists must use amalgam separators to remove mercury from their waste streams.

Taxes and Charges

Run-off Charge: Bellevue Utilities in Bellevue, Washington, manages storm and surface water systems to protect water quality and wildlife habitat. They believe water quality is determined by run-off quantity, so they charge landowners for the amount of runoff. Calculations are based on development intensity and impervious surface area (vegetated and unpaved land areas have less run-off than impervious areas with the same activities on site) (BUD, 2004).

Public/Private Partnerships

Wastewater Reclamation Plant: The East Bay Municipal Utility District and Chevron USA Inc. partnered to build a wastewater reclamation plant. East Bay financed construction of the $17 million treatment plant in North Richmond, while Chevron financed improvement of pipelines and associated facilities to convey reclaimed municipal wastewater to the company's refinery in Richmond, California for use in industrial cooling.

Treated Wastewater for Farming: About 72 million liters (19 million gallons) of treated wastewater is delivered to 769 hectares (1,900 acres) of city-owned farmland every day in Tallahassee, Florida. The city contracts out the farm operations to a private operator who grows and markets a variety of crops.

Land-Use Planning for Water and Wastewater Management

Grass Paving: The city required developers to manage run-off for their shopping mall and parking area development in Hartford, Connecticut. The projected cost for construction of a retention pond was more than $1 million, so instead the developers chose grass paving which cost about $500,000. This was more expensive than conventional paving, but the permeable surface parking lot (made of grass interspersed with paved sections) accommodated run-off effectively, thus eliminating the need to construct a detention pond.

Swales Instead of Culverts: In the early 1970s, developers Michael and Judy Corbett struggled to get approval for swales instead of culverts for storm water run-off at the subdivision they were building in Davis, California. By incorporating the swales into the landscaping they saved money and improved drainage performance. The use of swales and other permeable surface open water drainage channels are now recognized and accepted as best practices for storm water management (USEPA, 1999).

County Land Purchase: To protect a sensitive groundwater recharge area from development, Suffolk County, Long Island, New York spent $118 million to acquire 3,400 hectares (8,398 acres) of open space. The groundwater feeds the county's potable water supply (Brown, 1993).

Master Plans and Programs for Wastewater Management and Reclamation

Dual Distribution System: Palo Alto, California developed a Water Reclamation Master Plan which calls for a dual distribution system for large turf areas (such as golf courses and parks) that uses a blend of treated and reclaimed water. This system saves millions of gallons of treated water per year as the reclaimed water provides a portion of irrigation needs.

Water Reclamation and Reuse Programs: New York City's 2004 Comprehensive Water Re-use Program (CWRP) provides a 25 percent reduction in water service rates for property owners who treat and re-use water on-site for non-potable uses. In Florida, treated or reclaimed water is used for irrigation, wetlands creation, recharging groundwater, and urban non-potable uses such as toilet flushing, car washing and decorative lakes and fountains (NYCDEP, 2004; SFWMD, 2004).

Biological Sewage Treatment Facility: Denham Springs, Louisiana runs its processed sewage through two shallow 16-hectare (40-acre) ponds that have been lined, carpeted with stones, filled with water, and planted with lilies and other plants. Although it looks like a flower farm in summer, the biological sewage treatment facility can treat over 11 million liters (3 million gallons) of sewage per day. Compared with conventional processing, the city saved $1 million in initial construction costs and saves approximately $60,000 per year on operation and maintenance (MacLeish, 1990; Marinelli, 1990).

Wastewater for Community Economic Development

SAS Greenhouse: Bear River, Nova Scotia constructed a 303,030-liter (80,000-gallon) SAS providing sewage treatment for over 45 houses and discharging tertiary treated water to the local river. Instead of hiding the wastewater treatment plant on the edge of town they positioned it as a tourist attraction in the heart of town. Residents have benefited from the estimated 1,500 new visitors per year drawn by the SAS, as well as cleaner water and reduced greenhouse gas emissions estimated at 5,600 kg (12,300 lbs) per year (CMHC, 2000).

INTEGRATED RESOURCE PLANNING

Water-efficiency and ecologically responsible ways of managing water quality and wastewater are key to sustainable urban development, but there are a number of barriers to progress. One of the greatest barriers is the departmentalization of city, municipal or regional water and wastewater services. In many communities, water and wastewater treatment departments are totally separate; their staff, boards, billing, budgets, and goals should be coordinated so that mutual goals can be achieved while saving costs and reducing impact on the ecosystem. A planning department may issue building permits, while the water and sewage departments are worrying about water supply infrastructure, water quality and capacity for sewage treatment.

Integrated Resource Planning or Integrated Water Planning is a nontraditional planning and management strategy for long-range water resource issues that considers all water uses and water-related activities, within whatever political, administrative, economic, or functional boundaries they are defined (Child and Armour, 1995). It requires inter-governmental cooperation and strives for multiple-purpose and multiple-means projects including: use of zoning and other land-use management strategies; regulations; incentive programs; taxation; and whatever else works to achieve multiple goals for provision of water and sewage services, and other objectives (such as energy-efficiency, recreation, flood control, wildlife preservation, irrigation, and even economic development).

Integrated resource planning opens the door for community economic development and job creation associated with sustainable development. For example, while reducing operating and infrastructure costs for communities, many water-efficiency programs can create jobs and stimulate markets for water conserving products and technologies. SAS can offer other opportunities for jobs and economic benefits from tourism and educational programs, and it is possible to combine production of flowers, plants and herbs with greenhouse operations of a SAS.

TOOLS AND INITIATIVES

Public Involvement in Decision Making: In the 1980s, the Denver, Colorado Water Board began plans for the Two Forks Dam and Reservoir project. Environmentalists and citizens groups balked at the plans, and persuaded the federal government to veto the project in 1991, in favor of more cost-effective and environmentally benign water-efficiency initiatives. As a result, the Water Board adopted an Integrated Resource Planning process, publishing a public information newsletter, conducting workshops, participating in public forums and receiving input from a citizens' advisory council, as well as from stakeholder groups. According to Peter Johnson, former Director of the Bonneville Power Administration, "By involving the public in the decision-making process itself, we gained authority and legitimacy, avoiding costly lawsuits and political challenges, and arrived at creative solutions to seemingly intractable problems" (Jones, 1994; Denver Water, 2002).

Conservation Avoids Dam Construction: Ashland, Oregon initiated a Water Conservation program in 1991 to avoid the construction of a new dam. By 1994, the water conservation program had achieved daily water savings of over 1 million liters (290,000 gallons), delaying the need for an increased water supply until 2021. In addition to avoiding the cost of a US$12-million dam, the program has saved residents 514 MWh annually in avoided water heating as well as reducing wastewater volume by 162 million litres (43 million gallons) per year (Lealess, 1996).

RESOURCES

American Water Works Association is an international, nonprofit scientific and educational society dedicated to the improvement of drinking water quality and supply, and the largest organization of water supply professionals in the world. Website: www.awwa.org/

Canadian Water Resources Association is a national organization of individuals and organizations interested in the management of Canada's water resources. Website: www.cwra.org

Ecological Engineering Group purchased the rights to the SAS technology and markets it and other septic-sewer alternatives. They provide wastewater treatment plant design, engineering, construction and operating services. Website: www.ecological-engineering.com/

Environmental Protection Agency's Office of Water has a website that provides guidelines, standards, reports, and case studies on water quality and management with links to other sites. Website: www.epa.gov/ow/

Metropolitan Water District of Southern California is a consortium of 26 cities and water districts that provides drinking water to nearly 18 million people. An example of successful Integrated Resource Planning, the MWDSC website provides excellent educational resources and information on innovative water reuse and conservation programs. Website: www.mwdh2o.com/

The Water Stewards Network and Ocean Arks International is an organization associated with Ocean Arks international that is concerned about the mismanagement of water resources. Dr. John Todd of Ocean Arks originally developed the SAS. Websites: www.oceanarks.org/and www.waterstewards.org/

US National Environmental Services Center (NESC) provides information about drinking water, wastewater, environmental training, and solid waste management in communities serving fewer than 10,000 individuals. NESC programs include the **National Small Flows Clearinghouse (NSFC)**, which provides information on wastewater systems and the **National Drinking Water Clearinghouse (NDWC)**, which provides answers to water quality questions. Website: www.nesc.wvu.edu

WaterWiser is a partnership between the government and private sector which seeks to be the preeminent resource for water efficiency and water conservation information. Website: www.waterwiser.org

REFERENCES

Brown, L. 1993. *State of the World 1993*. New York: W.W. Norton and Co.: 35-41.

Bellevue Utilities Department (BUD). 2004. *Storm and surface water services and charges*. Available from www.ci.bellevue.wa.us/departments/Utilities/files/stormq&aforweb.doc

California State Water Resources Control Board (SWRCB). 2003. *2002 Municipal wastewater recycling survey*. Available from www.swrcb.ca.gov/recycling/recyfund/munirec/index.html

Canadian Mortgage and Housing Corporation (CMHC). 2000. *Canada's first solar aquatics facility tourist attraction*. Available from www.cmhc-schl.gc.ca/en/imquaf/himu/buin_31.cfm

Child, M, and A. Armour. 1995. "Integrated Water Resource Planning in Canada: Theoretical Considerations and Observations From Practice." *Canadian Water Resources Journal* 20(2).

City of Mesa. 2003. *Water development fee rebate*. Available from www.cityofmesa.org/utilities/conservation/landscape_rebate.asp

Colorado Springs Utilities. 2003. *Conservation*. Available from www.csu.org/environment/conservation/index.html

Denver Water. 2002. *Water for tomorrow — an integrated water resource plan*. (PDF file) Available from:www.denverwater.org/aboutdw/MasterDocIRPOnline.pdf

El Paso Water Utility (EPWU). 2004. *Conservation — turf rebate*. Available from: www.epwu.org/turf.html

Everett Public Works. n.d. *Water conservation plan*. Available from City of Everett (WA) website: www.everettwa.org/community/default.asp?sectionid=3&parentid=2&subid=1

Greater Vancouver Sewerage and Drainage District (GVS&DD). 2000. *Sewer use bylaw no. 164*. (PDF file) Available from: www.gvrd.bc.ca/sewerage/pdf/SewerUseBylaw164.pdf

Hough, M. 1995. *Cities and Natural Processes*. London/New York: Routledge.

Jones, A. 1994. *Public Involvement In Water Management.* Rocky Mountain Institute.

Lowe, M.D. 1991. "Shaping Cities: The Environmental and Human Dimensions." Worldwatch Paper 105. Washington, DC: Worldwatch Institute.

MacLeish, W.H. 1990. "Water, Water, Everywhere, How Many Drops to Drink?" *World Monitor.* December: 54-58.

Marinelli, J. 1990. "After the Flush: The Next Generation." *Garbage,* Jan/Feb: 24-35.

Metropolitan Water District of Southern California (MWDSC). 2004. *Conservation and the environment.* Available from: www.mwdh2o.com/mwdh2o/pages/conserv/conserv01.html

Mono Lake Committee. 2004. *Ultra-low flush toilet program.* Available from the Mono Lake Committee website: www.monolake.org/socalwater/ultralow.htm

National Round Table on the Environment and the Economy (NRTEE). 1996. *Water and Wastewater Services in Canada.*

New York City Department of City Planning (NYCDCP). 2002. *Chapter seven — housing and infrastructure in 2002 annual report on social indicators.* (PDF file) Available from www.nyc.gov/html/dcp/html/pub/socind02.html

New York City Department of Environmental Protection (NYCDEP). 2002. *Drought response.* Available from www.nyc.gov/html/dep/html/drought.html

New York City Department of Environmental Protection (NYCDEP). 2003. *New York City 2003 Drinking Water Supply and Quality Report.* (PDF file) Available from www.ci.nyc.ny.us/html/dep/pdf/wsstat03.pdf

New York City Department of Environmental Protection (NYDEP). 2004. *City introduces innovative new comprehensive water re-use program — April 2, 2004 press release.* Available from www.nyc.gov/html/dep/html/press/04-16pr.html

Pinkham, R., & Davis, B. 2002. *North Central Arizona Water Demand Study Phase 1 Report.* (PDF file) Available from the Rocky Mountain Institute library at www.rmi.org/sitepages/pid172.php

Roseland, M., and M. Jacobs. 1995. "Sustainable Development, Economic Instruments, and the Sustainable Management of Aquatic Resources and Ecosystems: A New Framework for Water Management in the Fraser Basin." Burnaby, BC: Science Council of BC.

Sherry Lealess. 1996. *Resource conservation in Ashland, Oregon.* Case study Available from Tools of Change at www.toolsofchange.com/English/CaseStudies/default.asp?ID=106

South Florida Water Management District (SFWMD). 2004. *Water reuse / reclaimed water.* Available from www.sfwmd.gov/org/wsd/wsconservation/waterreuse.html

United States Environmental Protection Agency (USEPA). 1999. *Urban storm water best management practices study.* (PDF file) Available from www.epa.gov/ost/stormwater/

United States Environmental Protection Agency, Office of Water (USEPAOW) 2002a. *Cases in water conservation: How efficiency programs help water utilities save water and avoid costs.* (PDF file) Available from www.epa.gov/owm/water-efficiency/utilityconservation.pdf

United States Environmental Protection Agency, Office of Water (USEPAOW). 2002b. *Water efficient landscaping — preventing pollution and using resources wisely.* (PDF file) Available from www.epa.gov/owm/water-efficiency/final_final.pdf

United States Environmental Protection Agency (USEPA). 2004. *Protecting water resources with smart growth.* (PDF file) Available from www.epa.gov/smartgrowth/pdf/waterresources_with_sg.pdf

CHAPTER 6

WASTE REDUCTION AND RECYCLING

Despite a growing awareness of the three "Rs" — reduce, reuse, recycle — North Americans produce an embarrassing amount of solid and hazardous waste. The US alone produced 483 million tons of solid waste in 2002 and per capita municipal solid waste rates are still climbing, despite the fact that more than 100 million Americans now recycle (Kaufman, Goldstein, Millrath, & Themelis, 2004; Lombardi & Goldstein, 2001). Until recent years, the conventional method of managing our waste stream was to bury it in a local dump or sanitary landfill located on the fringe of a community. In the late 1960s, higher regulatory standards and public resistance to facility siting began to create problems in accessing affordable landfill space (Blumberg and Gottlieb, 1989; Young, 1991). Solid waste management responded to these issues with "end-of-the-pipe" solutions such as incineration and export of wastes. Efforts focused on waste diversion, which simply cleans up the mess rather than preventing it in the first place. This approach neglects other options in the principles of waste management, which actually includes four Rs in a hierarchy of preferred options: reduce, reuse, recycle, and recover (RCBC, 1994b). Recovery and recycling are ranked as the lowest priorities, yet energy recovery (incineration for use as a fuel supply) and recycling programs have blossomed across the continent, while little has been done to promote source reduction or materials reuse.

The irony of the waste diversion strategy is that it only delays the onset of landfill crises in communities across the continent (RCBC, 1994b). Reuse and reduction offer the greatest opportunities for eliminating pollution and depletion of natural resources, yet they are often perceived to be at odds with economic development. How does a community (or business or individual) prosper by reducing and reusing? This may require a paradigm shift in perceptions of wealth, economic development, and quality of life, or at the very least, a more comprehensive means of measuring costs and benefits. Let us explore some of the elements of the waste management hierarchy.

SOURCE REDUCTION

The best way to reduce waste is by not creating it in the first place. Arguably, "re-think" should be at the top of any waste management hierarchy. As a society we need to rethink our indicators for quality of life. Current measures of success can be summed up in a bumpersticker: "the one who dies with the most toys wins." However, there is a vast difference between standard of living and quality of life. New indicators, such as how much time we spend with our friends and families, and how many walks we take per week, can replace our consumer-oriented lifestyles while enhancing our quality of life. By re-thinking our consumer habits, we may realize we just don't need so much *stuff!* This may be the ultimate way to achieve source reduction.

More typically, the definition of source reduction refers to reducing the amount of waste and byproducts that enter the waste stream. This can be done by: industries modifying processes and procedures to reduce the amount of waste associated with product manufacture; government offices and businesses choosing to double-side photocopy and correspond electronically; and consumers avoiding packaging at the store.

Source reduction strategies are available in all categories of the waste stream: agriculture, construction and demolition, industrial hazardous, industrial non-hazardous, mining, oil and gas, and municipal solid waste. Municipal solid waste typically consists of consumer discards such as durable and non-durable goods, containers and packaging, food scraps, yard trimmings, and miscellaneous organic and non-organic items. Municipal solid waste flows from households, commercial establishments such as stores and restaurants, institutions, office and support operations in industrial sectors. However, a large percentage of solid waste produced in the US and Canada is not directly generated by consumers. Despite being the focus of much public concern, municipal solid waste represents less than 2 percent of all solid waste regulated under the Recycling and Resource Recovery Act (World Resources Institute, 1993). Most waste production originates in the manufacturing and distribution phases of production of consumer products. Therefore opportunities for source reduction in municipal solid waste begin before products are even manufactured — citizens can choose to reduce the amount of waste they produce by changing their consumption choices and patterns.

For cities and towns, source reduction translates into lower costs for municipal waste management services and less burden on local landfills. For business and industry (and even government offices), source reduction can mean thousands, even millions, of dollars in savings by avoiding disposal costs. In an era of downsizing and budget cutbacks, businesses simply cannot afford to waste resources, and source reduction may be the most cost-effective means of reducing waste.

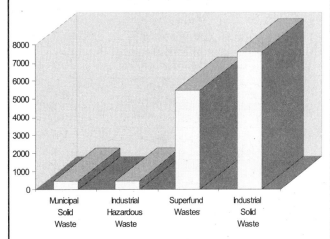

US Solid Waste and Its Sources
(output per year)

Source: Council on Environmental Quality, *United States of America National Report* (prepared for the United Nations Conference on Environment and Development, 1992). Exhibit 6h.1, p.333 — from World Resources Institute (1993), *The 1993 Information Please Environmental Almanac*

Note: Superfund (Resource Conservation and Recovery Act) wastes include discards from oil and gas operations (1.5 billion tons), mining (3.6 billion tons) cement kiln dust (4 million tons), and electric utility wastes (8.5 million tons)

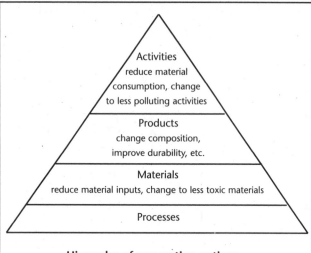

Hierarchy of preventive options

From Hirschhorn, J., T. Jackson, and L. Baas, "Toward Prevention: The Emerging Environmental Management Paradigm," in T. Jackson, Ed., *Clean Production Strategies*, Ann Arbor: Lewis Publishers, 1993

Product life-cycle and cradle-to-grave management are two systemic approaches to encourage source reduction. Conventional waste management is designed as if solid and hazardous wastes emerge out of nowhere, with no connection to previous actions and decisions, except those of the final consumer. Yet every product has a life history which remains generally unknown to the consumer, *and* unaccounted for by our economy. A product's life has many stages, beginning on the drawing board of the industrial designer, and continuing through resource extraction, manufacturing, retailing, purchase or consumption, and disposal. At each of these stages wastes may be produced, compounding the total ecological impacts of the product. Life-cycle analysis reveals the opportunities to reduce waste at each of these stages.

Cradle-to-grave management is a way of assigning responsibility for a product so the producer considers the pollution and waste associated with the product after it leaves the manufacturing plant. Responsibility for solid and hazardous waste starts at the beginning of the product's life when brand owners and designers make choices to determine the extent of environmental impact a product will have throughout its life cycle. They decide, for example, on the composition of the product, its durability, toxicity, and potential for reuse and recycling. Cradle-to-grave management is yet to gain widespread acceptance in North America, but 30 nations have implemented "Take Back" laws that place the financial or physical responsibility on industry for end-of-life management of their products and packaging (Lombardi & Goldstein, 2001).

Life-cycle analysis reveals the benefits of more durable goods for source reduction. When products last longer, we don't throw them away and replace them with another. Responsible product stewardship will encourage design and manufacture of products that have extendable lives, by being durable as well as reusable, repairable, and remanufacturable (or recyclable). The true cost of using hazardous substances are revealed as manufacturers bear the burden of disposal or diversion. Faced with reclamation, producers may find alternative ways to manufacture products. Communities can use regulatory measures, education programs, or technical assistance programs to help industry reduce toxic wastes.

REUSE

Reuse is another under-utilized component of the waste hierarchy. When waste is considered a resource and opportunities are sought for reuse, the life of products, packaging and other materials are extended and reduce waste. The possibilities and the potential to link job training with reuse and repair businesses are endless. Local governments can provide special zoning, financial incentives, and information to encourage reuse, lease and rental businesses.

We are far better at making waste than at making products. For every 100 pounds of products we manufacture in the United States, we create at least 3,200 pounds of waste (Hawken, 1997).

Recognizing the potential savings — both financial and environmental — some businesses are starting their own initiatives to reuse products and materials. In 2000, over 4.6 million tons of copy paper was shipped in the US. Environmental Defense has initiated a partnership with Citigroup to reduce the environmental impacts of copy paper. The two organizations are working together to increase the recycled content in copy paper, reduce copy paper use, and develop environmental evaluation criteria for paper suppliers (Environmental Defense, 2003).

By identifying the *service* needed instead of the *product*, many businesses have leased and rented their office equipment, recognizing savings in maintenance, repair, and upgrading costs. Reuse also offers business opportunities. Over 150 Habitat for Humanity ReStores exist in North America, selling quality new and used building materials to the public at significant discounts. In doing so, ReStores create a link between those who have good quality materials they no longer need, and those who use these materials for the renovation and upkeep of their homes (Center for Ecological Technology).

Reused, repaired, and rental goods are important players in facilitating a shift from a product-based economy to a service-based economy; not only does the local economy expand, but waste destined for the landfill diminishes. Using the example of businesses leasing office equipment, is it unreasonable to imagine widespread support for leasing/rental options for other goods? Interface Incorporated leases all its carpets in tile form and then recycle the materials. They aim to be the first truly sustainable company by 2020 (Interface, Inc.).

Bottle-deposit legislation provides a powerful mechanism for reuse and recycling, with successful implementation by the beer industry for years. On average, a beer bottle is reused 15-20 times before being reprocessed into a new bottle. The resulting energy savings are enormous. Bills requiring refillable bottles for certain types of beverage containers emerged in the early 1970s. Despite the environmental benefits of bottle reuse, industry has promoted and proliferated disposable bottles, rendering refillables out of style. As a result, many bottle-deposit systems simply recover materials to be recycled. As packaging and products have become increasingly diverse, a second generation of bottle-deposit legislation is needed to encompass a broader variety of beverage containers. The US could save about 600 thousand tons of aluminum metal annually if they implemented a national "bottle bill," and recycled 85 percent of their cans. In 30 years, the US has thrown in the trash over one trillion aluminum cans worth about $21 billion at today's market prices (Container Recycling Institute). The logic of deposits/refund can apply to most commodities; from large appliances to batteries.

The waste hauling and disposal industry has grown into a national oligopoly in which three firms dominate the collection, transfer and disposal markets, and react negatively towards recycling. These firms make ten times as much profit when disposing of waste compared to when they recycle materials (Seldman, 2003b).

BEVERAGE CONTAINER LITTER REDUCTIONS WITH DEPOSIT STRATEGY

Iowa 79%
Maine 86%
Mich. 41%
Vermont 76%
Oregon 83%
Calif. 45%
N.Y. 75%

Courtesy of the Recycling Council of British Columbia

A neighborhood recycling center

While reuse of consumer goods is an important waste management strategy, industrial reuse eliminates pollution and other byproducts from manufacturing processes. Many industries have had symbiotic relationships where wastes and materials are transformed internally or by others. For example, metal industries use scrap materials in the production process, and the growth of rubber, plastics, paper, and glass recycling industries has generated demand for previously discarded goods. "Industrial ecology" is the term used to describe a strategy for modeling industrial systems after ecological systems. In natural systems, very little is wasted. Industrial ecology strategies use one industry's wastes as another's raw materials. The goal is cost-savings and ecological responsibility through reuse to eliminate waste. Industrial waste exchanges are already in existence, and some communities in North America are planning eco-industrial parks where complementary businesses operate in the same industrial park to share byproducts and close the loop on industrial waste. (See also Chapter 12: Community Economic Development for more discussion of eco-industrial parks).

RECYCLING AND RECOVERY

It is easy to become confused about recycling given the barrage of information and media surrounding it. The term "recycling" is often used when only recovery or even collection are the activities taking place. Recovery refers to finding some way to extract energy or utility from waste materials. Waste-to-energy facilities that burn wastes for fuel to produce heat, or power for manufacturing processes, or electrical generation are popular options. However, while these facilities may reduce the use of fossil fuels, they often waste valuable resources, sending economic opportunities right up their smokestacks. Collection of recyclable materials, such as Blue Box programs, is the first step in a recycling program. Other mechanisms for capturing and collecting recyclable products and materials include bottle deposits, take-back programs, and eco-industrial parks. Ensuring cost-effective and environmentally sound recycling is another vital step in the waste management hierarchy.

Anti-recycling arguments also deserves further discussion. One argument, often supported by corporate interests, suggests that as more technologies become available for waste disposal, we will not need to go through the trouble or incur the costs of source separation and collection. This contention neglects to acknowledge benefits associated with recycling, including: reducing the extraction of virgin raw materials; creating new industries and jobs in local communities; and cost-savings. For example, in the area of paper manufacturing, mills recycling waste paper for newsprint, boxes, cartons, and other products may have lower capital and operating costs than new mills using virgin wood. The percentage of discarded materials recycled has risen from 5

If you're not buying recyclables, you're not recycling!

percent (8 million tons) in 1968 to 30 percent (75 million tons) today. Indeed recycling has become a part of daily life (Seldman, 2003), from only a few cities with curbside collection programs in 1970 to over 9000 programs in 2003.

Creating a strong market for recycled products is key to completing the recycling process and "closing the loop." Consumers close the loop when they purchase products made from recycled materials. Governments can promote buying recycled products through their own procurement programs and guidelines. Manufacturers can participate by using recycled materials in their products (USEPA, 2004).

Sacramento, California hosts an annual Recycled Products trade show to "showcase high-quality, competitively priced, recycled content and environmentally preferred products." Over 100 vendors display products ranging from office supplies to materials handling equipment, including Kelly Moore Paints (with 50 percent post consumer content) and US Cold Patch (a more environmentally friendly and longer lasting pothole repair compound) (Feinbaum, 2004).

COMPOSTING

Food residuals are often seen as a stand-alone component of waste management, but they too should be subject to the waste hierarchy. Berkley and San Francisco, California are increasingly relying on biodegradable bin liners to reduce contamination of non-biodegradable plastic bags in their commercial food scraps, food soiled paper, waxed cardboard, and plant materials. The bags have the potential to increase the collection of food scraps by more businesses ("Expanding Participation in Food Residuals Recycling Programs," 2004).

Local governments have discovered composting as a recycling technology that significantly reduces waste management costs and volumes. While some communities are offering curbside pick-up of yard wastes and food scraps, others are recognizing more cost-effective measures by providing low-or no-cost recycling bins for on-site recycling. Annapolis Royal, Nova Scotia has embarked on a "Zero Waste" by 2005 initiative. Using food- and waste-digesters (Green Cones) with more conventional back-yard composting units and "Earth Tubs", the majority of households and composting units now process all food and yard wastes. They estimate landfill diversion rates of 53 percent and have saved the town $15,000 per year by opting out of regional waste disposal (FCM, 2001b).

Restaurants, grocers, food manufacturers, breweries, and universities are only a sample of the kind of businesses and institutions that can reduce disposal volumes and costs through composting or other organic waste diversion strategies. Mid-scale in-situ composting technologies are offering options that were not previously available or affordable. Washington State University (WSU) collects and sells 24 different waste by-products maintaining composting and recycling rates near 53 percent. WSU composts 12,000 tons of organic material annually and is currently building a transportable, demonstration anaerobic digester that will convert dairy manure and municipal waste to biogas for electricity generation, and high-quality compost ("In Composting and Recycling, WSU gets 'A' for Effort," 2004).

The Blue Box has become the focus of attention over the past few years. It has become a convenient means for people to feel like they are doing something good for the environment. Although the Blue Box has increased the rate of diversion from local landfills, it has done little to promote source reduction or address over consumption. In addition, we must consider the distance the materials collected by Blue Box programs must travel to be processed (and associated impacts).

Who pays for curbside programs is also an important issue. Currently, most municipal recycling programs are funded by taxpayers, not industry. When local governments are forced to pay for recycling programs, recycling offers a hidden subsidy to industry, as they are able to continue making products without concern for the costs of disposal.

In 1968, the US recycling industry consisted of 8,000 companies that employed 79,000 people, with annual sales of 4.6 billion. By 2000, maintaining an average annual growth rate of 8.3 percent, 56,000 private and public facilities employed 1.1 million people and enjoyed 236 billion in annual sales (Seldman, 2003a).

TOOLS AND INITIATIVES

Education and Information

Guide and Directory: The Internet Consumer Recycling Guide provides a starting point for consumers in the USA and Canada searching for recycling information. The information is for regular folks with regular household quantities of materials to recycle. The goal is to help make recycling easy and automatic (Evergreen Industries & Obviously Enterprises, 2001).

Waste Reduction Awards Program: The California Waste Reduction Awards Program provides an opportunity for California businesses to gain public recognition for their outstanding efforts to reduce waste. The logo is used on products, in advertising, and on public educational materials to recognize waste-reduction efforts (California Integrated Waste Management Board).

Eco-Labelling: The European Union Eco-label is a voluntary scheme to provide manufacturers with an incentive to produce environmentally friendly products and services, while giving consumers the ability to differentiate their purchases on the basis of environmental criteria. Eco-labeling in the US and Canada still remains low (European Union Environment DG, 2004).

Precycle Program: Berkeley, California has a Precycle Program to encourage people to consider waste *before* they buy.

eCycling: eCycling is the reusing or recycling of consumer electronics. The National Safety Council projects that nearly 250 million computers will become obsolete in the next five years and by 2005 mobile phones will be discarded at a rate of 130 million per year (USEPA, 2004).

Collaboration and Partnerships

Reuse-A-Shoe: The US National Recycling Coalition and Nike have partnered to recycle all brands of athletic shoes into Nike Grind, a unique ground-up material that is used to resurface athletic fields, courts, tracks and playgrounds. Nike arranges for shipping once 5,000 pairs of shoes are collected, and shoes don't contain any metal (e.g., eyelets or cleats). Since the program began in 1993, 15 million pairs of shoes have been recycled (National Recycling Coalition).

Post-Consumer Innovation: Almost 140 North American publishers have agreed to eliminate the use of paper with Endangered Forest fiber. They are accomplishing this goal through meeting the following objectives within 3 to 5 years: 30 - 100 percent post-consumer recycled paper; processed chlorine free and a non-post-consumer recycled portion comprised of certified virgin pulp bleached using Processed Chlorine Free

(PCF) technologies; flax, straw, hemp,or kenaf; and fiber pulp verified to be free of endangered forest fiber (US Green Press Initiative).

Take-Back Program: The Rechargeable Battery Recycling Corporation (RBRC) started a nationwide take-back program, in 1994, for collection and recycling of used nickel-cadmium batteries, which includes all portable rechargeable battery chemistries. This is the first nationwide take-back program that involves an entire US industry (USEPA, 2004).

Economic Instruments

The most useful financial instruments, applied by national, provincial/state or local authorities, are those that target the production, manufacturing, and design stage of products. Disposal charges (tipping fees) help reflect true costs of disposal and recycling, and serve as financial incentives to reduce consumption.

Unit Charges: Charges can be levied to manufacturers to internalize recycling and disposal costs, or discourage use of certain products. British Columbia applies a $3-levy to used tires, in part to fund research and development for new uses for the discarded materials (RCBC, 1992a).

Tax credits: Financial incentives such as tax credits can encourage businesses to base their production on secondary (used or recycled) materials. California's Recycling Market Development Zones offer tax breaks to recycling-based businesses.

Deposit/Refunds: Deposits and refunds have been successfully used for beverage bottles for years, however the concept can be applied to other materials and products. Michigan recently passed legislation requiring a deposit system for nickel cadmium and mercury batteries. Consumers pay a $2-deposit, refundable when they return the battery, and retailers are responsible for delivering used batteries to an authorized disposal facility. A deposit on batteries helps rechargeable batteries become more cost-competitive.

In-House Waste Disposal Charge: Businesses and government can encourage waste reduction and recycling by implementing more accurate tracking of waste production and accounting for disposal costs. The City of Santa Monica (1996) charges each of their departments independently for waste disposal, creating an in-house incentive to decrease waste. Waste audits are an important tool that enable businesses and institutions to evaluate current practices and develop plans to minimize waste.

Pay As You Throw: Once limited to a few progressive communities, Pay As You Throw (PAYT) programs have spread to over 4200 communities serving over 27 million Americans. PAYT programs have decreased waste from 14 to 27 percent and increased recycling rates from 32 to 59 percent (Hui II, 1999).

Waste Taxes: Isolating the cost of disposal and recycling on tax bills highlights the costs to users and may provide an incentive to reduce. The City of Tulsa, Oklahoma developed a user-pay system charging waste taxes based on the amount of wastes generated. Waste taxes are charged monthly along with water/sewer taxes. If the waste portion of the bill is not paid, water service is halted. This provides an effective means of enforcement.

Variable Tipping Fees and Tax Incentives: Seattle uses both reduced tipping fees and tax incentives to encourage commercial recycling. The city charges no tip fees for loads of recyclables delivered to transfer stations. The per ton tip fee for a load of yard debris is 25 percent lower than the tip fee charged for trash delivered to these facilities. The city charges a tax on collection revenues, but excludes recycling collectables from this tax (USEPA, 1999).

Regulations and Legislation

Recycled Content Laws: Minimum recycled content requirements, such as those required by several states for certain paper products, create market opportunities for recyclables. In 1991, Germany passed a "refill law," whereby 72 percent of beverages must be sold in refillable containers (Fishbein and Saphire 1992).

Materials Ban for Landfill: Municipal governments can ban certain materials from local landfills to encourage recycling or avoid contamination of landfills by toxic wastes. The Greater Vancouver Regional District, BC banned gyprock (wallboard) from local landfills because under wet, oxygen-starved conditions it generates a toxic gas, hydrogen sulfide. Because extra charges are levied for disposal of this toxic waste, new local businesses have sprung up that recycle gyprock into new wallboard.

Post-Consumer Paint Stewardship Program: North America's first completely industry-funded collection program for paint began in British Columbia in 1994. A provincial regulation requires any company that sells paint to provide a stewardship program for old paint by providing return depots.

Germany's Green Dot System: Implemented in 1993, this system requires manufacturers, users, and distributors of packaging to take back used packaging from consumers for recycling. In order to sell in Germany, manufacturers *must* reduce the amount, weight, and dimensions of packaging to make less do more, reuse where possible, and make packaging easier to recycle. Even though packaging waste was reduced from 30 percent to 5 percent since 1990, Germany exports a large amount of its packaging waste to other countries because its recycling facilities cannot keep up (Dragicevic, 1997).

Guidelines, Policies, and Other Programs

Environmentally Preferable Purchasing (EPP): EPP is a concept that combines procurement and environmental sustainability into an environmentally conscious purchasing strategy. The program emphasizes the purchasing of recycled-content supplies, reducing the number of toxic chemicals, and minimizing energy consumption through more energy-efficient technologies (USEPA, 2001).

Development Permits and Building Codes: Permits and codes provide mechanisms to ensure builders and real estate developers incorporate waste reduction into their plans. Developers in Boulder, Colorado seeking residential building permits must score at least 20 points among several conservation categories. For example, designing homes and buildings that accommodate recycling (such as built-in recycling boxes in homes) earn two points. In tendering a contract for demolition of a prison outside

Vancouver, BC, the province required submissions of bids for salvage (or deconstruction) as well as demolition. The winning bid was for deconstruction. Despite requiring more labor by creating two additional jobs, the contractor saved money by reducing disposal costs and selling salvaged materials.

Materials Exchange: The Massachusetts Materials Exchange connects businesses with reusable materials and with others that can use them. In the past four years, the Massachusetts Materials Exchange has moved over 2,000 tons of materials, saving participants more than $100,000 in avoided disposal and purchasing costs (Center for Ecological Technology).

Toxic Round-Ups: New Jersey's, yearly or bi-annual "toxic round-up" events provide a central drop-off location for hazardous household wastes, and "toxic taxis" cruise neighborhoods for collection. If well advertised, such programs are very effective (Association of New Jersey Household Hazardous Waste Coordinators).

Resourceful Economic Development

Conservation and Job Creation: Materials for the Future Foundation in San Francisco links resource conservation and waste reduction with job creation and local empowerment. The Foundation works with youth organizations to establish computer reuse, repair, and recycling programs, and an affordable housing project in which youth are trained in deconstruction of old buildings and construction using salvaged materials. Grants are offered for development of businesses based on waste reduction (*Resource Recycling*, 1996).

Recycling and Reuse: The City of Montreal is recycling and reusing many types of waste materials that once languished in the city's landfill. Montreal has five eco-centres where residents can dispose of items, such as furniture or renovation waste, which is not accepted in regular garbage or recyclables. From 1997 - 2000, the eco-centres received almost 85,000 tonnes of materials produced by residents, saving $400,000 a year in tipping fees for each centre and creating one job for every 1,000 tonnes of materials collected (Brugmann, 1997; FCM, 2001, 2001a).

Recycling Market Development Zones and Loans: The California Integrated Waste Management Board promotes the re-manufacturing industry through the development of Recycling Market Development Zones and Loans. Recycling is combined with community economic development to create new businesses and jobs. The Board offers low interest loans, financial assistance, product-marketing, and permit assistance to businesses located within a zone. Local governments offer additional incentives, such as relaxed building codes and zoning laws, streamlined local permit process, reduced taxes and licensing, and a reliable supplement of secondary material feedstock (California Integrated Waste Management Board). The Loan program provides direct loans to businesses who use recycled content feedstock in their manufacturing process and are located within a designated Recycling Market Development Zone. Local governments in the zone are helped to finance public works infrastructure that directly supports businesses using post-consumer or secondary waste material.

Eco-Industrial Park: Kalundborg, Denmark is home of the world's first Eco-Industrial Park. Several businesses, including a power station, pharmaceutical manufacturer, plasterboard factory, fish farm, and oil refinery are linked through an innovative symbiotic relationship. Byproducts, such as water, steam, surplus gas, and other waste materials, are redistributed as fuel or resources for other businesses in the Park. The exchange of wastes provides mutual commercial benefits. (See also Chapter 10: Land Use and Urban Form.)

RESOURCES

Association of New Jersey Household Hazardous Waste Coordinators is a professional organization of public and private sector individuals involved in household hazardous waste management and related programs. Website: www.njhazwaste.com/

California Integrated Waste Management Board promotes a zero waste California in partnership with local government, industry and the public. Website: www.ciwmb.ca.gov/mrt/wpw/wpbiz/wpbiz4.htm

City Farmer is Canada's unofficial office of Urban Agriculture Website: www.cityfarmer.org

The Community Recycling Network UK is a membership organization promoting community-based waste management as a practical and effective way of tackling the UK's growing waste problem. Website: www.crn.org.uk

Global Recycling Network is the world's waste collection, disposal and recycling marketplace. Website: www.grn.com

US Environmental Protection Agency Municipal Solid Waste is a good source of MSW information Web ite: www.epa.gov/epaoswer/non-hw/muncpl/recycle.html

Worm Digest promotes the use of earthworms in waste management and sustainable agriculture. Website: www.wormdigest.org

REFERENCES

Association of New Jersey Household Hazardous Waste Coordinators, 2004, from www.njhazwaste.com/

Brugmann, J. (1997). Is there a Method in Our Measurement? The Use of Indicators in Local Sustainable Development Planning. *Local Environment*, 2(1): 59 -72.

California Integrated Waste Management Board, 2004, from www.ciwmb.ca.gov

Center for Ecological Technology. (n.d.). *What is The Massachusetts Materials Exchange?* Retrieved October 28, 2004, from www.materialsexchange.org/about.htm

City of Santa Monica. 1996. *Sustainable City Progress Report.* Santa Monica: Task Force on the Environment.

Container Recycling Institute. (n.d.). *A trillion aluminum cans trashed in America since 1972, recycling rate at lowest point in 25 years.* Retrieved October 27, 2004, from www.container-recycling.org/

Dragicevic, M. 1997. "German Waste Exports." Trade and Environment Database, American University, School of International Service, Washington, DC <gurukul.ucc.american.edu/ted/GERMWSTE.HTM>.

Environmental Defense. 23 June 2003. *Copy Paper: Hidden Costs, Real Opportunities.* Retrieved October 27, 2004, from www.environmentaldefense.org/pdf.cfm?ContentID= 2860&FileName=CopyPaper.pdf

European Union Environment DG. October 13, 2004. *Eco-label.* Retrieved October 27, 2004, from http://europa.eu.int/comm/environment/ecolabel/index_en.htm

Evergreen Industries & Obviously Enterprises. July 2001. *The Internet Consumer Recycling Guide.* Retrieved October 27, 2004, from www.obviously.com/recycle/

Expanding Participation in Feed Residuals Recycling Programs. 2004, Sep. *BioCycle, 45*: 43-45.

FCM. 2001a. Municipal Government and Sustainable Communities: A Best Practices Guide.

FCM. 2001b. Municipal Government and Sustainable Communities: A Best Practices Guide. *Eliminating Waste.*

Feinbaum, R. 2004, Aug. New Recycled Products on Display. *BioCycle, 45*: 31-32.

Fishbein, B., and D. Saphire. 1992. "Slowing the Waste Behemoth: Source Reduction is Overshadowed by Recycling's Success." *EPA Journal* 18 (3): 47-49.

Hawken, P. 1997. "Natural Capitalism." *Mother Jones.* March/April: 40-62.

Hirschhorn, J., T. Jackson, and L. Baas. 1993. "Towards Prevention — The Emerging Environmental Paradigm." In *Clean Production Strategies — Developing Preventive Environmental Management in the Industrial Economy,* T. Jackson, ed. Ann Arbor: Lewis Publishers.

Hui II, G. 1999, June 1, 2004. *Pay-As-You-Throw Continues to Grow [Electronic version].* Retrieved October 27, 2004, from www.epa.gov/epaoswer/non-hw/payt/ research.htm#comm

"In Composting and Recycling, WSU gets 'A' for Effort". 2004, Sep. *BioCycle: 45*, 22-24.

Interface, Inc. (n.d.). Retrieved October 28, 2004, from www.interfaceinc.com/goals/ vision.html

Kaufman, S. M., Goldstein, N., Millrath, K., & Themelis, N. J. 2004, Jan. "The State Of Garbage in America. *BioCycle", 45*: 31-41.

Lombardi, E., & Goldstein, J. 2001, Sep. Beyond Recycling...Zero Waste or Darn Near. *BioCycle, 42*: 75 -76.

National Recycling Coalition. (n.d.). *The NRC-Nike Reuse-a-Shoe Partnership.* Retrieved October 27, 2004, from www.nrc-recycle.org/partnerships/nike/index.htm

Resource Recycling. 1996. (15)11.

Recycling Council of British Columbia (RCBC). 1992a. "The Cost Of Recycling." *Reiterate: The Newsletter of RCBC,* May.

RCBC. 1994a. "BC Debates the Regulation of Plastics." *Reiterate: The Newsletter of RCBC,* February.

RCBC. 1994b. "Why We Must Reduce our Waste." *Reiterate: The Newsletter of RCBC,* May.

Seldman, N. 2003a, Nov. "From Solid Waste Management to Sustainable Economy". *BioCycle, 44*: 60-62.

Seldman, N. 2003b, Nov. "From Solid Waste Management to Sustainable Economy". *BioCycle, 44*: 60-62.

United States Environmental Protection Agency (USEPA) 1999. *Cutting the Waste Stream in Half: Community Record-Setters Show How [Electronic version]*.

USEPA. February 9, 2004. *Buy Recycled*. Retrieved October 27, 2004, from www.epa.gov/epaoswer/non-hw/muncpl/buyrec.htm

USEPA. May 18, 2004. *eCycling*. Retrieved October 27, 2004, from www.epa.gov/epaoswer/hazwaste/recycle/ecycling/index.htm

USEPA. August 22, 2004. *Product Stewardship: Batteries*. Retrieved October 27, 2004, from www.epa.gov/epr/products/batteries.html

USEPA. July, 2001. *WasteWise Update: Environmentally Preferable Purchasing [Electronic version]*: Solid Waste and Emergency Response. Retrieved October 27, 2004, from www.epa.gov/wastewise/pubs/wwupda15.pdf

US Green Press Initiative. n.d. Retrieved from http://greenpressinitiative.org/index.html

Young, J.E. 1991. "Reducing Waste, Saving Materials." In *State of the World 1991, Worldwatch Institute*. New York: W.W. Norton.

Energy Efficiency and Renewables

Energy production is big business, and its consumption fuels our economy just as it fuels cars, heats and cools our homes, and lights our office buildings. Yet what is the price to our communities, our ecosystem, and to the world around us?

Canadians and Americans consume more energy per capita than any other nation. Environmental impacts of our consumptive lifestyles include ozone layer depletion, acid rain, smog, potential climate change, and other forms of pollution and environmental degradation. Our addiction to energy also manifests itself in congested roads, urban sprawl, excessive heating, cooling, lighting, and ventilation expenditures in buildings, costly inefficiencies in commercial and industrial equipment, weaker local economies, and excessive taxes.

Citizens and their governments hold tremendous power to change our patterns of consumption and support sustainable ways of using energy resources. Designing more energy-efficient buildings, and retrofitting existing homes, office and civic buildings saves millions of dollars in energy expenditures, and frees up money for investment in schools, hospitals, community economic development, and a more secure future.

Reducing consumption is usually more cost-effective than expanding supply. By increasing efficiency, the same amount of electricity can serve more users without requiring massive capital investments to expand power plant capacity. If additional supply is needed, renewable energy production, such as wind power and photovoltaic (solar) power, as well as cogeneration are more sustainable options. For heating options, technologies such as ground-source heat pumps and district heating, are more efficient and environmentally responsible than most conventional heating systems.

By encouraging energy efficiency and clean, renewable or efficient energy supply strategies, communities foster local self-reliance and economic diversification. This is not science fiction — these are "off-the-shelf" technologies and techniques that are available today. All that is required is public and political will.

ENERGY EFFICIENCY

Energy-efficiency simply means "more bang for your buck." It implies use of products, such as refrigerators, lightbulbs, washing machines, computers, printers, copiers, industrial motor systems, air conditioners, space heaters, and ventilation systems that deliver the same service as other units, but with a fraction of the energy or electricity demands. Energy-efficient buildings use strategies and technologies, such as passive solar design, light shelves, light-tubes, and high-performance windows, to reduce energy consumption by minimizing or even eliminating the need for heating, cooling, ventilation systems, and day-time lighting.

To a homeowner this can mean hundreds, even thousands of dollars in savings every year from reduced utility bills. To a large commercial building owner or industrial operation this can translate into millions of dollars in energy savings. To a utility company, reductions in energy consumption can mean loss of revenues, but doesn't have to mean loss of profits.

Supply and Demand

Population growth, economic development, and increasing demands for electricity require costly expansions to energy-supply infrastructure. Faced with the cost of constructing multi-billion dollar power plants, and the uncertainty in planning future capacity needs, many utilities support initiatives to improve customer energy efficiency. Helping a customer reduce demand for electricity is often more profitable than building a new power plant. While the latter expands revenues, it is accompanied by long-term debt, higher operating expenditures, and the risk that an economic slump may reduce consumption, leaving an excessive supply.

Energy efficiency means doing more with less.

This strategy was termed "demand-side management" (DSM), referring to the focus on managing customer demand instead of simply expanding supply. Today, it is often referred to as energy productivity strategies or energy services.

Most electric utilities in Canada are Crown corporations (owned by the provinces), however, there are a few regionally-owned electric generators and a growing number of independent power producers. In the US, the Department of Energy owns and operates several large power generators, but there are also hundreds of larger shareholder-owned utilities, independent power producers, and many municipal-owned power generators as well. Regardless of whether a community owns its utility or purchases power from a large provider, investment in cost-effective DSM strategies is simply good business.

Energy and Local Economies

For many towns, 75 cents of every dollar spent on energy (electricity and fuel) leaves the community to pay generators, refiners and the coffers of large electric or gas utility companies. When a dollar is saved on energy, it can be re-invested in the local economy and circulate several times over. This strategy is termed "economic multipliers." (See Chapter 12: Community Economic Development for examples and discussion). "Plugging the leaks" in local energy expenditures saves individual homeowners and tenants money, and helps businesses reduce operating costs to increase their economic competitiveness (Hubbard and Fong, 1995).

Many individuals and companies are realizing these opportunities. They're purchasing more energy-efficient products and devices, retrofitting buildings, or requiring high standards of energy efficiency for new buildings. Citizens and local governments can play a strong role by organizing education and information campaigns, and by influencing equipment standards or policy and codes for energy-efficient building design and operations.

Governments can also save taxpayer dollars by reducing energy expenditures in libraries, hospitals, schools, community centers and civic buildings. Money saved on a school's utility bills can be spent on books and teachers' salaries instead, and savings in electricity and heating costs for public buildings can translate into lower taxes or redirection of tax dollars to community economic development, affordable housing programs, or environmental, cultural, or sports programs that enhance the quality of life for residents of the community.

Economic multipliers and government energy efficiency programs directly and indirectly create jobs for local citizens, and DSM initiatives address the regressive nature of low income people's energy use. Low income people tend to live in the worst housing stock, often characterized by drafty rooms, inefficient heating systems, and energy-guzzling refrigerators. DSM programs improve the comfort of homes and reduce utility bills, thereby increasing the standard of living for those who need it most.

> ### *Reducing the Heat Island Effect*
>
> Dark, heat absorbing materials, such as concrete and brick, absence of tree cover, waste heat from buildings, industry and automobiles all contribute to increasing temperatures in cities. In addition to exacerbating effects on public health, this urban heat island effect leads to significantly higher demand for air conditioning (Torrie 1997). Cities can counteract the heat island effect by planting more trees, increasing vegetated land within the city, and by using lighter color paints and building materials to reduce absorption of solar radiation. The U.S. National Academy of Sciences estimates that strategic use of white surfaces and vegetation could save $2.6 billion in energy costs (Lowe, 1991).

TOOLS AND INITIATIVES

Public Education and Information Programs

Conference and Trade Show: The Community Office for Resource Efficiency is a nonprofit organization that promotes renewable energy and energy efficiency in Roaring Fork Valley and the rest of western Colorado. CORE provides community energy education through forums, presentations, and newspaper and magazine articles. In 1994, CORE hosted a two-day exhibition and trade show to educate and inspire locals to pursue energy efficiency issues; its programs have since grown to include a solar production incentive, renewable energy mitigation fund, and efficient building program (CORE, 2004).

Interfaith Coalition on Energy: Since 1980, the Interfaith Coalition on Energy has helped religious congregations in Philadelphia reduce their energy use. The Coalition sponsors workshops to help congregations of any faith make their buildings more energy-efficient, and they publish a newsletter providing tips on energy-efficient strategies. The newsletter also offers information on where to buy products and services, and how to finance building retrofits and efficiency upgrades (ICE, 2003).

Workshops for Homeowners: The City of Ashland, Oregon offers workshops on energy efficiency for homeowners including a Home Energy, Duct, and Leakage

Analysis by an energy analyst. Complimentary programs include financing and rebates for energy upgrades and weatherization (City of Ashland, 2004; Lealess, 1998).

Builder and Architect Education Programs

Green Builder Program: The Austin Green Builder Program in Texas provides training in energy-efficient and environmentally responsible construction techniques. Participants receive guidebooks, product and service sourcebooks, and attend workshops and training seminars. Builders and developers can apply the Austin Green Builder rating system, awarding one to four stars to their houses. The program has won national awards for developing ecological building agendas and has been recognized as a top "success story" by the US Department of Energy (Austin Energy, 2004).

Leadership in Energy and Environmental Design (LEED): The LEED Green Building Rating System® is a voluntary, consensus-based national standard for assessing building performance and meeting sustainability goals. Developed by the US Green Building Council (USGBC), LEED accredits professionals and awards four levels of building certification. The USGBC also partners with other organizations, such as the City of San José and the Pacific Energy Center, to offer workshops and programs on renewable energy and energy efficient design (USGBC, 2004; City of San José, 2004).

Audits and Retrofit Programs

Audits and Upgrades: The Sacramento Municipal Utility District in California promotes audits and arranges complete residential efficiency upgrades for their customers. An inspector recommends an appropriate package of measures to improve efficiency, typically including: improved insulation, weather stripping, insulating the hot water tank, installing compact fluorescent fixtures, and replacement of electric resistance heating with a heat pump. For simply agreeing to the audit, the utility provides the homeowner with a free compact fluorescent light bulb, a high performance showerhead, and two trees (which can reduce air conditioning energy requirements). If the customer decides to proceed with the retrofit, part of the cost is an outright grant (about $800) from the utility, and the rest of the cost (typically $3400) is put on the customer's utility bill, amortized over 15 years. This extra charge is less than the immediate reduction in energy costs, so the customer comes out ahead with lower power bills (Millyard, 1992).

Energy Policy: In April 1990, the City of Portland, Oregon adopted an energy policy with the goal of "increasing energy efficiency in all sectors of the City by 10 percent by the year 2000 so as to enhance the livability, economic strength and well-being of the City's residents and businesses and reduce environmental problems...that contribute to global warming." By 2000, the city's Energy Office had achieved more than 90 percent of its goals, including reducing annual energy bills by $1.1 million, weatherizing over 22,000 apartments, and a 9 percent reduction in per-capita household energy use (ICLEI, 1991; PEO, 2000).

Conservation Power Plant: The Emerald People's Utility District in the Eugene-Springfield, Oregon area signed an agreement with Bonneville Power Administration to build a "conservation power plant" to generate millions of kilowatt-hours of energy savings. The District offers cash incentives and zero-percent loans for residential and commercial weatherization, retrofit and conservation efforts. Bonds are issued through the Oregon Department of Energy's Small Scale Energy Loan Program to finance program costs; the Power Administration pays the principal and interest on the bonds, recognizing the benefits in avoiding the cost of new power-plant construction. Customers pay a small levy to offset revenue losses to the utility, but these charges are more than offset by the savings accrued from retrofits (Conservation Monitor, 1993a; EPUD, 2003).

Codes, Bylaws, and Ordinances

Building Code: Osage, Iowa established higher-than-state standards of energy efficiency in their local building code. If, for example, commercial or residential buildings do not meet the city's standards for insulation levels, the building will not receive utility service. Since 1984, every building has complied with the energy-efficient standard.

Retrofit Ordinance: San Francisco, California enacted a comprehensive residential energy conservation retrofit ordinance in 1982. The ordinance required all existing residential buildings, including apartment buildings, to be brought up to an energy-efficiency standard at the time of sale. The cost of the measures could be included in the financing of the residential unit. A Resource-Efficient Building (REB) ordinance went into effect in 1999 to promote resource-efficient building standards in all City buildings and address the goals of the City's Sustainability Plan. Resource-efficient, or "green," buildings are structures that are designed, constructed, renovated, operated and demolished with minimal environmental impacts. They also exhibit high levels of economic and engineering performance, and save financial resources over the buildings' lifetime (Local Government Commission, 1990; SFE n.d.).

Solar Access Ordinance: Many local governments have adopted and implemented solar access ordinances. The City of Boulder's solar access ordinance guarantees access to sunlight for homeowners and renters in the city. This is done by setting limits on the amount of permitted shading by new construction. A solar access permit is available to those who have installed or who plan to install a solar energy system and need more protection than is provided by the ordinance (DSIRE, 2004).

Setting Examples with Public Buildings

What better way to demonstrate the benefits of resource conservation than through building and retrofitting more efficient schools, libraries, hospitals and civic buildings? The US government set a grand example with the Greening the White House program, which started in 1993. Through the Federal Energy Management Program (FEMP), energy service companies have installed energy-efficient lamps, motors, air conditioning systems and heating equipment in federal buildings, resulting in a reduction of building-related energy use of more than 25 percent per square foot compared to 1985 levels. FEMP helps federal agencies achieve greater energy efficiency and cost-effectiveness through four service areas: technical assistance, financing, policy and outreach (FEMP, 2004; *Green Business Letter,* 1997).

Passive Solar Building: The school board of Johnston County, North Carolina, realized they spend more taxpayer dollars on utility bills and building maintenance over the life of a building than they spent on constructing the building itself. They invested in better design at Four Oaks Elementary School where the passive solar building uses half the energy of a typical school and has low maintenance costs as well.

Energy Conservation and Savings Plan: The City of Phoenix, Arizona has saved several million dollars since they began auditing and retrofitting civic buildings in the late 1970s. As an incentive for participating in the energy efficiency program, departments and city agencies get to keep all (or a predetermined percentage) of the money they save from using energy more efficiently, and a professional energy manager monitors and documents all savings. In 1984, city council established the Energy Conservation Savings Reinvestment Plan. Under this plan, the city reinvests 50 percent of all documented energy savings (up to $500,000) to finance energy efficiency capital projects (DOE, 1992a).

City of Phoenix Yearly Utility Cost Savings from Energy Efficiency Projects

Facilities	Costs Before Retrofit	Costs After Retrofit	Savings in Dollars
Civic Plaza	$1,465,627	$1,046,748	$418,879
Parks	884,714	508,709	376,005
Municipal	923,796	609,744	314,052
Fire Stations	453,328	243,381	209,947
Cultural Centers	719,908	524,719	195,189
Plaza Municipal	565,568	399,591	165,977
Police and			
Public Safety	1,008,358	886,748	121,610
Branch Libraries	344,750	173,934	170,816

Guidelines, Certification, and Rating Systems

Certification Benefits: The US Green Building Council (USGBC) has developed the LEED Green Building Rating System® which evaluates building performance in six areas: sustainable sites, energy and atmosphere, materials and resources, indoor environmental quality, innovation and design process, and water efficiency. New or retrofitted buildings are awarded one of four certification levels (Certified, Silver, Gold, Platinum), which qualifies them for a number of state and local incentive programs, such as preferred mortgage rates. Similar programs exist in other cities and states in the US, such as the Home Builders Association of Kitsap County's Built Green certification and training program, and the national GoodCents utility marketing and certification program (USGBC, 2004).

Power Smart: BC Hydro's Power Smart was launched in 1989 as a cost-effective initiative to assist customers in conserving electricity and to help offset the province's growing demand for electricity. Programs such as the Power Smart Home Award and Power Smart Certification program recognize residents and businesses that have reduced their power consumption. By 2002, Power Smart programs had resulted in annual savings of over 2,500 GWh. Their new Power Smart Partner Program provides access to a variety of tools and financial incentives to become more energy efficient (BC Hydro, 2003).

Grants, Loans, Mortgages and Bonds

Upgrade Financing: When a development firm was constructing a multi-unit building for low-income residents, it approached the locally-owned utility company, Emerald People's Utility District in Eugene, Oregon for support. Realizing that people with lower incomes have a harder time paying their bills, the developer requested a lower rate for electricity supply for residents of the new building. Instead, the utility kept rates the same, but financed upgrades to the building's windows, lighting, and heating system so that occupants would enjoy lower monthly energy bills.

Zero Interest Loans: Some municipal utilities, such as the City of Ashland, Oregon and Fort Collins, Colorado have made zero-interest loans available for residential energy efficiency improvements or installation of solar hot-water heaters. Fort Collins' program initially started with a Community Development Block Grant, and the utility contributed by buying down the interest rates on the loans.

Municipal Bonds: Many local governments can also issue bonds to raise money to construct public buildings, bridges, or to repair roads. The City of Ann Arbor, Michigan issued $1.4 million in municipal bonds to finance energy improvements to 30 public buildings.

Financing Home Energy Improvements: Roaring Fork Valley's Community Office for Resource Efficiency (CORE) offers zero percent financing and community grants of $500 to $5,000 for projects targeting energy efficiency, renewable energy or education. Similarly, the Vermont Energy Investment Corporation (VEIC) offers technical assistance and energy improvement financing to low- and middle-income Vermonters, as well as providing consulting services on energy investment and improvement. The success of VEIC programs have led to their participation in national and international projects (CORE, 2004; RMI, 2003).

Energy-Efficient Mortgages: Neworld Bank in Massachusetts is one of dozens of financial institutions in North America offering energy-efficient mortgages for homes purchase or renovation. Typically homes are rated (see above) or there is a list of energy efficiency requirements that qualify a home for a reduced mortgage rate of 1 percent to 2 percent below prime. Energy-efficient mortgages may be supported directly by the financial institute, or backed by local governments, Community Development Corporations, or state, provincial, or federal energy-conservation programs. In the US, national secondary mortgage institutions offer energy-efficient mortgages, but few lenders and mortgage applicants are aware of the opportunity (RMI, 2003).

Rebate Programs

Rebates and Reductions: Waverly Light and Power has received national recognition for its innovative programs servicing the small community of Waverly, Iowa. Residents can receive rebates when purchasing efficient appliances and take advantage of reduced power rates based on the time of day, Good Home certification (see above), and total usage. Successful past initiatives include the "Waverly bucks" program whereby residents received rebates that could only be used to purchase energy-efficient products from local stores (WLP, 2004).

Utility Company Rebates: For years many utility companies (municipal and others), such as BC Hydro, Ontario Hydro, and Bonneville Power Authority, have offered rebates on energy-efficient lightbulbs, refrigerators, and other appliances. Pacific Gas and Electric (PG&E) in California, is one utility which continues to offer rebates. The utility pays up to $300,000 to commercial customers for upgrades of lighting, air conditioning, motors or refrigeration appliances; 100 percent equipment financing is also provided if needed. In 2002, PG&E's energy efficiency programs helped customers save more than $56 million in energy costs (PG&E, 2003).

Community Energy Services

Community Energy Services Corporation: The City of Berkeley, California established a Community Energy Services Corporation offering energy services, such as audits and project management to commercial, residential and public building projects. The non-profit corporation also helps people find financing for energy-efficiency initiatives.

ENVIRONMENTALLY RESPONSIBLE ENERGY SUPPLY

Energy efficiency is clean, cost-effective and widely available, but we still need some source of power supply. What are the options? Ecological impacts of large-scale hydro electric dams are no longer acceptable to the public, and most utility companies and communities in Canada and the US recognize that nuclear power generation is simply too expensive and short-sighted. (Where do we put the radioactive waste kept in "short-term" storage at nuclear facilities across North America?) Rising concerns about local and global pollution and climate change are spurring review of fuel choices and operating efficiencies of oil, coal and gas-fired conventional power plants. Pollution-abatement technologies and combustion efficiencies are improving some plants, but renewable energies offer opportunities for local-self reliance in energy production for electricity needs. Community-scale projects, using efficient technologies such as cogeneration or district heating, are other options to minimize consumption and reduce dependency on fossil fuels.

Renewable Energy Supply

Renewable energy sources are often regarded as new or exotic, but in fact they are neither. Until quite recently, in historical terms, the world drew most of its energy from the sun, either directly from sunlight or indirectly through the natural processes that generate winds, rivers, and plants. The advantages of renewable energy sources — particularly wind, solar, and biomass (plant) energy — are, if anything, more compelling today than ever before (ACORE, 2004; Lovins, 2002).

While renewable energies have not enjoyed the massive subsidies of the fossil fuel and nuclear power sectors, great strides in technological improvements, operating efficiencies and equipment costs have been made in recent years. In many parts of the US, wind technology is now directly cost-competitive with new supply costs for conventional power plants. In fact, all renewable technologies are cost-competitive, and even more economical when long-term operating costs and the financial benefits of environmental protection are factored into the equation. Thousands of Canadians and Americans use solar hot water panels or photovoltaic (solar electric) panels to provide domestic hot water and electricity for their homes, and increasingly utility companies and communities are capitalizing on this opportunity. Rooftops all over North America are ideal for installation of solar panels to provide sustainable energy supplies.

District Heating

District heating pipes heat, hot water, or steam generated at a central facility to each building in a community. By constructing systems to serve a large customer base, such as a whole neighborhood or community, energy-efficient heating systems, such as co-generation and ground-source heat pumps can compete with cheaper inefficient heating systems. District heating requires a certain level of density to be effective. For example, in Britain, 44 dwellings per hectare is considered the minimum density for economical operation (Lowe, 1991).

The source of district heat is often a hospital, university, hotel, or factory, that has its own cogenerating system. Cogeneration systems make electricity and steam together to power and heat buildings with one-third less fuel than is needed to produce each on its own; they are also well-suited to sophisticated pollution control equipment. Industries that generate excessive heat, such as pulp and paper mills, can harness waste heat for cogeneration; and industrial wastes, such as wood chips and sewage sludge may also be used as fuel sources. Some wastes are better suited than others for fuel; while burning wastes is still not without environmental impact, it may be more advantageous to burn than dump.

Ground-source heat pumps use heat pump technology to extract heat from the earth to heat buildings, swimming pools, or domestic hot-water supply. Water-source heat pumps use water sources such as ponds as a source of heat. The technology can also work in reverse to cool buildings or keep ice rinks frozen. Ground-source heat pumps use a series of closed-loop pipes containing heat-absorbing fluid that absorbs heat from the surrounding earth. These are not to be confused with geothermal systems that extract heat from hot springs or hot rock areas in the earth. While geothermal systems are effective, there are few places with suitable geology for this technology.

Renewable Energy Options

Photovoltaic (solar electric) power: Photovoltaic panels produce electricity for independent systems with batteries for storing energy, or supply electricity to the power grid.

Solar thermal energy. Solar hot-water systems typically provide water for showers and baths, heating swimming pools, hot tubs, or radiant heating (space heating). Some solar thermal projects are designed to convert heated water into electricity.

Wind power: Stand-alone turbines supply electricity for homes, farms, small communities. Wind farms are clusters of wind turbines generating power for the electrical grid.

Micro-hydro: Unlike large-scale hydro electric projects, micro-hydro exerts minimal disturbance of waterways. Small turbines typically use springs, creeks or municipal water supply lines to generate enough electricity for a single building or an entire town.

Biomass: Agricultural plants or organic wastes provide fuels, such as methanol or ethanol, which can be used as an alternative for most oil or gas needs. Biomass still contributes to air pollution and greenhouse gases. While not strictly a renewable technology, hydrogen gas is a clean, efficient technology that will soon be used in vehicles, and may be adapted for building and community heating and power generation.

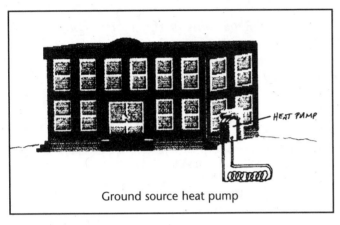
HEAT PUMP

Ground source heat pump

Ground-source and water-source heat pumps work effectively with only the moderate temperature increases found below the earth's surface or in bodies of water.

Ground-source heat pumps deliver three to five times more heat (or air conditioning) per unit of energy consumed than conventional space heating systems, so operating efficiencies are high. The mechanical heat pump action can be powered by electricity or natural gas, and the cost to install piping is the biggest expenditure. The capital cost is prohibitive for most homebuyers, but for community-scale projects, or large buildings, such as schools, nursing homes and housing complexes, the operating savings offset the investment.

Tools and Initiatives

District Heating Programs and Cogeneration

Cogeneration: Helsinki, Finland's has been operating a district heating program for over 50 years; in 2003 over it provided heat to over 12,000 customers. Their cogeneration process results in a 40 percent reduction in fuel requirements (Helsinki Energy Board, 2004).

Local Energy Supply Program: Saarbrücken, Germany has an aggressive Local Energy Supply program that requires conservation, district heating, and local energy supplies. Over 40,000 homes are served by district heating, and the homeowners can receive subsidies to install rooftop solar-energy panels.

District Heating: Enwave is one of the largest district energy systems in North America, providing heating and/or cooling services to over 130 institutional and commercial buildings in downtown Toronto, Canada. Enwave's innovative Deep Lake Water Cooling System uses the perennially cold water at depth in Lake Ontario to provide air conditioning and cooling services at competitive rates, offsetting more than 59 megawatts of consumption per year (Enwave, 2004).

Ground-Source Heat Pump Public Projects

Ground source heat pumps or geoexchange systems, have a long history of residential use in North America, and the past decade has seen a rapid growth in commercial and public use as well. The non-profit Geothermal Heat Pump Consortium, Inc. (GHPC), reports that there are over 900,000 geoexchange systems in the US, resulting in annual savings of more than 7 billion kWh (GHPC, 2004).

Commercial System: The Galt House, a waterfront hotel and office building complex in Louisville, Kentucky, uses over 4,700 tons of geoexchange to meet its heating and cooling needs. The cost of the installing the geoexchange system was $1,500 per ton compared to conventional system costs of $2,000 to $3,000 a ton, and operating energy savings have averaged $25,000 per month. The system is also very space-efficient, resulting in 25,000 square feet of additional commercial space compared to a conventional system (Liepe, 2001).

Renewables Demonstration Programs

Numerous communities and utilities are testing the reliability and compatibility of various solar and wind power products. The Million Solar Roofs Initiative (MSRI) is a partnership between states and local communities administered by the Department of Energy. Established in 1997, MSRI and its partners are working towards the goal of installing 1,000,000 new solar energy systems in the United States by 2010.

Wind Turbine: In 1993 the municipal-owned utility of Waverly became the first public power system in the Midwest to own and operate a wind turbine. By working with a local college, the cost of the pilot project was reduced because engineering technology students provided maintenance and collected data to monitor operating costs and efficiencies. Based on the success of the demonstration project, additional turbines were added in 1999, 2001 and 2002, and wind generation now provides energy for the equivalent of 761 homes (WLP, 2004).

Green Power Programs

Green power programs, also known as Green Tags, or renewable energy credits (REC), are cropping up all over. Community-scale power production, typically using renewable energy supplies, is fostering local self-reliance and greater environmental responsibility. Programs such as the US's federal Renewable Energy Production Incentive (REPI) and Canada's Wind Power Production Incentive (WPPI) provide a per-kWh price premium to green power producers. Other programs, such as the US Federal Government Green Power Purchasing Goal, are directed at increasing the market for renewable energy.

Cooperative Wind Turbines: Groups of families in Denmark cooperatively own and operate wind turbines scattered throughout the country. Typically, each family pays for its share of the project, financed by bank loans, and the cooperative sells excess electricity back to their utility. More than 150,000 Danish families are involved, representing over 80 per cent of the country's 6,300 wind turbines (Krohn, 2002).

Green Power: The Emerald People's Utility District (EPUD) offers three renewable green power options to their clients: 50 percent renewable, 100 percent renewable or 100 percent wind, at an average cost of $5-$15 per month. Renewable power comes from wind and microhydro fish-friendly installations. EPUD also produces 3.2 mW per year and $350-400,000 in revenue from methane gas extracted through its Short Mountain Landfill Gas Project near Eugene, Oregon (EPUD, 2003).

Photovoltaic Rooftop Program: Sacramento Municipal Utility Department (SMUD) is running a photovoltaic rooftop program. Participants in the program receive training and assistance to purchase and install a grid-connected system at a reduced price.

Microhydro Turbine: Many communities, such as the small town of Cedaridge, Colorado are tapping into their water supply pipeline for a low-cost source of clean, renewable energy. The town attached a microhydro turbine to the pipeline, providing a megawatt of power. Only the incremental cost of the turbine and power conversion equipment was required because the town had already paid for the pipeline. Apart

Sustainable Cities Project

With funds from the Urban Consortium Energy Task Force, the California Cities of San Jose and San Francisco, and Portland, Oregon developed sustainable energy plans. The cities collaborated but pursued independent courses to develop energy policies that meet their local needs and objectives. Key objectives were:

- to use energy effectively in achieving other municipal goals such as affordable housing, efficient transportation systems, economic development, and job creation;
- to protect and maintain the quality of life by reducing environmental problems associated with inefficient energy use; and
- to contribute to national security by reducing vulnerability to predicted oil shortages and price increases.

As part of the Sustainable City Project, the cities developed a planning guide to serve as a model for other communities. It describes a seven step process:

1. Conduct an environmental scan to identify the impacts of energy use and determine present and future energy resource needs.
2. Identify community goals and issues for policy planning.
3. Build support for a sustainable energy plan.
4. Identify and analyze options: costs, benefits, environmental effects, technological potential, and political acceptability.
5. Adopt policies and strategies to direct future actions.
6. Develop specific energy implementation plans.
7. Evaluate program success, including energy saved, positive environmental impacts, and specific lessons learned.

from maintenance costs, their power supply is essentially free.

COMMUNITY PLANNING AND MANAGEMENT ISSUES

While energy efficiency and green-power supply options offer many benefits for communities, greater benefits are possible if local governments integrate energy considerations into other planning decisions. Strategies and policies for land use, urban development, building sizes, architectural design and standards, transportation planning, environmental protection, air quality and economic development *all* influence energy issues. By integrating planning, communities can address multiple goals while maximizing cost-efficiencies. This requires cooperation among various governmental departments and non-governmental businesses and entities, and may require changes to conventional ways of planning and costing projects.

Least Cost Utility Planning

A number of cities, governments, and utilities in Canada and the US have implemented Least Cost Utility Planning or Integrated Resource Planning. Such planning for electricity supplies allows investments for energy efficiency and DSM (as opposed to supply-focused) to be on equal footing with investments for new generating capacity. Energy efficiency is treated as an alternative energy source (what Amory Lovins of Rocky Mountain Institute calls "negawatts" rather than "megawatts"), and substitution of non-conventional, decentralized, smaller generators for large, central generating plants is supported (a perfect application for renewable energy systems and cogeneration). Applications of this concept require close coordination among utility regulators, individual utilities and local governments. To ensure effectiveness, these programs commonly combine technical support and financial incentives for energy efficiency improvements targeted to residential, commercial and industrial consumers.

Strategic Planning

Many local governments use strategic planning to identify, rank, and implement energy and environmental policies and programs. Strategic planning is a systematic way to identify and accomplish priorities. It goes beyond goal-setting to focus on implementation and allocation of resources. As part of the Sustainable City Project, sponsored by US Department of Energy, Urban Consortium Energy Task Force (DOE, 1992b), three cities (Portland, Oregon, San Francisco and San Jose, California) developed sustainable city plans on the strategic planning process, and published a guidebook for other communities.

<u>TOOLS</u> <u>AND</u> <u>INITIATIVES</u>

Community Energy Management Projects

Local Advisory Committee: Faced with the decision to build another electric power plant, expand the existing diesel plant, extend a power line to hook up with the provincial utility grid, or pursue energy efficiency, Alberta Power collaborated with a local advisory committee to develop and implement goals for their energy-efficient project. The advisory committee, made up of the Jasper Chamber of Commerce, environmental groups, the school board, the local hospital, the Canadian Park Service, and Alberta Power, targeted all sectors including commercial, industrial and residential customers. Customers were offered audits, cash incentives, reduced prices on energy-efficient devices, and other options which helped the town achieve a 20-percent reduction in energy consumption in eight months (*Home Energy,* 1994).

Energy Conservation Division: Ashland, Oregon integrates energy-efficiency initiatives with town planning. Since the early 1980s, the department of community development has included an energy conservation division offering audits and rebates for homes and businesses. They provide weatherization assistance and energy smart building design assistance, and they've upgraded the efficiency of area and street lighting. The city also influences energy efficiency by the codes, zoning and standards it enforces for building and land-use development. Energy issues are considered in all stages of planning, land use and building decisions, and the city promotes pedestrian-oriented urban planning to reduce vehicle energy consumption as well. The program saves over 8 million kilowatt-hours per year (City of Ashland, 2004; Lealess, 1998).

Comprehensive Energy Planning

Energy Office and Energy Commission: Portland, Oregon prepared a comprehensive energy conservation policy in 1979. As a result, the Energy Office and Energy Commission were established to coordinate programs dealing with energy efficiency, transportation, land-use planning and water conservation. Funded by the City of Portland, several staff work with utilities, service providers, state energy agencies and other local government departments to operate programs such as the Block-by-Block Weatherization Program. A one-percent fee on all city government energy bills generates some of the revenue to operate the Energy Office. In the past decade, the office has helped weatherize 20,000 apartments and 2,000 low-income homes and has saved the city nearly $2 million per year in energy costs (POSD, 2004).

Planning for Community Energy, Environment and Economic Sustainability: Modeling software and energy planning computer programs, such as Planning for Community Energy, Environment and Economic Sustainability help communities such as San Diego and San Jose, California, Portland, Oregon and Vancouver, BC include energy decisions in building design and urban planning. The program quantitatively measures integrated actions to evaluate energy, environmental and economic benefits of decisions about energy supply options, building design, orientation and lay-out, as well as neighborhood density and lay-out, transportation decisions, and other urban planning issues.

Bonds to Finance Sustainable Energy Management

Energy Resource Management Plan: In Eugene, Oregon, the Water and Electric Board is financing the city's Energy Resource Management Plan with a $150-million bond issue. After a citizen-based resource planning effort, residents voted overwhelmingly in support of this initiative, which includes financing for energy efficiency, renewables, cogeneration and hydro power (Conservation Monitor, 1993b; EWEB, 2003).

RESOURCES

Alliance to Save Energy deals with various energy policy issues and provides publications on model building codes, energy education, updates on federal energy policy and more. Website: www.ase.org

American Council for an Energy-Efficient Economy conducts research on energy efficiency to stimulate the adoption of energy-conserving technologies and practices. Website: www.aceee.org

American Solar Energy Society promotes education in fields related to solar energy and publishes a variety of information on solar-related topics.
Website: www.ases.org

Database of State Incentives for Renewable Energy (DSIRE) a comprehensive source of information on state, local, utility, and selected federal incentives that promote renewable energy. Website: www.dsireusa.org

Energy Ideas Clearinghouse provides access to comprehensive and objective energy information, education, resources and technical assistance for increasing energy efficiency in the commercial and industrial sectors. Website: www.energyideas.org/

Rocky Mountain Institute is an entrepreneurial nonprofit organization that fosters the efficient and restorative use of resources. RMI publishes reports on energy policy and technologies, and consults for and provides information to the public and professionals on energy efficiency and other topics. In 2004, RMI developed an online Community Energy Opportunity Finder (CEOF) that mimics the preliminary analysis of an expert consultant in order to help your community identify potential energy savings and renewable alternatives. Websites: www.rmi.org and www.finder.rmi.org (CEOF)

The Source for Renewable Energy is a comprehensive online buyer's guide and business directory to more than 8,000 renewable energy businesses and organizations worldwide. Website: www.energy.sourceguides.com/index.shtml

US Department of Energy: Energy Information Portal is a clearinghouse for information on energy efficiency and renewable energy, as well educational resources. Website: www.eere.energy.gov

US Environmental Protection Agency has two main resources for energy-related issues. Clean Energy Programs are designed to improve the national foundation of information on renewable energy by creating networks between the public and private

sector, providing technical assistance, and offering recognition of environmental leaders. Energy Star is a government-backed program helping businesses and individuals protect the environment through superior energy efficiency
Websites: www.epa.gov/cleanenergy/index.htm and www.energystar.gov/

REFERENCES

American Council on Renewable Energy (ACORE). 2004. *Renewable energy in America: The call for phase II.* (PDF file) Available from www.acore.org/pdfs/ 04policy_summary_10_7.pdf

Austin Energy. 2004. *Green building program.* Available from www.ci.austin.tx.us/ greenbuilder/

BC Hydro. 2003. *Why power smart?* Available from www.bchydro.com/ powersmart/index/index3199.html

City of Ashland. 2004. *Conservation division.* Available from www.ashland.or.us/ SectionIndex.asp?SectionID=432

City of Portland Office of Sustainable Development (POSD). 2004. *Energy division.* Available from www.sustainableportland.org/default.asp?sec=energy&pg=menu_Com

City of San Jose. (2004). *Educational programs.* Available from www.ci.san-jose.ca.us/ esd/gb-educational-programs.htm

Conservation Monitor. 1993a. "Emerald PUD, PBA Reach Landmark Agreement." July/August.

Conservation Monitor. 1993b. "EWEB Voters Seek More Resource Independence." July/August.

Community Office for Resource Efficiency (CORE). 2004. Available from www.aspencore.org/

Database of State Incentives for Renewable Energy (DSIRE). 2004. *Boulder — solar access ordinance.* Available from www.ies.ncsu.edu/dsire/library/includes/ incentive2.cfm? Incentive_Code=CO08R&state=CO&CurrentPageID=1

Department of Energy, US (DOE). 1992a. "Energy Dollars Relieve Municipal Budgets." *Tomorrow's Energy Today for Cities and Counties,* NREL. December.

DOE. 1992b. *A Local Government Planning Guide For A Sustainable Future.* Urban Consortium Energy Task Force. December.

Emerald People's Utility District (EPUD). 2003. Available from www.epud.org/energy_ efficiency.htm

Emerald People's Utility District (EPUD). 2003. Energy efficiency. Available from the Energy Efficiency and Electricity Generation folders at www.epud.org/

Enwave. (2004). Available from www.enwave.com/enwave/

Eugene Water and Electric Board (EWEB). 2003. *Energy resource strategy 2000.* (PDF file) Available from www.eweb.org/energy/energy_plan/IERP_Strategy_2000.pdf

Federal Energy Management Program (FEMP). 2004. *2003 year in review.* (PDF file) Available from www.eere.energy.gov/femp/pdfs/yrinrview_2003.pdf

Geothermal Heat Pump Consortium, Inc. (GHPC). 2004. *Geoexchange heating and cooling systems: Fascinating facts.* (PDF file) Available from www.geoexchange.org/documents/ GB-003.pdf

Gouchoe, S., Everette, V., & Haynes, R. 2002. *Case studies on the effectiveness of state financial incentives for renewable energy.* (PDF file) Available from www.nrel.gov/docs/fy02osti/32819.pdf

Green Business Letter. 1997. June.

Helsinki Energy Board. 2004. *Annual report 2003.* (PDF file) Available from www.helsinginenergia.fi/en/index.html

Home Energy. 1994. "The Jasper Energy Efficiency Project." March/April.

Hubbard, A., and C. Fong. 1995. *Community Energy Workbook: A Guide to Building a Sustainable Economy.* Snowmass, Colorado: Rocky Mountain Institute.

Interfaith Coalition on Energy (ICE). 2003. Available from www.interfaithenergy.com/

International Council for Local Environmental Initiatives (ICLEI). 1991. *The Urban CO2 Project.* Toronto: ICLEI.

Krohn, S. 2002. *Danish wind turbines: An industrial success story.* Available from www.windpower.org/en/articles/success.htm

Lealess, S. 1998. *Resource conservation in Ashland, Oregon.* Available from www.toolsofchange.com/ English/CaseStudies/default.asp?ID=106

Liepe, P. C. 2001. Geoexchange systems heat and cool commercial buildings. *Environmental Design & Construction,* Available from www.edcmag.com/CDA/ ArticleInformation/features/BNP__Features__Item/0,4120,18817,00.html

Local Government Commission. 1990. "Model Ordinances for Environmental Protection." Sacramento, California: Local Government Commission.

Lovins, A. B. 2002. *Accelerating Renewables: Expanding the policy and marketing toolkit. American Council for Renewable Energy organizing conference keynote address, Washington, DC, 10 july 2002.* (PDF file) Available from www.rmi.org/images/other/Energy/E02-07_AccelRenewables.pdf

Lowe, M.D. 1991. "Shaping Cities: The Environmental and Human Dimensions." *Worldwatch* 105. Washington, DC: Worldwatch Institute.

Millyard, K. 1992. "A Preliminary Carbon Dioxide Inventory for the City of Ottawa." Ottawa: Friends of the Earth.

Pacific Gas and Electric (PG&E). 2003. *2002 Environmental report.* (PDF file) Available from www.pgecorp.com/corp_responsibility/pdf/env_rpt_02.pdf

Portland Energy Office (PEO). 2000. *1990 Energy policy: Impacts and achievements.* (PDF file) Available from www.sustainableportland.org/energypolicyupdate2000.pdf

Rocky Mountain Institute (RMI). 2003. *Community energy opportunity finder.* Available from http://finder.rmi.org/efficiency/initiatives/financing2.asp

San Franciso City and County, SF Environment (SFE). n.d. *Resource efficient building / green building.* Available from http://temp.sfgov.org/sfenvironment/facts/resource_bldg.htm

Torrie, R. 1997. Urban Energy Management and the Cities of APEC — Opportunities and Challenges (draft). Prepared for the National Round Table on the Environment and the Economy, March.

US Green Building Council (USGBC). 2004. *Leadership in energy and environmental design (LEED).* Available from www.usgbc.org/LEED/LEED_main.asp

Waverly Light and Power (WLP). 2004. Energy efficiency programs. Available from the Energy Efficiency and Renewable Energy folders at http://wlp.waverlyia.com

ATMOSPHERIC CHANGE
AND AIR QUALITY

M any scientists believe that the context for thinking about sustainable development for the next several decades will be global atmospheric change. Put simply, we are changing the composition of the earth's atmosphere. If the change continues at current rates, the world's weather may be significantly altered by the middle of the next century. While scientists are unable to say conclusively that recent storms and floods are a result of human-induced climate change, the insurance industry has been expressing serious concern about increasing weather-related losses since the late 1990s (ICLEI, 1997a). Nearly 50 percent of all insured losses in the US from natural catastrophes in the past 40 years have occurred since 1990 (EPA, 2000). Some models point to increased flooding, drought and peak winds as a result of higher atmospheric concentrations of greenhouse gases (IPCC, 2001).

Although atmospheric change is a complex technical issue, only a few basic concepts are required to comprehend its implications and design community strategies to reduce its threat. This chapter addresses the key areas of atmospheric change that concern communities — local air quality, potential climate change, and ozone layer depletion. The economic consequences of addressing climate change are then explored.

LOCAL AIR QUALITY

Local air quality obviously varies according to local conditions, but shares causes and solutions with broader atmospheric change issues. The release of atmospheric pollutants by human activity results in two local phenomena: smog and acid rain.

The combustion of fossil fuels, primarily from motor vehicles, produces a yellow-brown layer of pollution known as smog. It is especially evident over cities in summer months. Smog results from the reaction of nitrogen oxides and hydrocarbon gases with sunlight to produce ozone and other trace gases. Ground-level ozone inhibits photosynthesis in plants.

Sulphur dioxide, emitted from cement works, oil refineries, and various industrial sources, is a primary cause of acid rain. It can contribute to plant, forest, and crop damage, and deteriorate structures and materials.

CHAPTER 8

It is imperative that the insurance industry in the United States become cognizant of changes occurring in our climate and its causes.
Franklin W. Nutter, President, Reinsurance Association of America (ICLEI, 1997a).

What are the health effects of atmospheric pollutants? While we don't know all the answers yet, those that we do know give cause for concern. Nitrogen oxides (a byproduct of fossil fuel combustion from motor vehicles) can increase susceptibility to viral infections such as influenza, irritate the lungs, and cause bronchitis and pneumonia. Ground-level ozone (which reacts with nitrogen oxides in sunlight) irritates the lungs and respiratory system, reduces resistance to colds and pneumonia, can aggravate heart disease, asthma, bronchitis, and emphysema, and is associated with the symptoms of dry cough, chest tightness or discomfort, sore throat, headache, and eye irritation. Sulphur dioxide and particulate matter concentrations can provoke or exacerbate cough, phlegm production, chest tightness and wheezing associated with asthma and chronic bronchitis. Low-level exposure to carbon monoxide from motor vehicles may exacerbate heart disease, and compromise brain function (French, 1990; Kleinman et al., 1989).

CLIMATE CHANGE

Global warming is one possible consequence of atmospheric change. In essence, we might be giving the planet a fever by increasing the Earth's natural greenhouse effect. We know from personal experience that a fever allowed to rise unchecked poses serious health risks to the brain, the immune system, and many other key bodily functions. Likewise, an unchecked global fever poses serious health risks to food production systems (irrigation, growing seasons, crop failures, etc.) and many other key social and ecological functions that human civilization depends upon.

The greenhouse effect refers to heat retention in the earth's atmosphere. There has always been a natural greenhouse effect; without it the earth would be too cold for life. The problem now is what scientists call the enhanced greenhouse effect; in the last several decades we have dumped additional quantities of greenhouse gases into the atmosphere, which greatly increase its heat retention.

Six gases have been identified as greenhouse gases (GHGs) of particular significance including: carbon dioxide; methane; nitrous oxide; hydrofluorocarbons; perfuorocarbons; and sulphur hexafluoride (Cool Vancouver, 2003).

OZONE LAYER DEPLETION

In the upper layer of the Earth's atmosphere, the stratosphere is a thin shield of ozone that limits the amount of ultraviolet radiation that can reach the Earth's surface. Depletion of the ozone layer causes an increase in ultraviolet radiation, which is expected to result in higher incidences of skin cancer, cataracts, immune system disorders, damage to crops and plant life, and destruction of marine phytoplankton.

Halocarbons

There is now an effective consensus among the world's leading scientists and serious well-informed people outside the scientific community that there is a discernible human influence on the climate.
John Browne, Chief Executive of British Petroleum (Clover, 1997).

Ozone layer destruction is caused primarily by the release of a group of human-made chemicals known as halocarbons that have been used since the 1930s. CFCs, halons, and chlorocarbons including methyl chloroform and carbon tetrachloride drift up to the stratosphere where they destroy ozone molecules for 60-100 years. These gases also contribute to the greenhouse effect, trapping 20,000 times more heat, molecule for molecule, than carbon dioxide. Because it takes so long for ozone-depleting chemicals to reach the atmosphere, the ozone depletions now being observed are actually the result of releases prior to the 1980s. Most CFCs and related chemicals are still on their way up.

Ozone depleting chemicals are used as coolant materials in refrigerators, and in building and automobile air conditioners. They are also used as the blowing agent for foam products such as seat cushions, insulation, and foam containers, and they are used as cleaning solvents in the computer, aerospace, and metal products industries. Halon fire extinguishers and hospital sterilants also use ozone depleting chemicals, although in many jurisdictions they have been decommissioned and replaced with non-ozone destroying alternatives (Local Government Commission, 1990; DEFRA, 2000).

One pound of CFC-12 refrigerant, commonly known as R-12 and even more commonly as freon, can destroy 70,000 pounds of ozone. A 1994 United Nations Environment Program study estimated that every one percent decrease in the ozone layer results in at least a one-percent increase in the incidence of skin cancer (Sheff 1997). For these reasons, many communities have called for stricter actions. Making fast progress toward eliminating the release of ozone depleting chemicals is important since their ozone depleting capacity lasts for so long.

The cities of Irvine, California and Newark, New Jersey passed comprehensive bans on ozone-depleting compounds in 1989-90 when international agreements would have allowed their use for another decade. The leadership demonstrated by communities such as Irvine and Newark helped ensure that ozone depletion was put high on the agenda of senior governments.

On January 1, 1996, production of CFCs was to have ceased under the provisions of the Montreal Protocol of the Vienna Framework Convention on Ozone-Degrading Substances. Developing countries have a 10-year grace period before they must phase out production as well. The phase-out represents the culmination of diplomatic, scientific, and industrial work to forge an international consensus and to develop alternatives to these environmentally harmful substances (World Resources Institute et al. 1996). Consequently, communities no longer have to worry about taking a leadership role on ozone layer depletion, but they must concentrate on ensuring that these international agreements are enforced locally.

Carbon Dioxide

The recent progress witnessed in respect to ozone-layer depletion unfortunately does not apply to carbon dioxide (CO_2) emissions. Whereas phasing out ozone-degrading substances is essentially a technical problem, reducing atmospheric carbon dioxide emissions may require more fundamental long-term changes in how we organize our lives and our communities.

Given the uncertainty associated with the effects of atmospheric change, should decision-makers act now or wait for more information? Global warming and the destruction of the ozone layer are essentially irreversible processes. If we wait to see the proof of these phenomena, the costs of dealing with changes in agriculture, forestry, and weather patterns will be much greater than if we act now to start reducing the likelihood of these events occurring (City of Vancouver, 1990).

CFC Smuggling

CFCs are invisible, the harm they do is both technical and abstract, and the service they provide is blandly and selfishly appealing. In the first three years since the domestic manufacture of chlorofluorocarbons began to be phased out as a result of the Montreal Protocol, an estimated 60 million pounds of illegal CFCs, with a street value of $1.5 billion, were smuggled into the United States. CFCs were replaced with relative ease in high-tech degreasers and solvents, refrigerators and home air-conditioning systems by 1993. However, while post-1993 vehicles use alternative chemicals in their air conditioners, some 80 million older Freon-spitting vehicles in the US alone must have their coolant replaced every two to three years. R-12 smugglers sell the coolant to auto-parts stores and various middlemen, who resell it to service stations and air-conditioning repair shops. These businesses can buy a 30-pound canister of R-12 for $400, charge a customer as much as $80 per pound, and pocket the $2000 difference. R-12 smuggling is a bigger business than gun-running or smuggling prescription drugs. The dollar value of intercepted CFCs is second only to that of intercepted drugs (Sheff, 1997).

Global Warming as a Municipal Issue

The United Nations Intergovernmental Panel on Climate Change, a panel of world-renowned scientists, has concluded it is *certain* that "emissions resulting from human activities are substantially increasing the atmospheric concentrations of the greenhouse gases . . . resulting on average in an additional warming of the Earth's surface."

The major greenhouse gas forcing the rise in global temperatures is carbon dioxide (CO_2), produced largely through the burning of fossil fuels for energy use. The concentration of CO_2 in the atmosphere has risen about 25 percent since pre-industrial times and is continuing to rise at the rate of 0.5 percent annually due to human activities.

Critical scientific concerns about global warming are:

· Without action to reduce emissions of greenhouse gases from human activities, global warming may increase 2ºC to 5ºC, and sea levels may rise 30-100 centimeters (12-40 inches)over the next century.

· A continuous world-wide reduction of net CO_2 emissions of 1 percent to 2 percent per year would stabilize atmospheric concentrations of CO_2 by the middle of the next century.

· Many studies conclude that technical and cost-effective opportunities exist to reduce CO_2 emissions in industrialized nations.

· These nations must implement reductions even greater than those required on average for the globe as a whole to allow for increased emissions from developing countries.

Cities, among the most energy-intensive ecosystems on the planet, are major producers of CO_2. As over half the world's population now lives in urban areas, the reduction of fossil fuel use in cities is vital to the implementation of an international climate change convention. Furthermore, many of the actions necessary to reduce CO_2 emissions-licensing, building codes, land-use planning, zoning, transit, and transportation plans-fall under the jurisdiction of municipal or regional governments (ICLEI, 1991; IPCC, 1996, ICLEI, 2004).

Carbon dioxide lingers for 100 years in the atmosphere and accounts for about half of the greenhouse effect. Carbon dioxide is fully integrated into our daily activities since it is released largely from fossil fuel combustion and from burning forests and plants. While deforestation may have contributed as much as 40 percent to the increase of carbon dioxide earlier in the century, 80 percent of today's global carbon dioxide emissions are from fossil fuels — coal, oil and natural gas (City of Vancouver, 1990). In the United States, most carbon dioxide (98 percent) is emitted as the result of the combustion of fossil fuels (EIA, 2002). Fossil fuels will continue to be the most significant source of atmospheric carbon well into the 21st Century.

On a per person basis, Canada and the US are among the world's largest consumers of fossil fuels and among the largest producers of carbon dioxide. For example, despite its relatively small population (one-half of one percent of the world's population), Canada is responsible fully for 2 percent of global greenhouse emissions (Flavin, 1990). Canada ranks 27th out of 29 OECD nations when greenhouse gas emissions are measured on a per capita basis. Canadians produce 16.84 tonnes of carbon dioxide, per person, per year, 48 percent above the OECD average of 11.41 tonnes and more than four times the global average. Canada uses 33 percent more energy per unit of GDP than the United States (Boyd, 2001). If North Americans are to help in reversing climate change, we must reduce our carbon dioxide emissions and contribute to the development of cleaner and more energy-efficient technologies. Transportation, land use, energy, and greening the city are all directly concerned with the challenge of reducing our carbon dioxide emissions.

The US Environmental Protection Agency has estimated that merely to stabilize atmospheric concentrations of CO_2 at the current level, carbon emissions must be cut by 50 percent to 80 percent by the middle of the century. An important global action plan calls for the governments of all high- and medium-energy consuming countries to reduce their carbon dioxide emissions by 70 percent by 2030. Scientists and policy makers offered a short-term goal: cutting them by 20 percent by 2005 (e.g., IUCN et al., 1991; Toronto Conference Statement, 1988). Yet despite commitments signed at various conventions during the 1990s and the early 2000s, US and Canadian emissions continue to rise (EIA, 2004; EIA, 2002, Environment Canada, 2004).

In 1992, a global approach to addressing the challenge of climate change was launched with more than 155 countries signing the United Nations Framework Convention on Climate Change (UNFCCC). Since 1992, a number of United Nations conferences have taken place. The goals of the agreements were to limit greenhouse gas (GHG) emissions and protect carbon sinks and reservoirs.

In 1997, the *Kyoto Protocol* was established to create a future of lower GHG emissions, better energy efficiency, sustainable economic performance, and cleaner air, leading to an overall cleaner, healthier environment. The Protocol created various targets, for industrialized Annex 1 Countries that ratify the agreement, to reduce overall GHG emissions by a global average of 5.2 percent below 1990 levels in the commitment period of 2008 to 2012.

The Protocol comes into effect 90 days after at least 55 Parties to the Convention, which account for at least 55 percent of the total carbon dioxide emissions for 1990 from the Annex 1 Countries, have ratified, accepted, approved or acceded to the Protocol. The 55 percent requirement was satisfied for the Protocol's entry into force when Russia ratified the Protocol in 2004. Canada has ratified the Protocol; the United States has indicated that it will not ratify the Protocol.

While international bodies and national governments struggle to formulate policies to reduce carbon dioxide emissions, *it is at the community level where most of these policies will be implemented.*

Despite commitments signed at the Rio Climate Convention in 1992 to stabalize greenhouse gas emissions at 1990 levels by 2000, US emissions had increased 11 percent by 2002 and are projected to rise 25 percent above current levels by the year 2025 (EIA, 2004; EIA, 2002). Canadian greenhouse gas emissions had risen 9.2 percent over 1990 levels by 1996, and current Environment Canada forecasts suggest that by 2020, Canadian emissions of greenhouse gases will be 36 percent above 1990 levels (Duffy, 1997; Environment Canada, 2004).

In the face of such challenges, many communities have started developing initiatives to address the root causes of environmental deterioration and to contribute solutions toward a sustainable future. They recognize that net fiscal, economic, and ecological benefits will accrue to those who get their environmental house in order.

Methane

Methane has received less media attention than other greenhouse gases, but it does play a significant role in local air quality and global atmospheric change. Methane, released from rotting organic matter such as bogs, wetlands, and landfills, is responsible for about 18 percent of the greenhouse effect. Although methane's lifespan in the atmosphere is approximately 10 years (versus up to 100 years for carbon dioxide and CFCs) methane's heat-trapping ability on a molecule by molecule basis is 25 times greater than carbon dioxide, and its presence is increasing in the atmosphere at a significantly faster rate than carbon dioxide (City of Vancouver, 1990; 2003).

To initiate change, communities can construct methane gas collection systems for their landfills. When collected, methane can also be used as an energy source for the landfill or sewage plant, or sold to other users.

Public Transportation and Greenhouse Gases

Data from a study of 32 major world cities show that those cities with the highest public transport utilization (and these are virtually all rail-based systems) have the lowest greenhouse gas emissions. This is important as it is sometimes claimed that if we are going to use more public transport then it is not much better than the automobile when it comes to emissions per capita. However, this is because simplistic assumptions are being made about changing from one mode to the other. It is not just a matter of one trip by car being replaced by one trip on public transport. Once a mode is provided that can adequately compete with the automobile, then a range of other changes also occur. Only by considering these kinds of changes is it possible to do justice to the full benefit of rebuilding our cities around non-automobile modes.

The study data show that the cities with highest CO_2 emissions have the greatest provision for the automobile in terms of roads and car parking. The data also show that the cities with the lowest CO_2 emissions have the slowest moving traffic; this goes against the often stated theory that free-flowing traffic saves fuel and reduces emissions due to greater vehicle efficiency. A more realistic explanation is that congestion does indeed reduce vehicle efficiency but it also facilitates other modes, and most of all it keeps a city from sprawling and hence building in extra travel distances. The conclusion has been applied in the US, where the Environmental Protection Agency has now requested all new highway applications to consider the effect of increased vehicle miles of travel (VMT) on emissions from new highways, not just the effect of improved vehicle efficiency. This is an important step in recognizing the need for cleaner cities and not just cleaner cars.

In short, electric rail-based cities are clearly the way we should be heading in a greenhouse future (Newman, 1991; see also Newman and Kenworthy, 1999).

ECONOMIC BENEFITS OF ADDRESSING ATMOSPHERIC CHANGE

"No regrets" policies for reducing greenhouse gas emissions are policies which are either inexpensive (such as encouraging consumers to buy energy-efficient appliances) or worth implementing regardless of whether or not global warming proves to be a problem (such as reducing subsidies to fossil fuels). The Intergovernmental Panel on Climate Change calculates that cost efficient measures could allow global emissions to be reduced below year 2000 levels in 2010-2020 (IPCC, 2001).

A number of economic benefits arise from policies that reduce atmospheric and air emissions. These include:
• lower energy costs that come from conservation and energy efficiency;
• growth of businesses that sell energy-efficient technologies;
• growth of renewable energy businesses;
• more disposable income from increasing taxes on the inefficient use of energy and using that money to reduce taxes on income and capital; and
• reduced repair costs for damage to the environment and human health caused by climate change and other pollutants.

As stated in a declaration signed by over 2,000 economists across North America, including six Nobel laureates:

There are many potential policies to reduce greenhouse-gas emissions for which the total benefits outweigh the total costs ... For the United States and Canada, sound economic analysis shows that there are policy options that would slow Climate Change without harming North American living standards, and those measures may in fact improve productivity in the longer run (*The Economist*, 1997; David Suzuki Foundation, 1997).

TOOLS AND INITIATIVES

Cities for Climate Protection Campaign

The International Council for Local Environmental Initiatives (ICLEI) Cities for Climate Protection campaign is working with over 500 municipalities around the world representing 8 percent of the world's greenhouse emissions to develop local strategies to reduce energy consumption and CO_2 emissions (ICLEI, 2004). The cities have each pledged to develop a local action plan to reduce emissions. The cities — representing perhaps 10 percent of global greenhouse gas emissions — have each pledged to develop a local action plan to reduce emissions.

North America: The Canadian cities of Vancouver, Victoria, Regina, Toronto and others have set targets of freezing or reducing CO2 emissions below 1988 levels by 2005. Canadian Cities for Climate Protection represent 61 percent of Canada's population and range from major urban centres such as Calgary, Edmonton, Toronto and Vancouver to smaller towns such as Gondola Point, NB, Port Alberni, BC and Fort Smith, North West Territories (ICLEI, 2004a). There are more than 140 US cities and towns participating in Cities for Climate Protection ranging from major urban centres such as Atlanta, Chicago, Los Angeles, and Dade County, Florida, to smaller towns such as Austin, Texas, Maplewood, New Jersey, and Chittenden County, Vermont (ICLEI, 2004b).

Europe: Many European cities such as Frankfurt, Freiberg, and Hagen have set the more ambitious goal of halving CO_2 emissions by the year 2010. Hanover, Germany has proposed a comprehensive program that would include: switching fuels for electricity generation, retrofitting municipal buildings, strengthening energy performance standards in the building codes for new buildings, modifying land-use patterns, and improving waste management. Copenhagen has proposed a local energy tax and utility rate reform to reduce energy consumption (Sandborn, 1996).

Urban Carbon Dioxide Reduction Plans

In the early 1990s, the International Council for Local Environmental Initiatives established the Urban CO2 Reduction Project to help municipal governments world-wide develop effective strategies to reduce emissions of greenhouse gases (ICLEI, 1990; 1991; 1997b). Twelve international urban jurisdictions agreed to reduce emissions to 1988 levels by 2010. These cities include Portland, San Jose, Denver, Toronto, Minneapolis-St. Paul, and Dade County, Florida.

Minneapolis-St. Paul developed a six-part strategy which includes a municipal action plan, diversification of the local transportation sector, expanded urban reforestation efforts, energy efficiency measures, energy supply measures (promoting renewables), and 'precycling and recycling' (reducing product use and making products from secondary rather than raw materials), all of which now form part of a comprehensive city-wide sustainability plan (City of Minneapolis, 2003)

Portland also developed a six-part strategy which focuses on transportation, energy efficiency, renewable resources and cogeneration, recycling, tree planting, and lobbying for stronger federal actions with respect to vehicle fuel efficiency standards and tax incentives (City of Portland, 2001).

Toronto developed the "5 Best Measures" for action: retro-fitting city owned buildings for energy efficiency and conservation; expanding the existing district energy system for heating and cooling, energy and water-efficiency retrofits of all commercial and residential buildings; energy efficiency and conservation standards for new and existing buildings; and balancing employment and residential growth in the central area as part of an integrated land-use and transportation policy. These measures have been incorporated into a city-wide comprehensive sustainability plan (City of Toronto, 2000).

Dade County's strategy focuses on four areas. Transportation objectives include improvements to mass transit, transportation demand management, promoting increased bicycle use, and increasing fuel efficiency. The land-use objective is to reduce vehicle miles traveled by 5 percent through mixed land use. Energy objectives include increasing efficiencies of county operations, decreasing residential sector energy use, expanding community tree plantings and white surfaces, and promoting public participation in energy conservation. Solid waste objectives include recycling 30 percent to 50 percent of the county's waste stream, recovering and utilizing landfill methane, and reducing the generation of solid waste by up to 5 percent. Each year since adopting the strategy, the Department of Environmental Resources Management prepares a progress report assessing reduction efforts (DERM, 2001).

Airshed Quality Management

For especially significant environmental problems, local governments have the ability and will to take significant corrective actions. The Los Angeles South Coast Air Quality District plan is the most drastic, comprehensive, and expensive effort to improve air quality ever drawn up locally in the US While specific actions proposed were not mandated by the federal government, court decisions in response to the region's non-compliance with federal air quality standards were a major factor in the development of the local plan. Implementation of the plan will be a local responsibility (SCAQMD, 2003; Cone, 1997; OECD, 1990; SCAG, 1989; SCAQMD, 1989).

Auto-Use Restrictions: In early 1989, an extensive air quality improvement plan was adopted for the metropolitan area of Los Angeles, California. The program's first stage (1989-93) included tightening restrictions (at a cost of $2.8 billion per year) on the use of private automobiles and on pollution-causing industrial and household activities, including deodorants, hair sprays, perfume, nail polish removers, and bathroom cleaners. The second stage (1993-98) focussed on conversion to cleaner fuels for both mobile and stationary emissions sources. And the final stage optimistically anticipated the total prohibition of gasoline vehicles by the year 2007. A key to the success of the plan was a redirection of development patterns, employment and housing locations, and a substantial reduction in travel from homes to employment centres.

Current air quality management in the region divides strategies between stationary and mobile pollutant sources. Stationary sources include (i) household products such as automotive polishes, heavy-duty hand soaps, paint removers, metal polishes, spot removers, herbicides, lubricants, floor wax strippers and hair shine sprays; (ii) industrial emissions; and (iii) emissions from construction materials. Control of mobile source emissions focuses on a 5-part strategy: (i) technology-forcing emissions standards for new vehicles with a push toward zero emissions technology by 2010; (ii) reduce emissions from vehicles currently in use; (iii) fuel strategies including requirements for cleaner fuels, supporting alternative fuels and reducing petroleum dependency; (iv) reducing emissions from Federal and State mobile sources; and (v) pursue long-term advanced technologies measures (CARB, 2004; SCAQMD, 2003).

RESOURCES

Cities for Climate Protection (CCP) is a campaign of the International Council for Local Environmental Initiatives (ICLEI). The CCP is a performance-oriented campaign that offers a framework for local governments to develop a strategic agenda to reduce global warming and air pollution emissions, with the benefit of improving community livability. Five hundred local governments are participating the Campaign, representing 8 percent of global greenhouse gas emissions, and the numbers are growing.

REFERENCES

Boyd, D. 2001. "Canada vs. the OECD: An Environmental Comparison". Victoria, British Columbia: University of Victoria, Eco-Chair of Environmental Law and Policy

California Air Resources Board (CARB). 2004. Mobile Source Program. Retrieved from http://www.arb.ca.gov/msprog/msprog.htm

City of Minneapolis. 2003. *Sustainability Initiatives*. Retrieved from http://www.ci.minneapolis.mn.us/environment/docs/Sustainability-Initiatives-FINAL.pdf

City of Portland. 2001. *Local Action Plan on Global Warming*. Retrieved from http://www.sustainableportland.org/Portland%20Global%20Warming%20Plan.pdf

City of Toronto. 2000. *Clean, Green and Healthy: A Plan for an Environmentally Sustainable Toronto*. Retrieved from http://www.toronto.ca/council/etfepfin.pdf

City of Vancouver. 1990. *Clouds of Change: Final Report of the City of Vancouver Task Force on Atmospheric Change*. Two volumes. Vancouver: City of Vancouver.

City of Vancouver, "A Discussion Paper on Greenhouse Gas Reduction Planning for the City of Vancouver," (City of Vancouver, BC: Cool Vancouver Task Force, June 2003).

Clover, C. 1997. "Oil Firms Back Move From Fossil Fuels to Alternatives." *Daily Telegraph* (London), reprinted in *Vancouver Sun*, 23 May 1997: A1.

Cone, M. 1997. "California Takes Smog Fight Home." *Los Angeles Times*. Reprinted in *Vancouver Sun*, 25 July 1997: A17.

David Suzuki Foundation. 1997. "Preventing Climate Change." *Report,* April.

Department for Environment, Food and Rural Affairs. 2000. Phase out of halon 1301 and 1211 — EC Regulation 2037/2000. Retrieved from http://www.defra.gov.uk/environment/climatechange/ozone/halons.htm

Department of Environmental Resources Management, Dade County, Florida. 2001. *A Long Term CO Reduction Plan for Miami-Dade: Progress Report*. Retrieved from: http://www.co.miami-dade.fl.us/derm/globalwarming/library/co2report-2001.pdf

Duffy, A.1997. "Canada Faces a Diminished Role." *Vancouver Sun*, 21 June, p. G4.

Environment Canada. 2004. *Climate Change Overview*. Retrieved from http://www.ec.gc.ca/climate/overview_2020-e.html

Environmental Information Administration (EIA). 2002. *Emissions of Greenhouse Gases in the United States*. Retrieved from http://www.eia.doe.gov/oiaf/1605/1605a.html

Environmental Information Administration (EIA). 2004. *Annual Energy Outlook 2004 with Projections to 2025.* Retrieved from http://www.eia.doe.gov/oiaf/aeo/emission.html

Environmental Protection Agency (EPA). (2000), *Preparing for Global Warming - Smart Insurance.* Retrieved from http://yosemite.epa.gov/oar/globalwarming.nsf/UniqueKeyLookup/SHSU5BVQZ9/$File/smart_insurance.pdf

Flavin, C. 1990. "Slowing Global Warming." In *State of the World 1990: A Worldwatch Institute Report on Progress Toward a Sustainable Society*, L.R. Brown, ed. New York/London: W.W. Norton. pp. 17-38.

French, H.F. 1990. "Clearing the Air." In *State of the World 1990*, L. Brown, ed. New York/London: W.W. Norton.

Intergovernmental Panel on Climate Change (ICPP). 2001. *Climate Change 2001: Synthesis Report.* Retrieved from: http://www.ipcc.ch/pub/un/syreng/spm.pdf

Intergovernmental Panel on Climate Change (IPCC). 1966. IPCC Second Assessment Synthesis of Scientific-Technical Information Relevant to Interpreting Article 2 of the U.N. Framework Convention on Climate Change 1995, January draft. Geneva: World Meterological Organization/United Nations Environment Program.

International Council for Local Environmental Initiatives (ICLEI). 1990. The Urban CO_2 Project proposal. Cambridge, Mass.: ICLEI.

ICLEI. 1991. The Urban CO_2 Project. Toronto: ICLEI.

ICLEI. 1997a. "Cities for Climate Protection Campaign." *Campaign Update* 3 Winter.

ICLEI. 1997b. Cities for Climate Protection Campaign, "Cities in Action." <www.iclei.org>.

ICLEI. 2004. *Cities for Climate Protection.* Retrieved from http://www.iclei.org/ccp/

ICLEI. 2004a. *Cities for Climate Protection, Regional Campaigns, CCP-Canada.* Retrieved from http://www.iclei.org/ccp/canada_pcp.html

ICLEI. 2004b. *Cities for Climate Protection, Regional Campaigns, CCP-US.* Retrieved from http://www.iclei.org/us/ccp/

Kleinman, M. T. et al. 1989. "Effects On Human Health of Pollutants in the South Coast Air Basin" El Monte, Calif.: South Coast Air Quality Management District/ California State University Fullerton Foundation.

Local Government Commission. 1990. *Model Ordinances: Addressing Ozone Layer Destruction.* Sacramento, Calif.: Local Government Commission.

Newman, P. and J. Kenworthy. 1999. *Sustainability and Cities: Overcoming Automobile Dependence.* Washington, DC: Island Press.

Newman, P. 1991. "Greenhouse, Oil and Cities." *Futures* May: 335-48.

Organization for Economic Cooperation and Development (OECD). 1990. *Environmental Policies for Cities in the 1990s.* Paris: OECD.

Reuter. 1991. "Mexico City Street-Vending Machines to Sell Oxygen." *Vancouver Sun*, 8 February: A8.

Sandborn, C. 1996. "Lessons From the Cities Summit: Toward Democracy and Sustainability." In *Urban Green Governance: The Views from the United Nations Conference on Human Settlements*, M. M'Gonigle, ed. Victoria: University of Victoria Faculty of Law, Eco-Research Chair.

Sheff, D. 1997. "The Chilling Effect." *Outside* 22(8) August: 90-125.

South Coast Association of Governments (SCAG) and South Coast Air Quality Management

District (SCAQMD). 1989. *Air Quality Management Plan: South Coast Air Basin.* Los Angeles: SCAG/SCAQMD.

South Coast Air Quality Management District (SCAQMD). 1989. *The Path to Clean Air: Attainment Strategies.* El Monte, Calif.: SCAQMD.

SCAQMD, Governing Board. 2003. *2003 Air Quality Management Plan.* Retrieved from http://www.aqmd.gov/aqmp/ AQMD03AQMP.htm

Toronto Conference Statement. 1988. Presented to The Changing Atmosphere: Implications for Global Security, Environment Canada, Toronto, 27-30 June.

US Energy Information Administration (EIA). 2002. "Emissions of Greenhouse Gasses in the United States 2002". Retrieved from http://www.eia.doe.gov/oiaf/1605/ggrpt/ carbon.html

World Conservation Union (IUCN), United Nations Environment Program (UNEP), and World Wide Fund for Nature (WWF). 1991. *Caring for the Earth: A Strategy for Sustainable Living.* Gland, Switzerland: IUCN/UNEP/WWF.

World Resources Institute, UNEP, United Nations Development Program, and World Bank. 1996. *World Resources 1996-97: The Urban Environment.* New York: Oxford University Press.

CHAPTER 9

Transportation Planning and Traffic Management

In 1970, Americans collectively drove a trillion miles per year, and by the mid-1990s this figure reached more than two trillion per year. There are more than 220 million registered automobiles in the US alone, and their numbers will soon overtake the country's population.

As cities sprawl farther into distant suburbs, an hour per day in the car has become the national norm. The average family takes 10 car trips a day. Our obsession with the automobile is clearly unsustainable, and has become an addiction.

The National Transportation Board predicts that delays caused by congestion will increase by 5.6 billion hours between 1995 and 2015, wasting 7.3 billion gallons of fuel; 70 percent of all daily peak-hour interstate travel now occurs under stop-and-go conditions, with a measurable "rush hour" stretching through most of the day (Motavalli, 2002).

Unsustainable transport systems not only are a major contributor to atmosphere change, but also lead to increasing congestion, longer commuting times, increasing demands for shorter work hours to compensate for longer travel hours, and higher prices due to reduced worker productivity. In fact, the primary objective of conventional traffic management has been to move vehicles in and around communities as rapidly and efficiently as possible using strategies such as designation of one way streets, synchronization of traffic signals, road widening, and construction of left-hand turn bays.

Governments face increasing difficulties in funding expansion of transportation infrastructure to meet these continuous increases in demand. Even if the enormous financial challenge of meeting demand for such infrastructure could be met, our transportation dilemma would be far from solved. In the words of Whitelegg (1966): "If we build a freeway system or an extended airport system to meet some prediction of future demand, then we should not be surprised to discover that these investments hasten our progress in that direction. Our plans and analyses boomerang so that our efforts are rewarded by the return of the problem, usually with some force and destructive impact."

The term "automobile dependency" was coined in the 1980s by Australian researchers Peter Newman and Jeffrey Kenworthy to help define our transportation challenges. Rather than try to eliminate cars altogether, an idea which few people consider realistic, we should focus on breaking our addiction to, or dependence upon, the automobile. Almost 88 percent of daily commuters use private vehicles, and the majority of drivers want to move at the same times of day. In 2000, less than 5 percent of all commuters traveled by public transit (Downs, 2004). This chapter examines the costs, both environmental and social, of our current transportation system, the myths of technical fixes, and ways to move toward sustainable transportation.

TRUE COSTS OF DRIVING

Driving a car incurs more costs than gas, insurance, maintenance and parking. For the US as a whole, the total costs from motor vehicles (e.g., air pollution, crashes, noise, time stuck in traffic, run-off into waterways, pollution from manufacturing vehicles, tires, and batteries, and pollution from disposing of them, etc.) include: $20 billion in taxpayer subsidies; $290 billion in social and environmental damage; and $415 billion in costs borne by drivers. The total cost is $725 billion annually (Komanoff, 1995).

There is no clear relationship between the benefits of a car trip and the social costs incurred. Car-related taxes paid by motorists can add up to much more than government spending on roads, but the taxes are usually levied on the car itself, not on its use. One of the most significant barriers to more sustainable transportation systems is the manner in which motorists pay (or are subsidized) for their motor vehicle use. Higher fixed costs of motor vehicle acquisition combined with lower incremental user costs (e.g., free parking, free roads, and in some countries like the US, very low motor fuel taxes) encourage rapid growth of motor vehicle use (Replogle, 1996).

How Fast Are We Really Going?

There may be more costs involved in driving than most of us realize, but at least we get high-speed mobility for our pains, don't we? One study (B. McCann, 2000) found that households in more automobile dependent communities devote more than $8,500 annually, or 20 percent of household expenditures, to surface transportation. Communities with more diverse modes of transportation spent less than $5,500 annually, or 17 percent. Canadians spend over $9,000, on average, to travel 18,000 kilometres with their cars per year (Canadian Automobile Association, 2004).

Traffic, Health and Sprawl

During the 1990s, there was no standard definition for sprawl. Experts compared it to obscenity: "hard to define, but obvious when you see it" (Schmidt, 2004). Urban sprawl is having profound impacts on human health and traffic management, yet it is only recently that sprawl is more clearly defined and studied.

In a landmark report in 2002, "Measuring Sprawl and Its Impact," sprawl included the outcome of related factors, including limited options for walking or biking. The report ranked 83 metropolitan areas according to a "sprawl index" derived from 22 separate measures (Schmidt, 2004).

Perhaps our age will be known to the future historian as the age of the bulldozer and the exterminator; and in many parts of the country the building of a highway has about the same results upon vegetation and human structures as the passage of a tornado or the blast of an atom bomb. Nowhere is this bulldozing habit of mind so disastrous as in the approach to the city. Since the engineer regards his own work as more important than the human functions it serves, he does not hesitate to lay waste to woods, streams, parks, and human neighborhoods in order to carry his roads straight to their supposed destinations (Mumford, 1964).

Americans continue to own more cars and drive more miles in them [than their European or Japanese counterparts]: the average American car driver travels almost 20,000 kilometers (about 12,400 miles) a year, whereas the European one does only 14,000 kilometers. This does not have much to do with the size of the country: most trips are urban, with an average length of about 14 kilometers, the same as in Britain and somewhat less than in Germany. Part of the answer is that buses and trains in America account for barely 3 percent of travel mileage, whereas in Europe the figure is over 15 percent. The rest of the answer lies in the sprawling low-density structure of American suburbs, which involve greater distances between homes and shops, schools and other amenities (Economist, 1996).

Another area of growing interest is the link between sprawl, commuting times and health (McCann & Ewing, 2003; Frank, Andresen, & Schmidt, 2004). In communities where people are more likely to drive than to walk, residents are generally less physically active. The less active these residents are, the more they weigh and the worse their health.

Planners and health professionals are starting to advocate for smart growth and urban growth boundaries to keep sprawl in check while offering more opportunities for residents to enjoy physical activity, however their efforts are often met with resistance. Researchers have found that for every 30 minutes added to a daily commute, drivers have a three percent greater chance of being obese than those who drive less.

According to a study by the Texas Transportation Institute, the average US driver spent 51 hours stuck in traffic in 2001; up 4 hours from 1996. The study estimated the cost in wasted time and gas at $69.5 billion. Los Angeles led the list of most congested cities, with 90 hours per driver, followed by San Francisco (68 hours), Denver (64 hours), and Miami (63 hours) (*Miscellaneous Facts, 2004*).

Traffic and Social Networks

Street reclaiming: Street reclaiming involves reducing vehicle traffic volumes and speeds and creating more attractive street environments. It is a process for increasing the social, cultural, recreational and economic activity in neighborhood streets. Street reclaiming is intended to change way that people think about and use public streets by encouraging interaction and increasing residents' involvement in their community. Key components encompass a resident-led interactive planning process with transportation, aesthetics, and participatory interactions to guide street design and neighborhood development (Engwicht, 1999).

Aging and Mobility

Current transportation priorities focus almost entirely on driving. As people grow older, they often become less willing or able to drive, making it necessary to depend on alternative methods of transportation. As the number of older people increases, so too will their mobility needs. Alternatives to driving are sparse, particularly in some regions and in rural and small town communities. Unfortunately, the United States is currently ill-prepared to provide adequate transportation choices for its rapidly aging population.

A recent report by the Surface Transportation Policy Project presents their findings based on the National Household Transportation Survey of 2001 and places them in the context of other research on mobility in the aging population (STPP, 2004).

The City of Vancouver constructed a Wellness Walkway that incorporates ideas for enhancing accessibility in the public realm for people with physical challenges related to sight and mobility. Features of the walkway include sidewalk tinted "sandstone" to reduce glare and aligned curb ramps with directional grooves. Corner bulges installed on all corners to shorten crossing distances, accessible benches enabling easier transitions for people with walking disabilities, and a variety of street trees, fragrant flowering plants and shrubs to enhance sensory stimulation (Duncan, 2000).

TECHNICAL FIXES

Ah, but soon we'll have electric cars, low- or zero-emission vehicles, alternative fuels, hydrogen buses, smart highways, mental telepathy, the transporter from Star Trek ("Beam me up, Scotty!").

Segway

When an American inventor unveiled the Segway human transporter in 2001, it was supposed to herald a transport revolution. As it turned out, in the first two years only 6,000 human transporters were sold. Predictions that the Segway would prove to be as significant a breakthrough as the personal computer were evidently wide of the mark.

Technology and TDM

The history of transportation consists, in part, of faster modes that expand human activities: steamships, railroads, bicycles, automobiles and air travel. Some faster modes are likely to become more common in the future, yet we should consider the overall value these modes can provide to society, and the problems they create.

Can technology address common transport problems such as road and parking congestion, crash risks to motorists and pedestrians on local streets, and provide adequate travel options for non-drivers? It would be wasteful for a community to devote an excessive portion of its resources to these modes, when more fundamental transportation problems exist.

Perhaps the next trend in transportation is not a new mode or service, but a paradigm shift in how to think about transportation problems and solutions. Perhaps this shift is an incremental approach that consists of management innovations that result in more efficient use of existing transportation systems. This is not as radical as it may sound. Many important revolutions result from more effective use of existing technologies and resources, rather than new technology.

This means that the best solutions to transport problems may consist of management innovations that encourage efficiency and improve basic mobility services (for example, walking and cycling conditions, road system management and public transit services), rather than a new mode or breakthrough technology (Litman, 2004). Transportation Demand Management (TDM) is how we may achieve this.

Telecommunications

Now that the era of electronic communications is in high gear, many large employers are implementing or considering options for telecommunications. Telecommuting has potential to substitute for some of the commuting that goes on in and between our communities, and so may lead to a reduction in vehicle trips generated. Telecommuting also has potential to *increase* vehicle trips in our communities. People

The amount of road space to be provided in a city is not an engineering question. It is first and foremost a question of social justice. Auto-dominated cities create a group of people we may call 'access-to-exchange-disadvantaged' (ATED). People who are ATED are often elderly, poor, disadvantaged, handicapped, children, parents without access to a second car and those who choose not to own a car. Between 40 and 60 percent of the population in most Western cities are ATED (Engwicht, 1993).

working from home may need to make more trips per day than they would simply going to the workplace and having all their working requirements in one place. Working from the "electronic cottage" may also encourage flight from urban centers and thus promote further sprawl development of the countryside with its attendant problems. Therefore, telecommuting should be incorporated as only one component of a comprehensive commuter trip reduction program.

REDUCING AUTOMOBILE DEPENDENCY

Automobile dependency is defined as high levels of automobile use, automobile-oriented land use, and a lack of travel alternatives (Newman & Kenworthy, 1991, 1999).

Four forces are at work to influence the choice of fuel for the future: oil depletion, global warming, urban pollution, and urban congestion (Economist, 1996).

Efforts to relieve traffic congestion alone do little to reduce polluting emissions or the amount of fuel consumed. Cities must now stress reduction of single-occupancy vehicle trips as the only sound way to achieve improved air quality, reduce energy consumption contributing to atmospheric change, and relieve traffic congestion.

Sustainable transportation planning and traffic management initiatives are usually motivated by goals to reduce the number of automobile trips; increase opportunities for non-automobile trips; increase opportunities for non-auto transportation including bicycles, walking, rail, buses, and alternative vehicles; and reduce the use of gasoline and diesel fuel in conventional buses, autos, and trucks.

Sustainable transportation policies reduce reliance on fossil fuel burning and single-occupancy motor vehicles. They also favour a broader mix of active (or self-propelled) transportation, public transit, ride-sharing and car-pooling, and clean-powered vehicles (BEST, 2004).

Sustainable transportation is to development what preventive medicine is to health — anticipating and managing problems before they arise. Sustainable transportation requires us to rethink how we measure transportation and integrate land management along with communication strategies. Transportation planners and engineers receive professional rewards for implementing capacity expansion projects, but are seldom acknowledged for finding ways to avoid the need for such projects. Sustainable transportation focuses on quality of access, rather than simply measuring quantity of access. Mobility is seldom an end in itself (VTPI, 2004).

A comparison of global cities over the period 1980-90 reveals large differences in automobile dependence with strong implications for the future sustainability of cities in different countries. The study demonstrated there are significant statistical relationships between key transport and land-use variables. Urban density is a key determinant of auto and transit use, as well as the relative role of transit (auto use increases and transit decreases with decreasing density). Road provision, parking, and non-motorized mode use are all also strongly associated with the pattern of auto-dependence across cities. To reduce automobile dependence, the follow-

ing directions should be pursued:

- *Land-use objectives*: more transit-oriented, higher density, mixed land uses, which help to halt the growth in auto-based development;
- *Private transport objectives*: stabilized or lower car use and less emphasis on infrastructure for cars;
- *Public transport objectives*: higher quality transit systems, especially rail, which are more competitive with cars; and
- *Non-motorized mode objectives*: greater safety and amenity for walking and cycling and increased use of these modes (Kenworthy and Laube, 1996).

In general, local initiatives should aim to encourage transit over personal automobile use by: reducing the subsidies to private vehicles; identifying means for managing transportation demands, especially of commuters; and emphasizing bicycle and pedestrian networks as valid components of a regional transportation strategy.

Management Strategies

Transportation system management (TSM) is one option toward more sustainable transportation. TSM aims to affect the supply of transportation services by attempting to increase the person-carrying capacity of the road system without building additional road capacity, or by simply allowing congestion to worsen, thereby discouraging vehicle travel. Measures such as high occupancy vehicle (HOV) and transit-only lanes, queue jumpers, preferred parking for HOV vehicles and toll-free privileges for HOVs help to increase the person-carrying capacity of the road system without the need for additional road capacity.

HOV and transit-only lanes are the most common means of increasing road capacity. However in congested urban centers, transit-only lanes are more efficient since they have the capacity to carry far more people. At freeway speeds, for example, a full bus or rail car can carry as many people as a lane of car-pool traffic up to a kilometer long (Leman et al., 1994).

Walkable Communities

Walkability is a key to an urban area's efficient surface transportation. Walking remains the cheapest form of transport for everyone as every trip usually begins and ends with walking. The design and construction of a walkable community provides the most affordable transportation system any community can plan and maintain. Walkable communities put urban environments back on a scale for the sustainability of resources (both natural and economic) and lead to increased social interaction and physical fitness, while diminishing crime and other social problems. Walkable communities are more livable communities and lead towards the whole, happy and healthy lives of every resident (Walkable Communities, 2004).

Transportation Demand Management

Transportation Demand Management (TDM) offers many potential benefits. In fact, many transport problems are virtually unsolvable without some form of TDM strategy. Conventional solutions, such as increasing roadway capacity or improving vehicle design, often reduce one problem but exacerbate others, particularly if they increase total vehicle travel. When all costs and benefits are considered, an integrated TDM program that includes an appropriate set of complementary strategies is often the most cost-effective way to improve transportation.

Many transportation professionals are skeptical that TDM is effective because it requires consumers to change their travel behavior. They argue that North Americans have a love affair with cars, and so will not voluntarily reduce their driving. As a result, they favor technological fixes (for example, wider roads, increased parking capacity, vehicle design improvements) over TDM strategies. However, given appropriate options and incentives, people are often willing to shift their behaviours (VTPI, 2004d).

For distances under 2 kilometers (1.2 miles) pedestrian traffic can play a large role if provided with safe and attractive conditions. Pedestrian improvements should not be limited to small islands in the form of pedestrian zones, but rather should be included as part of the area-wide road network.

Cycling

Bicycles are ideal for use in highly congested urban centers and thus can play an important role in sustainable transportation strategies. They avoid air pollution and high levels of fuel consumption associated with low-vehicle operating speeds and short distance, cold start trips. Bikes also help reduce congestion since they demand far less space than motor vehicles. Experience in Davis, California and Toronto, Ontario suggest that where cycling facilities are improved, the number and frequency of cycling trips increases dramatically (Toronto City Cycling Committee, 1994).

Best practices for employee cycling program development include the following: creating a clear, consistent and positive message about the benefits of non-motorized travel; identifying and overcoming barriers to non-motorized transport; finding opportunities for cooperation with other organizations; working with local planners, employers and employees who cycle to design and improve cycling facilities and services; utilizing cycling, walking and recreational organizations to enlist volunteers; emphasizing cycling skills and safety education (Cleary & McClintock, 2000).

Since 1956, the League of American Bicyclists has declared May to be National Bike Month in the US (TLAB, 2004). In Canada, Bike Month is traditionally held in May or June. Communities, corporations, clubs, and individuals are invited to join in sponsoring bicycling activities in order to increase awareness and acceptance of bicycling.

The Thurston County, Washington State Bicycle Commuter Contest encourages individuals to bicycle to work, to school, and to run errands throughout the month of May. The contest is a participatory event for Thurston County residents and employees since 1988. Participants keep track of how often and how far they commute by bicycle, and win prizes in a variety of categories. In 1999, 574 participants rode a total of near-ly 15,000 miles (Climate Solutions, 2004).

Eugene, Oregon has a well-planned and well-used cycling network that includes 30 miles of off-street paths, 89 miles of on-street bicycle lanes, and 5 bicycle/pedestrian bridges spanning the Willamette River. This has resulted in 8 percent of commute trips by bicycle (Eugene, 2004).

It is a daunting challenge for many communities to find the space or finances to build separate bicycle paths. But many communities have a large network of quiet residential side-streets running parallel to main arteries. These residential streets can provide the basis for a network of bicycle routes that will be both safe and perceived as safe — leading to a significant increase in cycling.

TOOLS AND INITIATIVES

Automobile Restrictions

Car Free Living: Freiburg, Germany — Lunchtime at the Vauban kindergarten, and parents start pulling up to pick up their children. But there's no convoy of minivans or station wagons. Despite a bitter cold wind, these moms and dads roll to the door on bicycles, helmets on their heads and pant legs wrapped with reflective bands. Not because their cars are in the shop, but because they're not welcome in the neighborhood.

The Vauban development — so far, 280 new homes on a former military base — is Germany's biggest experiment in "auto-free living." Once dismissed as an "eco-freak" fantasy, the concept is moving off the drawing board and winning real-world converts, even in the land of high-speed autobahns and the Volkswagen "people's car."

"I simply like it better," says Ruthild Haage-Rapp as she bundles two fidgeting 2-year-olds, Simon and Maria, into their seats in a green-and-pink trailer attached to her dusty bicycle. "The children can play in the street," she says. "It's quiet. You can stand by your kitchen window without all the noise from the street. Then the inconvenience is worth it." (Geitner, 2000).

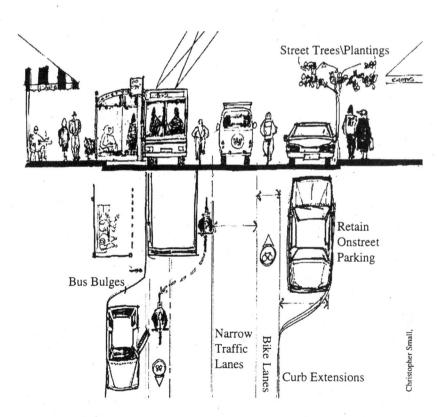

Traffic calming on a commercial street

Street Trees\Plantings

Retain Onstreet Parking

Bus Bulges

Narrow Traffic Lanes

Bike Lanes

Curb Extensions

Christopher Small,

Traffic circles work to slow traffic in residential neighborhoods. This Vancouver traffic circle was built by the city and planted by local residents

Car Sharing

Car sharing has become increasingly popular within the last decade with the service available in many North American cities (sometimes called car co-ops or car clubs). In Bremen, Germany, the car-sharing program *Cambio* has taken the concept one step further by collaborating with the city's transit authority and was the same pass for the transit system as an electronic key to Cambio's cars. In the future the electronic key will also act as a payment card for taxis (Fenton, 2003). Other car sharing programs include <www.carsharing.com>, <www.zipcar.com>, <www.flex-car.com> and <www.cooperativeauto.net>.

Road Pricing

Road pricing that reduces total vehicle travel can reduce road and parking costs, increase road safety, protect the environment, and encourage more efficient land use. The central London congestion charging scheme has reduced car congestion by 30 percent, and the volume of traffic within the zone was reduced by 15 percent, with a 28 percent reduction in crashes. Direct impact of congestion charging on business activity has been small, with reduced road traffic emissions and fossil fuel consumption (Transport for London, 2004).

Express Toll Lanes: State Route 91 in Orange County, California has 10 miles of express toll lanes privately constructed and funded by variable electronic tolls on State Route 91. The Express Lane uses "FasTrak" electronic transponders to collect tolls that vary from $0.75 to $3.50 per trip, depending on the level of congestion. In 1998, more than 9 million tolled trips were made on the facility, resulting in revenues of approximately $20 million (State of California, 2000).

Traffic Calming

Traffic calming is used widely in Europe and Australia, and increasingly in North America. Traffic calming measures include installation of stop signs, speed bumps, and/or traffic circles to slow or calm traffic, allowing roads to better accommodate a range of different road users and activities.

Former West Germany's traffic calming schemes have multiplied into the thousands since they were started in the 1970s. Originally intended for residential areas, the technique is now spreading over whole cities. Traffic calming greatly improves the quality of life in neighborhoods where it is implemented, and is gathering popularity in many countries, including Italy, Japan, Australia, Sweden, and Switzerland. Such restraints are so well-received in

This formerly two-lane road was "calmed," and the excess road space converted into park space

Denmark that local residents themselves are often willing to pay for the measure. The city of West Palm Beach, Florida (population 80,000) has developed "second generation traffic calming." Rather than considering traffic calming design as an added feature, traffic calming measures are designed when a street is built or reconstructed. This approach has proven to be more cost effective and equitable, toward improving a community's walkability.

Collision Decrease: Residents in neighborhoods with suitable street environments tend to walk, cycle and take transit more, and drive less. Traffic roundabouts which replace conventional intersections, raised landscaping in center medians, and speed reduction strategies can reduce total crashes by 39 percent, injury crashes by 76 percent, and fatal crashes by 90 percent (VTPI, 2004e).

Layout Change: For more than two decades Dutch cities like Delft, Groningen, and Maastricht have calmed traffic by changing the layout of the residential street, transforming it into a *woonerf*, or "living yard." In the *woonerf*, cars are forced to navigate slowly around carefully placed trees and other landscaping. Since motor traffic cannot monopolize the entire breadth of the street, much of the space becomes more open to walking, cycling, and children's play. Automobiles are free to enter the *woonerf*, but only as guests, while non-motorized traffic has priority. Experience with traffic calming has shown that it is most effective if widely implemented, so that motor traffic problems are not simply diverted to nearby streets. Traffic has been calmed on over 30 percent of residential roads in Maastricht.

Parking Measures

Ending the widespread employer practice of providing free or heavily subsidized parking to employees is a promising option for relieving both congestion and air pollution. By one estimate *free parking induces more travel than free gasoline would*. Parking costs can be considered unfair if applied selectively. For instance, if parking costs are imposed on lower income employees in commercial centers, but are not passed on to higher income employees or those working in suburban sites.

Parking charges represent a greater share of income for lower income motorists, but are not necessarily more regressive than alternative sources of paying for parking facilities, such as general income taxes. Higher-income people tend to receive the majority of parking subsidies since automobile ownership and use tends to increase with income (VTPI, 2004b).

Reduction in Required Parking: Several cities have found that parking programs pay. Sacramento, California grants developers a 5 percent reduction in required parking for providing bicycle facilities, 15 percent reduction for providing marked car/van-pool spaces, and 60 percent reduction for purchasing transit passes for tenants of new offices.

Preferential Parking for Car-Pools: Portland, Oregon and Seattle, Washington are leaders in on-street preferential parking programs for car-pools. Among the incentives: poolers are allowed to park downtown all day at specific metered locations; are exempted from hourly parking limits and meter fees; and enjoy spaces closest to building entrances.

In the US, each car consumes 4,000 square feet of parking space (including at home), which is almost three times the living area of the average family home (Renner, 1988).

Increased Parking Rates: The Canadian federal government increased its parking rates for federal employees in Ottawa, resulting in: a 23 percent reduction in employees driving to work; a 16 percent increase in transit ridership among federal employees; and an increase in average vehicle occupancy from 1.33 to 1.41 passengers.

HOV Pricing Strategies: Preferential high-occupancy vehicle (HOV) pricing strategies are also highly effective. Differential parking rates paid by the employer are applied, with two-person car-pools receiving a 50-percent reduction, three-person car-pools discounted 75 percent, and van-pools reduced 100 percent. A California study found that HOV lanes carry an average of 2,518 passengers per hour during peak hours, which only represented two-thirds of their capacity (substantially more people than a congested mixed-flow lane and roughly the same number of people as a typical mixed-flow lane operating at maximum capacity). Other studies indicate that HOV lanes produce mode shifts to ridesharing (VTPI, 2004a).

Area Wide Traffic Management

The aim of area wide traffic management is improving transportation efficiency by reducing over-reliance upon motorized vehicles within urban centers (VTPI, 2004f). Components of area-wide traffic management are also emerging in North America. Some cities have closed off streets to cars or designed pedestrian malls that offer no access to vehicles. In Canada, Calgary has several blocks devoted to a pedestrian mall, and more than 16 kilometres of passages connecting many buildings in the downtown area. Montreal has 30 kilometres of underground car-free passages that link about 60 large commercial, administrative, and apartment buildings in downtown.

The demand for traffic control was recognized at least as early as the first century A.D., when congestion caused Julius Ceasar to ban wheeled traffic from Rome in the daytime (Rajan, 1996).

In the United States, Minneapolis, Minnesota has 8 kilometres of enclosed overhead passageways in the commercial/retail heart of the city. Stanford University in California has designated 16 blocks on campus as car-free during the day, with only pedestrians, bikes, and some buses allowed. The heart of the commercial district in old downtown Boston and New Orleans includes several car-free streets ("People Over Cars," 2004).

Go Green Choices: In the workplace, Go Green Choices (GGC) provides training, education and support to companies in Greater Vancouver. Strategies are outlined with participants, or Go Green Coordinators, who are encouraged to use a range of comprehensive transportation strategies to address their organization's unique needs and realities. Strategies include: cycling, walking, transit, ridesharing, telecommuting, variable work hours, parking management and various types of incentives.

The key to the program's success is its ability to get people talking about alternatives to driving alone and exploring their transportation choices. Since the program's inception in 1997, GGC has trained over 300 Coordinators and currently supports over 100 businesses in Greater Vancouver (BEST).

SMART Movement: The SMART Movement is designed to "Save Money And The Air". They guide large organizations to reduce employee car trips and are based in Toronto, Halifax and Victoria, Canada (SMART Movement).

TravelSmart Australia: TravelSmart Australia brings together the many community and government based programs that request commuters to use alternatives to traveling alone (Australia).

Bus Bulges are a good way to speed up buses and improve the sidewalk environment. The curb is extended to meet the buses so they do not have to pull in and out and wait for traffic.

Transport Innovation

Improved transportation efficiency hinges upon improved public transport. Substantial volumes of car traffic can potentially be transferred to bus and rail; yet a number of different strategies are needed, including service innovations, payment innovations, and rail system development.

Curitiba, Brazil: One of Curitiba's best-known planning successes is its urban transportation system, which is a model for cities around the world wanting to implement eco-efficient transportation with environmental benefits. The city pioneered the idea of an all-bus transit network with special bus-only avenues that were also used to channel the city's growth. The transit system is rapid and cheap, and is currently being integrated within the metropolitan region, which encourages people to leave their cars at home. (Curitiba has more car owners per capita than anywhere in Brazil.) Since 1974, when the city boasted a single bus line, the population has doubled, yet auto traffic has declined by 30 percent. Curitiba has the highest public ridership of any Brazilian city (about 2.14 million passengers per day), and registers the country's lowest levels of ambient pollution and per-capita gasoline consumption (MacLeod, 2004).

In addition, an inexpensive "social fare" promotes equality, benefiting poorer residents settled on the city's periphery. A standard fare is charged for all trips, meaning shorter rides subsidize longer ones. One fare can take a passenger 70 kilometers.

After 25 years, Bogotá, Columbia has instituted a Curitiba-type transit system; and now 83 world cities are replicating the Curitiba bus system, including Seoul, Korea (Lerner, 2004).

Transit Marketing

Discounted Transit Passes: Discounted passes may encourage occasional riders to use transit more frequently and if implemented when fares are increasing, may avoid ridership losses. Discounts and targeted promotions that provide information on services and incentives may increase transit ridership by up to ten percent or more (VTPI, 2004e).

Regional Transit: Waterloo's regional transit system provides a seamless network and fare structure across three cities, including specialized transit service to three rural communities. The Grand River Transit has increased ridership from 4 to 12 percent in ridership jurisdictions (FCM, 2001).

Tax Exempt Transit Benefits: Commuter Check is a transit fare savings program that operates through employers. Commuter Checks are purchased by employers as either a company-paid benefit or by using pre-tax employee paid contributions. For example, the San Francisco Bay Area Commuter Check program began in 1991 and has expanded by approximately 35 percent per year. However, since pre-tax employee-paid options became available in 1998, the rate of growth has exceeded 100 percent. In 1999, over 35,000 employees and 2000 employers participated (Commuter Check).

U-PASS Progam: Since 1991, the U-PASS program has provided the campus community in Seattle, WA with an array of flexible, low cost transportation choices. Despite 12 years of population growth, university-related peak traffic levels remain below 1990 levels. Over three quarters of the campus population commutes using an alternative to driving alone. Because the U-PASS program reduces vehicle trips, the university has saved over $100 million in avoided construction costs of new parking spaces. The U-PASS program prevents roughly 8.2 million vehicle miles traveled and 3,300 tons of carbon dioxide from being emitted annually. The U-PASS program is a model for other regional pass programs and has set the standard in the region (U of W, 2003).

Free or Inexpensive Transit

Eliminating Fares: In November, 2000, residents of the Forest Glen neighborhood in the city of Boulder voted to form a General Improvement District (GID) to provide RTD transit passes for all neighborhood residents. All Forest Glen residents are eligible to receive an RTD Eco Pass, including home owners and renters. These passes are paid for by residents in Forest Glen as part of their annual property tax. The RTD Eco Pass

Encouraging wheelers, walkers, and bus riders helps make
a pleasant street environment
From: City of Vancouver (1996)

*They say everyone has a
BMW in Curitiba. You know,
BMW: Bus, Metro, Walking
(Lerner, 2004).*

allows unlimited riding on all RTD buses, Light Rail service to Denver International Airport, and Eldora Mountain Resort buses (VTPI, 2004a).

Non-Motorized Modes

Bike Stations: Chicago has joined Berkley, Palo Alto, Long Beach and Seattle with bike stations, as bicyclists are now enjoying an important and much sought-after cycling amenity: the new Millennium Park Bicycle Station.

The bicycle station, the first such facility in the MIdwest, opened as part of the Millennium Park grand opening. The 16,448 square foot heated facility includes free indoor parking for 300 bikes; showers and lockers; bicycle rental and repair; and a cafe. Chicago has earned an international reputation for promoting and improving bicycling, and was named best large city for cycling in Bicycling magazine in 2001 ("New Millennium Park Bicycle Station Opens", 2004).

BikeShare: BikeShare is a bike lending program launched in 2001 by the Community Bicycle Network. BikeShare pass holders can sign out a bike from one of several hubs in the downtown Toronto area, use the bike for up to three days at a time, and return it to their choice of hub. An online database is used to track the location and use of each bike. In 2004, the project offered 170 bikes at 14 hubs, and expects to operate at its capacity of about 450 pass holders (CBN, 2003).

Berkeley, California has developed such a good public transportation system that it continues to deliver almost one in five residents to work every day — four times the national and state average.

RESOURCES

Alt-Transp List is an Internet list to exchange information with 200 plus alternative transport professionals and activists. Members send and receive e-mail messages concerning transport related issues. To subscribe, e-mail *Majordomo@flora.org* with the body (not subject) of the message being: *subscribe alt-transp*, followed by your e-mail address. For more information, simply send the message: *help*.

Better Environmentally Sound Transportation (BEST) strives to make our communities healthier places to live by promoting sustainable transportation and land-use planning, and pedestrian, cycling and transit-oriented neighbourhoods.
Website: www.best.bc.ca

The Center for Neighborhood Technology has a unique mission: To invent and implement new tools and methods that create livable urban communities for everyone. TravelMatters offers a trio of resources — interactive emissions calculators, online emissions maps, and a wealth of educational content — to emphasize the close relationship between more efficient transit systems and lower greenhouse gas emissions.
Website: www.travelmatters.org/

Cities and Automobile Dependence: An International Sourcebook, by Peter Newman and Jeffrey Kenworthy (Gower Technical, 1989; 1999), is based on extensive research. This landmark study examines urban form, transport and energy use in 32 cities in North America, Europe, Asia, and Australia.

The data cover approximately 100 parameters for 1960, 1970, and 1980, and include parking, car ownership and use, roads, congestion, public transport, modal split and energy consumption; city form is characterized by central, inner and outer area population and employment data. The study confirms that the shorter distances inherent in medium- and high-density urban areas correspond with much more walking and cycling. For example, West European cities, averaging 85 people and jobs per hectare (2.47 acres) walked or cycled to work 21 percent of the time compared to Australian and American cities, which indicated only a 5 percent walking and cycling rate.

Newman and Kenworthy have produced numerous smaller studies based upon more recent census and other data, which update the original work. They are affiliated with the Institute of Science and Technology Policy at Murdoch University in Western Australia.

Conservation Law Foundation offers an interactive web site focused on sustainable transportation, and includes downloadable resources, electronic discussions, and a library of related sites.
Website: www.tlcnetwork.org/index.html

The Create a Commuter Program, envisioned, designed, and implemented by the Community Cycling Center, is the first comprehensive project in the USA designed to provides low-income adults with fully-outfitted commuter bicycle in Portland, Oregon.
Website: www.communitycyclingcenter.org/create-a-commuter.html

Environmental Defense Fund's National Transportation Program has an excellent resource site with many US transportation case studies.

Website: www.edf.org/

Institute of Science and Technology Policy was established in 1988 to help create a better understanding of the roles and effects of science and technology. Search for their materials in your library or through their web site.

Website: wwwistp.murdoch.edu.au:80/istp.html

Sustrans — the sustainable transport charity — works on practical projects to encourage people to walk, cycle and use public transport in order to reduce motor traffic and its adverse effects.

Website: www.sustrans.co.uk

US Department of Transportation's Bureau of Transportation Statistics has a web site that links many US transportation problems and solutions, such as the US Surface Transportation Policy Project. The site's table of contents is a massive library of transportation-related statistics and reports.

Website: www.bts.gov/

Vélo Québec is working to make Québec more bicycle-friendly and is a leading cycling organization in North America.

Website: www.velo.qc.ca

Victoria Transport Policy Institute specializes in progressive transportation decision making theory and practice. Their goal is to develop practical tools for incorporating social and environmental values into transportation decision-making. These tools include documents available free for downloading, documents for sale, and transportation cost-analysis software. This Institute is an extremely useful resource to bring a sustainability perspective into a transportation debate.

Website: www.vtpi.org

Walkable Communities, Inc. is a non-profit corporation, established in the state of Florida in 1996. It was organized for the express purposes of helping whole communities, whether they are large cities or small towns, or parts of communities, i.e. neighborhoods, business districts, parks, school districts, subdivisions, specific roadway corridors, etc., become more walkable and pedestrian friendly.

Website: www.walkable.org/

REFERENCES

BEST. 2004. Personal communication. Vancouver, BC

BEST. n.d.. *Go Green Choices (GGC)*. Retrieved October 5, 2004, from http://best.bc.ca/programsAndServices/ggc.html

Canadian Automobile Association. 2004. *2004 Edition Driving Costs*.

CBN. (July 18, 2003). *What is Bikeshare?* Retrieved October 17, 2004, from www.community-bicyclenetwork.org/bikeshare.html

City of Vancouver. 1996. *City of Vancouver Transportation Plan: Newsletter Number 4.* Spring.

Cleary, J., & McClintock, H. 2000. The Nottingham Cycle-friendly Employers Project: lessons for encouraging cycle commuting. *Local Environment.* Carfax Publishing Company. Vol. 5: 217-222).

Climate. Solutions. n.d. *Bicycle Commuter Contest 2004.* Retrieved October 23, 2004, from www.climatesolutions.org/

Commuter Check. n.d. *San Francisco Bay Area Commuter Check Program.* Retrieved October 17, 2004, from www.commutercheck.com/home.html

Downs, A. 2004. *Traffic: Why It's Getting Worse, What Government Can Do.* Retrieved October 11, 2004, from www.brookings.edu/comm/policybriefs/pb128.htm.

Duncan, A. 2000. *Wellness Walkways-Status and Next Phase for Implementation.* No. 7172 RTS No.00958 CC File No. 5767 P&E. Vancouver: City of Vancouver.

The Economist, 2004. "A long road ahead of it." 371. June 12: 13.

Engwicht, D. 1993. *Reclaiming Our Cities and Towns: Better Living with Less Traffic.* Gabriola Island, BC: New Society Publishers.

Engwicht, D. 1999. *Street Reclaiming; Creating Livable Streets and Vibrant Communities.* Gabriola, BC: New Society Publishers.

Eugene, C. O. 2004. *Eugene: City of Bicycles.* Retrieved October 27, 2004, from www.ci.eugene.or.us/PW/transportation/bike/bikeindex.htm

FCM. 2001. Municipal Government and Sustainable Communities: A Best Practices Guide 2001, F.C. M. S. C. A. 2001. Federation of Canadian Municipalities (FCM).

Fenton, B. 2003. One Smart Card, One Less Car. *Alternatives Journal,* 29(3): 25.

Frank, L. D., Andresen, A., & Schmidt, T. L. 2004. Obesity Relationships with Community Design, Physical Activity and Time Spent in Cars. *Journal of Preventive Medicine,* 27(2): 87-96.

Geitner, P. 2000. Auto-Free Living in Vauban.

Government of. Australia. 2003. *TravelSmart Australia.* Retrieved October 5, 2004, from www.travelsmart.gov.au/about.html

Kenworthy, J.R., and F.B. Laube. 1996. "Automobile Dependence in Cities: An International Comparison of Urban Transport and Land Use Patterns with Implications for Sustainability." *Environmental Impact Assessment Review* 16: 279-308.

Komanoff, C. 1995. "Charting the True Costs of Driving." In *Beyond the Car: Essays on the Auto Culture,* S. Zielinski and G. Laird, eds. Toronto: Steel Rail Press.

Leman, C., P. Schiller and K. Pauly. 1994. *Re-Thinking High Occupancy Vehicle Facilities and the Public Interest.* Annapolis: The Chesapeake Bay Foundation.

Lerner, J. 2004. Personal communication. Vancouver, B.C.

Litman, T. 2004. *The Next Big Thing, Online TDM Encyclopedia.* Retrieved October 5, 2004, from www.vtpi.org/tdm/tdm51.htm

MacLeod, K. 2004. *Orienting Urban Planning to Sustainability in Curitiba, Brazil.* Retrieved October 6, 2004, from http://www3.iclei.org/localstrategies/summary/=curitiba2.html

McCann, B. 2000. *Driven to Spend; The Impact of Sprawl on Household Transportation Expenses.* Retrieved October 11, 2004, from www.transact.org

McCann, B., & Ewing, R. 2003. *Measuring the Health Effects on Sprawl : A National Analysis of Physical Activity, Obesity, and Chronic Disease*: Smart Growth America, Surface Transportation Policy Project (STPP).

Miscellaneous Facts. 2004. World Almanac Education Group Inc.

Motavalli, J. 2002. Getting Out of Gridlock. *E Magazine: The Environmental Magazine*, 13: Mar/April: 34.

Mumford, L. 1964. *The Highway and the City*. New York: New American Library.

Newman, P., and J. Kenworthy, 1989. *Cities and Automobile Dependence: An International Sourcebook*. Brookfield, Vt.: Gower Technical.

Newman, P. 1991, 1999. "Succesful Ageing, Transport, and Urban Design." Presented to Conference on Succesful Ageing, Canberra, Australia. November.

"New Millennium Park Bicycle Station Opens". 2004. Retrieved October 5, 2004, from www.josta.de

People Over Cars. 2004. *Canada & the World Backgrounder*, 69(6), 28-31.

Public Innovation Abroad. 1990a. 14 (3) March.

Rajan, S.C. 1996. *The Enigma of Automobility: Democratic Politics and Pollution Control*. Pittsburgh: University of Pittsburgh Press.

Renner, M. 1988. "Rethinking the Role of the Automobile." Worldwatch 84. Washington, DC: Worldwatch Institute.

Replogle, M. 1996. Overcoming Barriers to Market-Based Transportation Reform. Presented to OECD International Conference, Toward Sustainable Transportation, Vancouver, BC, March.

Schmidt, C. W. 2004. Sprawl: The New Manifest Destiny. *Environmental Health Perspectives*, 112(11): 620-628.

SMART Movement. Retrieved October 5, 2004, from www.pollutionprobe.org/Reports/SMART.pdf

State of California, Dept., of Transportation. 2000. *Continuation Study to Evaluate the Impacts of the SR 91 Value-Priced Express Lanes*. Retrieved October 17, 2004, from http://ceenve.calpoly.edu/sullivan/sr91/sr91.htm

STPP. 2004. *Aging Americans: Stranded Without Options*. Retrieved October 17, 2004, from www.transact.org/report.asp?id=232

The League of American Bicyclists. 2004. Retrieved October 15, 2004, from www.bikeleague.org

Transport for London, G. O. U. K. 2004. *TfL Publish C-Charge Annual Report*. Retrieved October 6, 2004, from www.tfl.gov.uk/tfl/pn_releases.shtml

Toronto City Cycling Committee. 1990. "Bike to the Future: A Vision for a Bicycle-Friendly Toronto." Toronto: City of Toronto Cycling Committee.

U of W. 2003. 2003 *U-PASS Annual Report:* University of Washington, Transportation Office.

VTPI. 2004a. *HOV Priority, Strategies to Improve Transit and Ridesharing Speed and Convenience*. Retrieved October 4, 2004, from www.vtpi.org/tdm/tdm19.htm

VTPI. 2004b. *Parking Pricing, Direct Charges for Using Parking Facilities*. Retrieved October 6, 2004, from www.vtpi.org/tdm/tdm26.htm

VTPI. 2004c. *Public Transit Encouragement*. Retrieved October 6, 2004, from www.vtpi.org/tdm/tdm112.htm

VTPI. 2004d. *Sustainable Transportation and TDM, Planning That Balances Economic, Social and Ecological Objectives.* Retrieved October 5, 2004, from www.vtpi.org/tdm/tdm67.htm

VTPI. 2004e. *Traffic Calming, Roadway Design to Reduce Traffic Speeds and Volumes.* Retrieved October 5, 2004, from www.vtpi.org/tdm/tdm4.htm

VTPI. 2004f. *Transportation Management Programs, An Institutional Framework for Implementing TDM.* Retrieved October 7, 2004, from www.vtpi.org/tdm/tdm42.htm

Walkable Communities, Inc. 2004. *Welcome to Walkable Communities, Inc.* Retrieved October 17, 2004, from www.walkable.org/

Whitelegg, J. 1996. "The Information Society and Sustainable Development." *Journal of World Transport Policy and Practice* 2:4.

LAND USE AND URBAN FORM

L and use permeates virtually every aspect of sustainable communities. Many of the goals discussed in previous chapters depend in large measure upon how we organize our use of land and the form that use takes.

Conventional land-use practices spread our destinations, increase our need for space and travel, and bring a host of related problems. The cost of real estate in cities, for example, is often too high to accommodate green space, biological wastewater treatment facilities such as wetlands, or fields of photovoltaic (PV) panels. By integrating planning and design for multi-purpose use, these ideas can become affordable. For example, PVs on rooftops take up no extra space, nor do rooftop gardens. Wetlands can process sewage and provide wildlife habitat, recreation areas, and drainage for stormwater run-off. Parks can provide recreation and edible landscaping. "Whole-systems" or "multi-purpose" design and planning is critical to sustainable land use.

Sustainable land use can help invigorate communities, and provide considerable environmental, economic, social, and cultural benefits. Redeveloping and reusing existing buildings and land can also revitalize economies and communities that are falling into decay. Sustainable community planning can recognize and respond to the diversity of interests and desires in our communities by encouraging land uses that cater to a range of incomes, ages, physical abilities, and cultural backgrounds.

LAND USE AND TRANSPORTATION

Transportation and land use are inextricably related. To encourage people to use the transportation system more efficiently, we need to adopt land-use policies that reduce our needs for transportation and let us meet those needs in more energy-efficient ways.

Per capita gasoline consumption in US and many Canadian cities is now more than four times that of European cities, and over ten times greater than Asian cities such as Hong Kong, Tokyo, and Singapore. The biggest factor accounting for these differences in energy use appears to be not the size of cars or the price of gasoline, but the efficiency and compactness of land-use patterns. Cities with low "automobile dependence" are more centralized; have more intense land use (more people and jobs per unit area); are more oriented to non-auto modes (more public transit, foot traffic, and bicycle usage); place more restraints on high-speed traffic; and offer better public transit (Newman and Kenworthy, 1999). These patterns can be seen within communities as well.

For example, it has been found that neighbourhood urban design impacts auto ownership rates and mileage per car, just as much as more common socioeconomic indicators such as income and family size. In a study that examined nearly 3,000 neighbourhoods in Chicago, Los Angeles and San Francisco, Holtzclaw et al. (2002) found similar relationships between urban density and automobile ownership rates and mileage per car. The study shows that people who live in more dense and convenient communities are less dependent on cars and that those communities are also more liveable because they tend to have cleaner air and water and more protected open space. The results suggest that the dependence on the automobile can be addressed through policy measures at the municipal level that increase residential density, improve transit access and promote pedestrian and bicycle friendliness.

Through zoning and other techniques, land-use patterns and densities dictate travel volume, direction, and mode. In the US and Canada, our dispersed land-use patterns are typified by the low density suburb. The problem with the low-density land-use pattern is not just its high energy use. This settlement pattern has a complimentary set of environmental and social problems that all stem from its dispersed land use:

- high per capita auto emissions (both smog and greenhouse gases are directly related to the amount of gasoline used);
- high per capita water use (e.g., for lawn irrigation);
- high land requirements in both the block size and the road system required to service it (road provision is much greater in low-density areas than in medium density areas);
- high stormwater pollution from the extra urbanized land (low-density areas can have double the stormwater pollution of medium density areas);
- high domestic heating energy due to the lack of a shared insulating effect when buildings are grouped (50 percent differences can be found);
- poor recycling rates due in part to the large cost involved in collection compared to a compact housing system (European cities have four to six times the recycling rates of North America.);
- high physical infrastructure costs (utilities, pipes, poles, roads, etc.); and
- high social infrastructure costs (cars are required for participation in social life) (Newman and Kenworthy, 1999).

Costs for social infrastructure deserve more attention than they have received. When our communities require cars for participation in social life, who is marginalized and excluded? Clearly, it is the non-drivers. And who are the non-drivers? They are our children, our senior citizens, our physically challenged, and our very poor (who are predominantly women). Add up the numbers, and we may be talking about half the population of our communities (Engwicht, 1993).

All of this suggests a new approach to transportation and land-use planning in North America. In the absence of comprehensive planning, transportation has, almost by default, guided land use. Instead, land-use planning should guide transportation,

As our populations become increasingly concentrated into urban areas, they are simultaneously becoming less concentrated within those areas. In other words, "our cities and towns are not just growing in population, but at the same time they are spreading out and changing their structure into a looser, more widespread urban pattern" (Richardson, 1991).

and transportation should be designed to accommodate and support planned growth, inducing the needed changes in urban form (Cervero, 1991; Replogle, 1990).

DENSITY AND HOUSING

Denser land use could help solve many of the environmental, social, and aesthetic problems of sprawl, yet widespread misconceptions about increased density — even moderate density — often prevent communities from adopting compact land-use strategies. Contrary to popular belief, augmenting the density of development does not necessarily create a harsh physical environment. For example, Copenhagen and Vienna — two cities widely associated with urban charm and livability — are of moderate density (measured by the number of residents and jobs in the city, including its central business district and outer areas).

Why Los Angeles Still Has Smog

It is no wonder that Los Angeles still has smog more than 30 years after the battle to reduce it first began — the battle has concentrated on making vehicles cleaner and more efficient, it has done nothing to make them less needed. The principle that is often forgotten here is the Jevons principle. The Jevons principle was first enunciated in 1865 when an assessment was made that improving U.K. coal-burning efficiency would save coal — Jevons predicted that it would in fact lead to greater coal use as the efficiencies would lead to more economic uses for coal. The same principle seems to apply to our present assessment of transport fuel use. The price mechanism and urban sprawl ensure that for every increase in technological efficiency there is a rapid increase in the use of vehicles (Newman, 1991a).

Housing Forms and Density

Low Density — Single Family Form
about 0.6 FAR

Low Density — Attached Form
0.6 FAR

Medium Density — Ground-Oriented
0.7 to 1.1 FAR

Comprehensive Townhouse Development
about 0.6 FAR

Medium Density — Apartment
1.2 FAR

High Density — Apartment
about 2.0 FAR

FAR = Floor Area Ratio = Floor Area. Therefore Maximum Floor Area = FAR x Lot Area
Lot Area

Copenhagen has 19 people per acre and Vienna has 29 people per acre. By contrast, low-density cities such as Phoenix (five people per acre) often are dominated by unwelcoming, car-oriented commercial strips and vast expanses of concrete and asphalt. People often assume that low density ensures more green space and easier living, yet as Chapter 4: Greening the City shows, with appropriate planning and design, dense urban areas can lend themselves to greater vitality, more inviting spaces, and even higher use of trees and other plants (Lowe, 1992; Beatley, 2000).

Although municipal officials will attest that the numbers of household units per building or per hectare can be the subject of intense debate, those numbers are relatively unimportant in terms of human well-being. Instead, the most important indicator that links overcrowding to human stress and psychosis is the number of people per room. Although many people mistakenly equate density with overcrowding, there is a world of difference between high-density living in high-rise residential blocks with low numbers of people per room (such as New York City), and overcrowding in low-rise shanty town developments, with high numbers of people per room (such as Rio de Janiero or parts of Mexico City).

There are areas of high-density populations with low levels of social disorder (such as parts of Boston), while there are areas of low-density population with high levels of social disorder (such as parts of Los Angeles). This seems to indicate that the real issues at stake are more likely to be a combination of social and economic factors, such as low income, poor education, and social isolation. These complicating factors surrounding urban density should make us wary of falling for the implicit environmental determinism which is sometimes found in arguments both for and against high-density living (Haughton and Hunter, 1994).

THE COSTS OF SPRAWL

The flight of employment and people to the suburbs has underscored concern about the costs of sprawl. Preservationists are realizing that if suburbs drain city life there will be no impetus to protect historic buildings. Environmentalists are realizing that sprawl destroys rural environments, and that air quality is deteriorating due to commuter traffic. Concerned citizens everywhere sense that abandoned city neighborhoods and faceless suburban developments reduce a vital sense of community.

It has long been an axiom that development enhances the local tax base. However, extensive research now suggests that the costs of sprawl may exceed the benefits of low-density development. The Real Estate Research Corporation (1974) conducted a massive study for the US government, *The Costs of Sprawl*, which still stands as a classic. Three community types were analyzed: the "low-density sprawl" community (entirely single-family homes, 75 percent in traditional grid-pattern, typical of suburban development); the "combination mix" community (20 percent of each of five types of dwellings, half in planned unit developments, half in traditional subdivisions); and the "high-density planned" community (40 percent highrises, 30 percent walkups, 20 percent townhouses, and 10 percent clustered single family homes, all clustered together into contiguous neighborhoods). A major conclusion of the study was that sprawl is "the most expensive form of residential development in terms of economic costs, environmental costs, natural resource consumption, and many types of personal costs ... This cost difference is particularly significant for that proportion of total costs which is likely to be borne by local governments."

A Melbourne, Australia study suggests that it is cheaper for cities to pay developers to build near downtown cores than it is to pay for the cost of sprawl in terms of infrastructure development and remediating pollution from automobiles. Given its findings of lower road, sewer and education costs, the study showed a net benefit of CDN$32,000 for every household created downtown rather than in suburban Melbourne. With three million residents spread over 2,500

> ### *Land Use Terms*
>
> **Urban containment:** the physical and functional separation of urban and rural areas, and planning processes that aim for efficient forms of towns and cities with minimal impact on surrounding areas (Gayler 1990).
>
> **Densification:** increasing the numbers of housing units or commercial facilities built per acre of land, with the goals of increasing the efficiency of land use and reducing the overall impact of growth.
>
> **Urbanization:** creation of urban landscapes in formerly rural areas.
>
> **Urban areas:** characterized by human residential, commercial, and industrial structures and activities, and can include low-density suburban areas as well as urban cores where human activity is intense.
>
> **Compact cities:** urban areas that make efficient use of land for all purposes through densification and mixed land uses. Compact cities contrast with sprawl.
>
> **Sprawl:** an inefficient, extensive use of land for urban activities. The term suburban is often used to describe sprawling urban development (BCRTEE, 1994).

square kilometers (965 square miles), Melbourne considered a property tax holiday, bargain prices on city land and density zoning inducements to lure developers downtown (Neilson, 1990). The costs of sprawl were confirmed in a more recent study by Carruthers and Ulfarsson (2003) of 283 metropolitan countries in the US where it was found that the per capita cost of public service provision decreased with higher density and increased with the spatial extent of the urbanized land area.

The effectiveness of compact urban development can be fully achieved only if governments remove the conflicting incentives posed by other (often national) policies such as artificially low gasoline prices. For example, in the US, subsidies to the oil industry, protection/military costs of oil supplies, public funding for road construction and maintenance and the true environmental, health and social costs of private automobile use have been estimated as being between $558.7 billion and $1.69 trillion per year — a cost per gallon of between $5.60 and $15.14 (International Centre for Technology Assessment, 2004). Demand management tools such as increased fuel taxes could provide an enormous increase to investment in public transit, while reflecting the true cost of automobile use.

Despite the absence of supportive national policy frameworks, communities can do a great deal to create more energy-efficient travel patterns by concentrating activities in specific areas and developing a mix of land uses in those areas. Our objectives should be to create travel patterns that can be effectively served by more energy-efficient travel modes, such as public transit, bicycling, and walking; and to reduce the average length of daily automobile trips where other modes are not feasible.

CHANGING THE PATTERN OF GROWTH

Land-use planning rarely addresses long-term or life-cycle costs, so taxpayers often end up paying the hidden costs of development infrastructure (roads, sewage, etc.). Citizens in many communities see something wrong with this picture, but the solutions commonly proposed rarely speak to the underlying issues.

Future growth can provide the opportunity to preserve farmland and natural areas and reduce rising car dependency and traffic congestion. By promoting policies that encourage residential intensification and by creating more compact urban areas through infill development, adaptive reuse and brownfield development, communities can reduce infrastructure costs, revitalize urban areas in decline, and create more transportation choice (Tomalty, 2003).

Sustainable communities require that we go beyond the notion that land is a mere commodity. However, even in conventional economic terms, land is a peculiar commodity in that its supply cannot increase, no matter how high the price. As demand for land grows, the wealth of landowners tends to grow regardless of how well or badly they use the land. In his 1879 classic *Progress and Poverty*, Henry George proposed a solution to this dilemma: taxing away the value of land produced by anything other than private efforts. Such a land-value tax would keep private landowners from unfairly capturing the benefits of natural resources, urban locations, and public services. George also believed that this tax would force landowners either to put their land to its "highest and best" use themselves, or make it accessible to someone who would (Freyfogle, 2003).

Several economists have since called for differentiated treatment of land and buildings in property taxation. Whereas a higher tax on buildings encourages holding land unused or allowing buildings to deteriorate, a higher tax on land often encourages efficient use of the property. Since land is not produced, a tax on land is a cost of ownership, not a cost of production. By making land ownership more costly (less desirable), a tax on land results in *lower* land prices. Taxing land values helps make many infrastructure investments (like roads and subways) self-financing (Rybeck, 1996).

Local governments typically assess vacant properties at far less than their market value, effectively rewarding property owners for keeping their land idle. Property owners may respond better to tax-based financial inducements such as land value taxes to intensify land use and encourage the redevelopment of vacant land, and as a result reduce the incentive for urban sprawl. However, such tax strategies need to be combined with clearly defined growth boundaries to prevent spurts of sprawled growth (Gihring, 1999).

Since the higher land tax cannot be avoided or passed on to space users, land owners are motivated to generate income from which to pay the tax. The greatest economic imperative to develop land will exist where land values are highest, adjacent to existing infrastructure and amenities. At the same time, a reduction in the tax rate applied to buildings makes that development more profitable. Away from infrastruc-

One of the great mysteries of the American suburb is this: How, with such low-density development, have we produced such extraordinarily high traffic? How have we achieved the traffic of a metropolis and the culture of a cow town? (Duany and Plater-Zyberk, 1992)

ture where land values are low, taxes will be low and there will be less economic motivation for development. The result is more compact development that can be served by existing infrastructure, at lower costs to taxpayers and the environment. Compact development also enhances opportunities to walk, cycle, carpool, or use transit in lieu of single-occupant vehicles (Rybeck, 1996).

Even a reduced version of this tax could meet all local needs by capturing much of the gain from rising land values. To put this land tax into local hands would free localities from depending on state/provincial and federal financial help and its accompanying control (Daly and Farley, 2004).

NEW URBANISM

New Urbanism is the name given to an emerging set of planning principles designed to reinvigorate communities and provide a meaningful alternative to suburban sprawl.

An example of New Urbanist design

Variations on New Urbanism include "neo-traditional town planning," "pedestrian pockets," "transit-oriented developments," "complete communities" and LASTING communities — Livable, Affordable, Safe, Transit-Oriented, Inclusive, Neighborly, Growing.

New Urbanism has attracted considerable media attention, including a *Newsweek* cover story describing "15 Ways to Fix the Suburbs." The *Newsweek* list, in this order, is to give up big lawns, bring back the corner store, make the streets skinny, drop the cul-de-sac, draw [urban growth] boundaries, hide the garage, mix housing types, plant trees curbside, put new life into old malls, plan for mass transit, link work to home, make a town center, shrink parking, turn down the lights [use more smaller street lamps rather than fewer larger ones], and "think green" [don't pave the planet] (Adler, 1995).

Although New Urbanism is often characterized as a new model for suburban development, re-urbanization of existing urban areas is one of its principal tenets. Indeed, most New Urbanist principles have been deduced from successful cities that are made up of several independent neighborhoods, or "urban villages."

Urban villages provide a lifestyle with minimal car dependence and the kind of densities that make rail highly viable. Evidence suggests that those cities that have tried to build urban villages have found them to be an extremely attractive lifestyle option. The characteristics of these urban villages are:

- mixed land use, with commercial offices and shops on main spines, surrounded by residential;

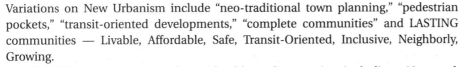
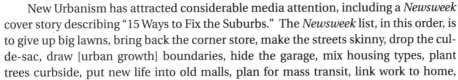

Greenfields and Brownfields

Pristine rural areas are called "greenfield" sites, while urban areas are referred to as "brownfield" sites because they often contain pollutants left behind by past uses. Brownfields are abandoned, idle or underutilized commercial or industrial properties where past actions have caused known or suspected environmental contamination. Left abandoned, brownfields adversely impact a neighbourhood's image and quality of life and may pose risks to human health and the environment. With proper support and partnerships between developers and all levels of government, brownfield redevelopment in urban areas (instead of development of greenfield sites on the periphery) could generate up to $7 billion of public benefits per year (NRTEE, 2003).

- high density so that everything within the "village" is within walking and cycling distance;
- considerable landscaping including gardens on top of buildings and on balconies;
- a mixture of public and private housing with an emphasis on families and hence quite large internal home spaces;
- extensive provision for children in good view of dwellings;
- community facilities such as libraries, child care, senior centers, and in a few cases, small urban farms;
- pedestrian links with parking lots placed underground and traffic calming on any peripheral roads;
- public spaces with strong design features (water, street furniture, playgrounds, etc.); and
- a large degree of self-sufficiency for the community with rail links to the rest of the city (Newman, 1991; Newman and Kenworthy, 1991, 2001).

Land Use Zoning

NOT this: *Isolation of home from work and services by exclusive zoning*	**THIS:** *Proximity of home to work and services by mixed-use zoning*
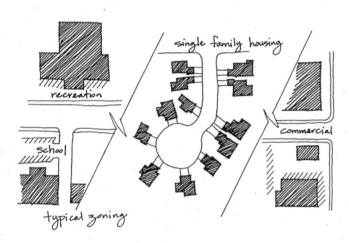	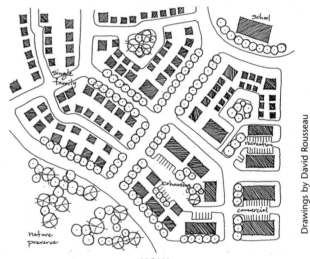

Drawings by David Rousseau

WHY NOT:
- Excessive commuting requirements; increases automobile dependency
- Empty residential areas in daytime and commercial areas at night; encourages crime
- Decreases contact among people; does not build community or support services
- High commuting costs and traffic congestion

"All that is not specifically required is strictly forbidden."

HOW:
- Design neighborhood centers within walking distance
- Flexible, mixed use zoning encourages participation in the community
- Increased hours of occupancy supports local services
- Design for local and in-home employment

"All that is not considered grossly objectionable is permitted."

New Urbanism is perhaps most succinctly described in the charter developed by the Congress for the New Urbanism, a group formed in 1992 comprising architects, urban designers, planners, and landscape architects from across North America. Their 1996 charter states that: neighborhoods should be diverse in use and population; communities should be designed for the pedestrian and transit as well as the car; cities and towns should be shaped by physically defined and universally accessible public spaces and community institutions; and urban places should be framed by architecture and landscape design that celebrate local history, climate, ecology, and building practice. In practice, New Urbanism means:

- designing communities with a connected and permeable public framework of streets and open spaces as the main structuring element of the community;
- facilitating easy movement through all parts of the community by foot, bicycle, public transit, and automobile, without favoring any particular mode;
- fostering community activity through ensuring that buildings enhance pedestrian comfort in the way that they relate to the public streets, and thereby pro-

Subdivision

NOT this: *Subdivision of entire parcels into individual lots* | **THIS:** *Cluster designs with commons*

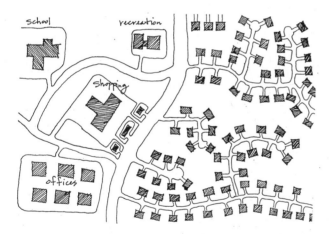

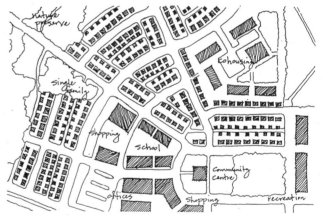

WHY NOT:
- Lack of common space impairs community self-image
- Residents isolated behind fences and in automobiles do not meet or watch out for their neighbors
- Heavy emphasis on the private domain does not encourage participation
- Utilities are widely extended and services dispersed

"All residential land is either private or dedicated to the automobile."

HOW:
- Thoughtful public and semi-public space integrated with private lots
- Design for meeting places and good visual supervision
- Provide small neighborhood parks, community gardens and playgrounds
- Cluster designs allow compact utility networks and concentrated services

"A community must have commons."

viding an attractive, safe, and inviting public realm;

- accommodating and integrating a diverse and wide range of land uses, densities, and building types within each neighborhood to include the full range of activities found in any healthy community, and to facilitate the provision of public transit;
- integrating the natural environment into the new community; and
- creating universally accessible public open spaces and community institutions that provide a sense of place and act as landmarks of community identity (Russell, 2004).

With increasing attention and publicity, New Urbanism has also earned its share of criticism. For example, a number of developments identified as "new urbanist" have frequently been built on previously undeveloped sites on the periphery of developed areas, without ecological design techniques (e.g., passive solar) or infrastructure (e.g., greywater water recycling), something critics have called "sprawl with porches" (Pollard, 2001). The "neo-traditional" new town of Celebration in Florida, created by

Housing Types

NOT this: *Limited housing types: single family detached*

THIS: *Many housing types*

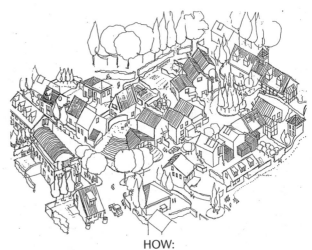

WHY NOT:
- Poor range of affordability
- Leads to limited social and economic mix among residents; ghettoization
- Inappropriate to aging residents and community-minded people
- Has highest individual land requirements
- Financially unstable due to dependence on only one market sector

"Everyone wants to live in a suburban home and can afford it."

HOW:
- Provide apartment and townhouses as a more affordable option
- Design mixed single-family and multi-family neighborhoods for diversity and social enrichment; healthier communities
- Provide supported seniors housing, co-housing and other options
- Design for mini-lots and strata lots to conserve common land
- Better financial stability by serving several market sectors

"Many people prefer townhouses, apartments and collective housing, particularly at some stage of their life."

the Disney Corporation is one such example. Celebration illustrates a principle defect with New Urbanism, the failure to recognize that a community's form and function is primarily shaped by its transportation system, which in this case is the suburban highway and freeways of South Florida (Marshall, 2003). And although traditional neighbourhood developments may be "designed" to encourage a mix of housing types and a diversity of income levels, they offer no mechanism to ensure any stock — never mind an adequate, permanent stock — of affordable housing. For example, it is now difficult for the schoolteachers, babysitters and service workers required by the Celebration community to find affordable residences there (Duany, 2004).

For New Urbanist development to be sustainable, it must incorporate energy-efficient land-use planning. There are several policies that communities can use to promote energy-efficient land use, such as:

- encourage greater density through multiple unit residential developments;
- integrate work, residence and shopping in mixed-use development;
- encourage residential clustering;
- zone higher-density development along established transit routes;
- decentralize commercial and community services to reduce travel distances, creating self-contained communities with a better balance between employment and population;
- place controls on outlying shopping centers, strip development, and urban sprawl;
- encourage the infilling (development) of existing vacant land in built-up areas;
- ensure that major public facilities have provision for walking and bicycling access to transit; and
- encourage the development of high-quality walking and bicycling facilities, including development design guidelines to support transportation alternatives to private automobile use, such as provision of on-site lunchrooms, day-care facilities, automated bank teller machines and other facilities (Sheltair, 2001).

Portland, Oregon provides an example of a larger city-region experimenting with land-use policies to control energy demand — in this case within the framework of a mandatory state planning goal requiring that land use be managed to conserve energy. One of the main objectives of the Portland Energy Conservation Demonstration Project, completed in 1977, was to examine the links between energy saving and urban form. An energy zone map, dividing the city into five zones based on relative energy

Location-Efficient Mortgages

The Location Efficient Mortgage (LEM) is tailored to expand homeownership opportunities for residents by leveraging the availability of the region's public transportation resources. LEM provides additional home purchasing power to working families because it allows homebuyers to benefit from the potential savings realized by living in a densely populated community served by efficient public transit. Fannie Mae (the US Federal National Mortgage Association) has begun a $100 million LEM pilot program in Chicago, Seattle, Los Angeles County and San Francisco to increase potential home-owner's purchasing power. For example, in a dense Chicago neighbourhood, a two-person household with an annual income of $60,000 and one car would qualify for a LEM equivalent of $350 a month, helping them to qualify for a mortgage $53,854 greater than under traditional mortgage underwriting guidelines (Fannie Mae, 2000; Krizek, 2003).

LEM mortgages could help both buyers and existing owners since some of the increased borrowing power would be capitalized in higher property values. This could create an incentive for neighbourhoods to improve their "location efficiency" by supporting increased density, mixed uses and better transit service (Durning, 1996).

efficiency, was produced to guide new development to energy efficient locations; and an energy conservation policy was adopted by city council after extensive public consultation in 1979. The project included commitments to develop land-use policies using density and location to reduce the need to travel, and to improve the efficiency of the transport system and reduce its consumption of non-renewable fuels. More specific objectives related to the location of new developments and encouragement of energy-efficient transport modes. These strategies were then incorporated into the city's draft comprehensive plan (Owens, 1990; Kasowski, 1991; Lowe, 1991a; Sheehan, 2001; Gibson and Abbott, 2002).

One of the main obstacles to creating New Urbanist communities is the conventional development standards behind most zoning codes. Kunstler (1996), a proponent of New Urbanism, explains the down side of zoning as follows:

> What zoning produces is suburban sprawl, which must be understood as the product of a particular set of instructions. Its chief characteristics are the strict separation of human activities, mandatory driving to get from one activity to another, and huge supplies of free parking. After all, the basic idea of zoning is that every activity demands a separate zone of its own. For people to live around shopping would be harmful and indecent. Better not even to allow them within walking distance of it. They'll need their cars to haul all that stuff home anyway. While we're at it, let's separate the homes by income gradients. Don't let the $75,000-a-year families live near the $200,000-a-year families — they'll bring down property values — and for God's sake don't let a $25,000-a-year recent college graduate or a $19,000-a-year widowed grandmother on Social Security live near any of them. There goes the neighborhood! Now put all the workplaces in separate office "parks" or industrial "parks," and make sure nobody can walk to them either. As for public squares, parks and the like — forget it. We can't afford them, because we spent all our money paving the four-lane highways and collector roads and parking lots, and laying sewer and water lines out to the housing subdivisions, and hiring traffic cops to regulate the movement of people in their cars going back and forth among these segregated activities.

Like most tools, zoning can be used for different purposes. Although historically, zoning bylaws are an inflexible instrument written to create certainty and offer only one way of doing things, a new set of zoning bylaws is being developed that allow for more flexible requirements that can encourage more compact growth patterns and developments that support goals of integrating land uses, intensification and housing diversity, and pedestrian-oriented streetscapes (Smart Growth BC, 2005). A few of the many zoning tools include:

- *Planned unit development* gives developers incentives to meet pre-determined land-use goals;
- *Floating zoning* permits special uses within a jurisdiction in accordance with development criteria;
- *Bonus or incentive zoning* provides developers with bonuses and incentives to achieve increased development density;
- *Mixed-use zoning* requires a wide array of types of development aimed at reduc-

ing distances between houses and jobs;

- *Land banking* allows outright purchase of land by the public sector well in advance of any development to ensure appropriate land use; and
- *Transit zoning districts* target development in areas with transit systems already in place (Congress for New Urbanism, 2004; Gordon, 1991).

Related tools include:

- *Transfer of development rights* allow landowners to get development value from their land even if they choose not to develop it;
- *Conservation land trusts* consist of local, regional, or state/provincial organizations directly involved in protecting important land resources for the public benefit;
- *Location-efficient mortgages* aid urban housing affordability;
- *Growth management ordinances* control one or more of the familiar components of land-use planning: the rate, location, type, density, amount, timing, and quality of development; and
- *Building permit allocation* allocates housing permits on a merit system that awards points for recreational amenities, landscaping and open space, design quality, impact on the local infrastructure, and energy efficiency (Heyerdahl, 1991; Land Trust Alliance, n.d.; Abberger, 1991; American Planning Association, 1991b; Durning, 1996; Russell, 2004).

Alternative Development Standards are helping many communities meet environmental concerns and social needs while reducing the spiraling costs of new infrastructure. Features of the Standards, often referred to as "traditional neighborhood design," include grid road systems and narrower road widths, smaller lots, use of curbs and sidewalks, and car access to houses from rear lanes (BCMMAH, 1997).

SOCIAL BENEFITS OF COMPACT COMMUNITIES

Clustered, pedestrian-friendly, transit-oriented communities are a key to reducing automobile dependency. As discussed in the previous chapter, achieving sustainable transportation requires technological, economic, and social solutions. Technological solutions, however, invariably forget that if gains in efficiency of motor vehicles are merely used to travel more, we do not have sustainable transportation. Economic solutions are often politically unacceptable due to the physical layout of our cities; and those who suffer most from user-pay schemes are those who can afford it least.

Social solutions can penetrate to the ultimate problem of automobile dependence. New Urbanism focuses on changing priorities in physical planning to ensure non-auto infrastructure; changing land use patterns to minimize the need for travel;

and changing lifestyle values so that greater emphasis is on the community rather than private or isolated values (Newman and Kenworthy, 1999).

Comparative studies of residential satisfaction in low-density versus higher-density equivalent communities show that the relative disadvantages of low-density communities for working women are increasing as the percentage of employed women rises. For women who can't afford a second car, or who have difficulty making childcare arrangements, or who have specialized employment needs, low-density communities are much less satisfactory.

One of the most frustrated population groups in low-density suburbia is adolescents. When young people are entering a stage in which they are seeking more and more independence from their parents, they find themselves in an environment where getting together with friends is made difficult by distance, paucity of public transport, separation of housing from shopping centers, and so on. One study found American suburban teenagers more often bored and engaging in vandalism than their counterparts in Sweden living at higher density with easy access to shops, clubs, public transport, and so on. Teenagers in clustered housing are more likely to find others of the same age living within walking distance and may have access to shared facilities or hanging-out places where they can spend time together, out of sight of home, yet not far away (Cooper, Marcus and Sarkissian, 1986).

TOOLS AND INITIATIVES

New Urbanism

Auto-Free Development: In Scotland, Edinburgh Council established a 120-unit housing development that incorporated a massive reduction in space for the car, where trees replaced pavement and where the use of recycled materials, low technology processes (passive ventilation) and the use of nontoxic materials was promoted. Since the development was opened in 2000, it has been calculated that residents have saved £250 per year in heating and hot water. Only 26 percent of households own a car, compared to the city average of 55 percent (Young, 2004). The GWL-terrein project in Amsterdam is another example that actively discourages the use of the car by only providing limited parking spaces which are located on the perimeter of the development and explicitly incorporating car-sharing services. The Hollerand development in Bremen, Germany was one of the first of the car-reduced developments that led to the widely successful Bremen car sharing club that has since been successfully replicated at locations throughout Europe and North America (Beatley, 2000).

Re-urbanized suburbs: Chattanooga, Tennessee's smart growth initiative is focussed on the redevelopment of an existing suburban shopping mall that is being transformed into a mixed-use development with offices, residences and retail spaces carved out of the mall and its former parking lot (Beatley, 2000).

Affordable Rental Housing: Boston's Dudley Street Neighbourhood is a small neighbourhood near downtown that has experienced the problem of severe inner-city disinvestment. In response, the community mobilized and created the Dudley Street

Neighbourhood Initiative (DSNI), which, through negotiation with the City, was granted eminent domain authority over all abandoned land in the neighbourhood. So far, DSNI has transformed more than 600 of 1,300 vacant land parcels into affordable rental and leased housing facilities with playgrounds, gardens and community facilities. The vision is to create an "urban village" with mixed-rate housing, jobs and tight community control over land through a community land trust that maintains affordability through 99-year leases to land and by restricting resale prices (Fannie Mae, 2000).

Urban Villages

Recent Examples: Urban villages appear to be succeeding and they are now appearing in such places as Arabella Park, Zamilla Park and Germering in Munich; Potsdamer Platz in Berlin; New Centrum in Den Haag; Der Seepark in Freiburg; and Java-eiland in Amsterdam. These are nearly all private developments with very high popularity. Examples of urban village style developments in North America include False Creek in Vancouver, BC, River Place in Portland, Oregon, and Mission Bay in San Francisco (Newman, 1991; Newman and Kenworthy, 1999; Beatley, 2000).

Smart Growth

Smart growth is growth that helps to achieve these six goals: neighbourhood livability; better access and less traffic; thriving cities, suburbs and towns; shared benefits; lower costs and lower taxes; and keeping open space open. To achieve smart growth, communities should: mix land uses; take advantage of existing community assets; create a range of housing opportunities and choices; foster "walkable," close knit neighbourhoods; promote distinctive, attractive communities with a strong sense of place, including the rehabilitation and use of historic buildings; preserve open space, farmland, natural beauty, and critical environmental areas; strengthen and encourage growth in existing communities; provide a variety of transportation choices; make development decisions predictable, fair, and cost-effective; and encourage citizen and stakeholder participation in development decisions (Smart Growth America, 2005).

Energy-Efficient Land-Use Planning

Auto-Use Reduction: Partly as a result of Portland's energy-efficient land-use planning, the number of jobs in downtown Portland has increased by 30,000 since the 1970s, with only a scant increase in traffic; in addition, 40 percent of commuters to the downtown area use public transportation. Between 2000 and 2001, local per capita emissions of carbon dioxide, the primary cause of global warming, decreased 2 percent and are now more than 7 percent below 1990 levels. For comparison, national per capita emissions have increased by 0.7 percent over the same period (Office of Sustainable Development, 2002 and 2004).By encouraging high-density development along transit routes and limiting urban sprawl, Portland is showing that at least some reductions in car use are possible (World Resources Institute et al., 1996).

Residential Intensification Programs

Residential intensification means the creation of new residential units or accommodation in existing buildings or on previously developed, serviced land, generally including: creation of rooming, boarding and lodging houses; creation of accessory apartments; conversion of non-residential structures to residential use; infill; and redevelopment.

Guelph, Ontario: The City of Guelph implemented official plan and zoning by-law changes to permit accessory units as a right in all low-density areas of the city. The registration process was made simple and free. An average of 75 new apartments were built and registered per year, for a total of 600 units since 1995. The new units serve as a major source of affordable rental stock and represent approximately one-third of the residential intensification in the city (Tomalty, 2003).

Ottawa Ontario: All residential developments in the downtown core are exempt from development charges, building permit fees, planning application fees and the requirement to pay for parkland. This has resulted in 64 new housing projects, accounting for 4,300 units either built, under construction, or in the approval process (Tomalty, 2003).

Toronto, Ontario: The Metropolitan Toronto Planning Department (1987) estimated that the conversion aspect alone of a residential intensification program could produce 39,000 new housing units, the equivalent of 11 years of rental housing production (both private and social units).

Jobs/Housing Balance

The jobs/housing balance is a useful developer's tool, although no rule of thumb or actual values are available. Basically, when jobs and housing are not in balance, transportation problems are the likely result. Land-use planners can look at the range of incomes and housing costs to determine how far people have to move away from their jobs to find housing they can afford. The imbalance between the location of jobs and housing is the most important determinant for longer commuting and suggests that higher quality and affordable housing growth close to the job-rich communities reduces traffic congestion and air pollution (Sultana, 2002; Weitz, 2003).

Redirecting Development: New Jersey's Urban Enterprise Zone (UEZ) program provides incentives to increase economic activity on vacant land and structures, using such things as business tax deductions for hiring zone residents, unemployment insurance rebates and sales tax exemptions for the sale of goods and services that will be used within the zone. Since it was created in 1984, the UEZ program has generated more than 58,000 new jobs, more than 6,500 businesses and $12.5 billion in private investment in areas throughout the state that had previously been suffering from disinvestments (Leigh, 2003). By encouraging job creation on vacant land that is already connected to nearby residential neighbourhoods, the jobs/housing balance can be improved.

Proximity Planning

Striking a balance between jobs and housing, as discussed above, is not enough unless the people who work in a given area have the option of also living in that same area. This requires policies to encourage access by proximity.

Clouds of Change: Vancouver's Clouds of Change program makes "access by proximity rather than access by transportation" a central focus of city planning (City of Vancouver, 1990).

Land Stewardship Guidelines

Halton, Ontario: The Regional Municipality of Halton, Ontario has advanced land stewardship as the first guiding principle for land-use planning in Halton (Regional Municipality of Halton 1991): "In this regard, we submit that the ownership rights of land are not absolute and the best and highest use of land is not an unfailing principle as there are other balancing factors to be considered. This is not meant as a denial of property rights, but an affirmation of a social responsibility .... The extent to which an individual realizes the economic benefit of a land use change should be balanced by the community's desire in preserving the environment or certain land forms in the landscape."

New Forms of Land Ownership

In recent years, land trusts and limited equity cooperatives have experimented with distributing the costs and benefits of land development in much the same way as proposed by Henry George, but through new forms of land ownership rather than taxation.

Common Property: In Boston's Dudley Street Neighborhood Initiative, for example, the project made the land in an inner-city redevelopment area the common property of a nonprofit group, while allowing private ownership of homes and other buildings.

Social Increment: Similarly, Connecticut's Equity Trust dedicates the "social increment" in property values (for example, the portion of a home's sale price that is due to the increase in land values rather than housing construction costs) to social purposes, such as subsidizing the purchase price for future homeowners (Ingerson, 1997).

Dual Property Tax System

Land Levy: Fifteen US cities levy a higher charge on land than on buildings to spur the regeneration of their blighted land. When Pittsburgh introduced a sharply graded dual tax system in 1978, the number of vacant lot sales, new building permits, and new dwellings quickly increased. At the same time, demolitions declined (Lowe, 1992).

Building Permit Allocation

Growth Management Ordinance: Boulder, Colorado experienced extreme growth pressures of around 6 percent per year between 1960 and 1970. As a result, in 1967, the city implemented one of the first greenbelt systems in the US to serve as a natural growth boundary by defining the limits to the city with open space and parkland. This was followed in 1976 with a cap on new residential developments designed to keep the annual growth rate at 1.5 to 2 percent per year. Under the cap, residential building permits were limited to 450 building permits per year, originally allocated under a point system based on availability of urban services, affordability and energy efficiency (the point system was discarded in 1981 as it was found to be too bureaucratic).

When the annual growth rate was reduced to 1 percent per year in 1995, the city council acted to create a larger share of affordable housing. New housing developments are now allocated according to a formula of 25 percent market housing, 55 percent affordable housing (based on size and other criteria) and 20 percent permanently affordable housing maintained through deed restrictions. The allocation of affordable housing is combined with a housing trust fund that uses an excise tax on new construction to subsidize affordable housing. Despite the significant growth pressure experienced in Boulder, the city has managed to manage and control growth by recognizing the financial and ecological limits to growth and adopting policies consistent with those limits (Fodor, 1999).

RESOURCES

Cyburbia contains a hierarchical resource directory of thousands of internet sites related to planning, urbanism and other topics related to the built environment. Website: www.cyburbia.org

Land Trust Alliance is a national organization that represents over 1,300 land trusts across America. They provide training, research, lobbying services and strategic planning to help leverage and connect the work of all of its member land trusts. Website: www.lta.org

Lincoln Institute of Land Policy is a nonprofit school that studies and teaches about land policy, including land economics and land taxation. Its major goals are integrating the theory and practice of land policy and understanding the forces that influence it. The Institute offers courses and workshops in various cities, has an impressive publications list, and publishes the quarterly newsletter, *LandLines*. Website: www.lincolninst.edu

The National Center for Smart Growth Research and Education is a non-partisan center for research and leadership training on Smart Growth and related land use issues nationally and internationally. It conducts independent, objective research in four general areas: land use and the environment; transportation and public health; housing and community development; and international development issues. Website: www.smartgrowth.umd.edu/

Smart Growth America is a coalition of nearly 100 advocacy organizations that have a stake in how metropolitan expansion affects our environment, quality of life and economic sustainability. Smart Growth America's coalition is working to support citizen-driven planning that coordinates development, transportation, revitalization of older areas and preservation of open space and the environment. Website: www.smartgrowthamerica.com

Smart Growth BC is a provincial non-governmental organization devoted to fiscally, socially and environmentally responsible land use and development. Working with community groups, businesses, municipalities and the public, they advocate for the creation of more liveable communities in British Columbia. Website: www.smartgrowth.bc.ca

REFERENCES

Abberger, W. 1991. "Growth Management Through Land Acquisition." In *Balanced Growth: A Planning Guide for Local Government*, J.M. DeGrove, ed. Washington, DC: International City Management Association.

Adler, J. 1995. "Bye-Bye, Suburban Dream: 15 Ways to Fix the Suburbs." *Newsweek* May 15: 40-53.

Beatley, T. 2000. *Green Urbanism: Learning from European cities*. Washington, DC: Island Press.

British Columbia Ministry of Municipal Affairs and Housing (BCMMAH). 1997. *Taking Action*. Victoria, BC: BCMMAH.

British Columbia Round Table on the Environment and the Economy (BCRTEE). 1994. *State of Sustainability: Urban Sustainability and Containment*. Victoria, BC: Crown Publications.

Carruthers, J. I., & Ulfarsson, G. F. 2003. Urban sprawl and the cost of public services. *Environment and Planning B: Planning and Design*, 30(4), 203-522.

Cervero, R. 1991. "Congestion Relief: The Land Use Alternative." *Journal of Planning Education and Research* 10(2): 119-29.

City of Vancouver. 1990. *Clouds of Change: Final Report of the City of Vancouver Task Force on Atmospheric Change*. Vancouver: City of Vancouver.

Congress for the New Urbanism, & Crawford, P. 2004. *Codifying new urbanism : How to reform municipal land development regulations*. Chicago: American Planning Association.

Cooper Marcus, C., and W. Sarkissian. 1986. *Housing as if People Mattered: Site Design Guidelines for Medium-Density Family Housing*. Berkeley: University of California Press.

Daly, H.E. & Farley, J. 2004. *Ecological Economics: Principles and Applications*. Washington: Island Press.

DeGrove, J.M., ed. 1991. *Balanced Growth: A Planning Guide for Local Government*. Washington, DC: International City Management Association.

Duany, A., and E. Plater-Zyberk. 1992. "The Second Coming of the Small Town." *Wilson Quarterly*. Winter. Reprinted in *Utne Reader* 1. May/June: 97-100.

Duany, A. 2004. *Celebration controversies*. www.intbau.org/essay8.htm

Durning, A.T. 1996. *The Car and The City*. Seattle: Northwest Environment Watch.

Engwicht, D. 1993. *Reclaiming Our Cities and Towns: Better Living With Less Traffic*. Gabriola Island, BC: New Society Publishers.

Fannie Mae. 2000. *Home buyers leverage public transit to increase home-buying power*. Retrieved from www.fanniemae.com/newsreleases/2000/0785.jhtml?p=Media&s=News+Releases

Fannie Mae. 2000. *Boston's Dudley triangle*. Retrieved from www.fanniemaefoundation.org/programs/bb/v1i2-boston.shtml

Fodor, E. 1999. *Better, Not Bigger: How to take control of urban growth and improve your community*. Stoney Creek, CT: New Society Publishers.

Freyfogle, E. T. 2003. *The land we share: Private property and the common good*. Washington, DC: Island Press.from

Gayler, H. 1990. "Changing Aspects of Urban Containment in Canada: The Niagara Case in the 1980s and Beyond." *Urban Geography* 11(4): 373-93.

Gibson, K., & Abbott, C. 2002. Portland, Oregon. *Cities*, 19(6): 425-436.

Gihring, T. A. 1999. Incentive property taxation. A potential tool for urban growth management. *Journal of the American Planning Association*, 65(1): 62-79.

Haughton, G., and C. Hunter. 1994. *Sustainable Cities*. Regional Policy and Development Series 7. London: Jessica Kingsley.

Heyerdahl, B. 1991. "TDRs: An Innovative Approach to Growth Management." In *Balanced Growth: A Planning Guide for Local Government*, J.M. DeGrove, ed. Washington, DC: International City Management Association.

Holtzclaw, J., Haas, P., Clear, R., Dittmar, H., & Goldstein, D. 2002. Location efficiency: Neighborhood and socio-economic characteristics determine auto ownership and use - studies in Chicago, Los Angeles and San Francisco. *Transportation Planning and Technology*, 25(1): 1-27.

International Centre for Technology Assessment. 2004. *The real price of gasoline*. Retrieved from www.icta.org/projects/trans/realpricegas.pdf

Ingerson, A.E. 1991. "Urban Land as Common Property." *LandLines* 9(2): 1-3.

Kasowski, K. 1991. "Oregon: Fifteen Years of Land-Use Planning." In *Balanced Growth: A Planning Guide for Local Government*, J.M. DeGrove, ed. Washington, DC: International City Management Association.

Krizek, K.J. 2003. Transit Supportive Home Loans: Theory, Application, and Prospects for Smart Growth. *Housing Policy Debate*, 14(4): 657-677.

Kunstler, J.H. 1996. "Home From Nowhere: How to Make Our Cities and Towns Livable." *Atlantic Monthly* 278 (3) September: 43-66.

Land Trust Alliance. n.d. Land Trusts. Washington, DC: Land Trust Alliance.

Leigh, N. G. 2003. *The state role in urban land development*. Washington: Brookings Institution Centre on Urban and Metropolitan Policy.

Lowe, M.D. 1991a. "Portland Bypasses Progress." *Worldwatch* 4(5) Sept./Oct.: 9, 30.

— — — . 1992. "City Limits." *Worldwatch* 5(1) Jan./Feb.: 18-25.

Marshall, A. 2003. A tale of two towns tells a lot about this thing called new urbanism. *Built Environment*, 29(3): 227-237.

Metropolitan Toronto Planning Department Policy Development Division. 1987. "Housing Intensification." In *Metropolitan Plan Review Report No. 4*. Toronto: Planning Department

National Round Table on the Environment and the Economy (NRTEE). 2003. *Cleaning up the past, building the future: A national brownfield redevelopment strategy for Canada*. Ottawa: NRTEE.

Neilson, L. 1990. Economic Perspective on Better Urban Space. Presented to Globe '90 Conference, Vancouver, BC, 20 March.

Newman, P. 1991. Urban Villages — Concept for the '90s. Presented to ECODESIGN Conference, RMIT, Melbourne, Australia, 18-20 October.

Newman, P. 1996. Reducing Automobile Dependence. Presented to OECD International Conference, Toward Sustainable Transportation, Vancouver, BC, March.

Newmand, P. & Kenworthy, J. 1999. *Sustainability and Cities: Overcoming automobile dependence*. Washington: Island Press.

Newman, P., & Kenworthy, J. 2001. Transportation energy in global cities: Sustainable transportation comes in from the cold? *Natural Resources Forum*, 25(2): 91-107.

O'Brien, F. 1990. "Toward a Greener, Cleaner Planet and a New Environmental Perspective." *Canadian Building* May.

Office of Sustainable Development. 2002. *Global warming update*. Retrieved from www.sustainableportland.org/engery_global_warming_2001_emissions.pdf

Owens, S.E. 1990. "Land Use Planning for Energy Efficiency." In *Energy, Land, and Public Policy*, J.B. Cullingworth, ed. New Brunswick, N.J.: Transaction Publishers: 53-98.

Pollard, T. 2001. Greening the American dream? If sprawl is the problem, is new urbanism the solution? *Planning, 67*(10): 10-15

Real Estate Research Corporation. 1974. *The Costs of Sprawl*.Volume I: Detailed Cost Analysis. Washington, DC: US Government Printing Office.

Regional Municipality of Halton (Ontario). 1991. *Land Stewardship and Healthy Communities: A Vision for the 90's and Beyond*. Official Plan Review Report B4 draft, January.

Replogle, M. 1990. "Sustainable Transportation Strategies for World Development". Presented to the World Congress of Local Governments for a Sustainable Future, United Nations, New York, 7 September.

Richardson, N. 1991. "Sustainable Development and Land Use Planning". Presented to Association of Municipal Clerks and Treasurers of Ontario and Intergovernmental Committee on Urban and Regional Research Management Symposium, Implementing Sustainable Development in Municipalities, Hockley Valley, Ontario, 8-10 May.

Russell, J. 2004. New urbanist essentials. *APA Planning Advisory Service Reports*, (526): 9-24.

Rybeck, R. 1996. Tax Reform Fights Sprawl. Prepared for OECD International Conference, Toward Sustainable Transportation, Vancouver, BC, March.

Sheehan, M. O. 2001. City limits: Putting the brakes on sprawl. *Worldwatch Paper*, (156): 1-85.

Sheltair Group. 2001. *Green municipalities: A guide to green infrastructure for Canadian municipalities*. Ottawa: Federation of Canadian Municipalities.

Smart Growth America. 2005. "What is Smart Growth/ How is Smart Growth Achieved?" www.smartgrowthamerica.com/

Smart Growth BC. 2005. "Alternative Development Fact Sheet and Background." Retrieved from www.smarthgrowth.bc.ca/index.cfm?group_IO=3405Sultana, S. 2002. Job/housing imbalance and commuting time in the Atlanta Metropolitan Area: Exploration of causes of longer commuting time. *Urban Geography*, 23(8): 728-749.

Tomalty, R. 2003. *Residential intensification case studies: Municipal initiatives*. Ottawa: Canada Mortgage and Housing Corporation.

Weitz, J. 2003. Jobs-housing balance. *APA Planning Advisory Service Reports*, (516): 1-41.

World Resources Institute, United Nations Environment Program, United Nations Development Program, World Bank. 1996. *World Resources 1996-97: The Urban Environment*. New York: Oxford University Press.

Young, R. 2002. *Innovation — the lessons from Slateford Green*. Retrieved from www.canmore-housing.org.uk/pdf forms/sg_review.pdf

CHAPTER 11

HOUSING AND COMMUNITY DEVELOPMENT

Reducing the environmental impact of housing and urban development is critical for the survival of our planet, but improving livability and fostering community is imperative for the survival of humanity. Mobility and migration have splintered many communities that were long based on blood ties, cultural heritage and life within a narrow geographic region. Yet new challenges have arisen to connect people — to share common interests, share burdens, and develop healthy relationships with other members of the human community. In other words, "Community is a group of people who commit themselves for the long-term to their own, one another's and the group's well-being" (Shaffer and Anundsen, 1993).

Despite myriad opportunities for social interaction, cities and towns are lonely places of isolation for many people. Community development requires good urban design to foster connection and neighborliness, and programs, policies, and initiatives to encourage healthy human interaction, including safety, respect, and social equity. Social equity means more than equal opportunity. It implies opportunities for adequate housing, healthcare, education, employment, and mobility. Homelessness alone strikes thousands of people in North America, and millions more live in abject poverty and subsistence housing.

Sustainable community development implies that we address not only the "hard" urban environmental issues such as transportation, land use, air quality, and energy conservation, but also the "soft" issues such as social and environmental justice.

MORE THAN A ROOF OVER OUR HEADS

Housing is a key factor influencing both environmental and social aspects of community development. Many, many people in North America live without adequate housing, or lack any form of permanent and secure shelter. In addition to these inequities, even those fortunate enough to have a home may live in a neighborhood lacking "a sense of place."

Affording a Home

A growing number of people cannot afford housing. Subsidized programs provide assistance to some, while others are leaving the city to find lower-cost housing in suburbs and small towns. Residents of low-cost housing are often stereotyped as jobless people who bring with them numerous social problems. While unemployment is a growing problem, many *employed* people don't earn enough to afford adequate housing. A survey of low-income residents of Contra Costa County, California, indicates most families who need affordable housing are simply hardworking people caught in the squeeze between rising housing costs and eroding wages. As real estate prices escalate and the cost of living continues to increase, many people working as secretaries, clerks, nurses aides, and truck drivers may not earn enough money to afford market-rate housing, and if they are supporting children or other family members, their financial stress magnifies.

A variety of strategies exist to finance affordable housing development and to support people seeking ways to lower housing costs. Community Development Corporations, credit unions, community development banks, and various other government and non-governmental agencies provide funding for construction, rents and mortgages, or in-kind support for affordable housing construction. (See also Chapter 12: Community Economic Development.) Unfortunately much of the affordable and lower-cost units built in the last few decades have failed to provide healthy, safe, and nurturing environments for residents. Single-mothers and the aged or infirm are groups whose needs are often neglected in housing design and planning. By "designing as if people mattered" (Cooper-Marcus, 1986), architects, planners, and developers honor the needs of all people and seek to provide places where all can thrive.

Alternative housing development strategies, such as cooperatives and cohousing, are planned with the participation of future residents. This enables residents to influence design so that it represents their needs. The focus is on community in these and other forms of shared-living communities, but they also offer opportunities for lower costs. Shared space such as gardens and common areas enable people to live comfortably in more compact space, and sharing of cars, computers, laundry service, and childcare can reduce living expenses.

Co-housing has been rapidly gaining popularity throughout North America as a result of dissatisfaction with the design of conventional residential developments. This housing alternative is serving the needs of people of varying incomes, in providing tan-

Social Sustainability

Social sustainability is another way of discussing social capital (see chapter 1). It requires social equity and responsible citizenship. Socially sustainable community members are able to:

- achieve and maintain personal health: physical, mental and psychological;
- feed themselves adequately;
- provide adequate and appropriate shelter for themselves;
- have opportunities for gainful and meaningful employment;
- improve their knowledge and understanding of the world around them;
- find opportunities to express creativity and enjoy recreation in ways that satisfy spiritual and psychological needs;
- express a sense of identity through heritage, art and culture;
- enjoy a sense of belonging;
- be assured of mutual social support from their community;
- enjoy freedom from discrimination and, for those who are physically challenged, move about a barrier-free community;
- enjoy freedom from fear, and security of person; and
- participate actively in civic affairs (BCRTEE, 1993).

Municipal Initiatives to Promote Affordable Housing

Municipalities can plan for and promote affordable housing in many ways, including the following:

- *Development Approval Process*: Accelerate the approval process and fast-track applications for rentals, special needs housing, and non-market housing.
- *Financing for New Developments*: Generate new funds for affordable housing projects through municipal initiatives.
- *Intensification of Existing Areas*: Re-zone to allow higher density housing in existing areas, e.g., secondary suites.
- *Intensification in New Areas*: Regulate zones to encourage compact forms of residential land use.
- *Land Use*: Lease or provide municipal land for affordable housing at lower than market rates.
- *Partnerships*: Collaborate with nonprofit or private organizations, churches, developers, etc.
- *Protect Existing Housing Stock*: Regulate existing housing stock to ensure it remains as affordable housing.
- *Technical Support and Housing Information*: Collect, maintain, and disseminate information regarding affordable housing in the community.
- *Zoning Regulations*: Develop creative zoning to promote affordable housing programs, e.g., mixed-land use or density bonuses (BCMCAWS, 2004).

---

gibles, such as shared facilities, help with child care, and meal preparation, as well as intangibles, such as a sense of community, support and a feeling of security (Fromm, 2000). With co-housing, residents share common areas and management of the complex, and abide by agreed-upon guidelines, but individuals are able to decide the degree to which they participate in community activities.

Creating a Community

To create a "sense of place" and foster connection among people, the physical characteristics of neighborhoods must draw people together and encourage an atmosphere of peace, security, and pride among residents of a community. In addition to thoughtful building design, clean streets, gardens and trees, and places to gather can create a village-like atmosphere even in inner-city neighborhoods. Ideally, closeness to other people is mirrored in a closeness to nature and integration of ecology into community living.

However, the physical design of housing and neighborhoods alone cannot create communities. Government policies and the actions and initiatives of local citizens are critical. Churches have often been the center of community, but in more recent times, people have also sought connection through involvement in neighborhood groups and activities, and participation in other non-government organizations such as environmental groups.

While responsible participation in governance is important, getting to know your neighbors is a simple first step. Getting involved and creating opportunities for inclusiveness are even bigger steps. True and rich community is a mix of young and old, rich and poor, men and women of varying ethnicity and abilities sharing their lives.

TOOLS AND INITIATIVES

Affordable Housing Programs

Housing Scholarship Program: Allied Housing Inc., a nonprofit housing corporation, manages the Housing Scholarship Program in the Tri-Valley region of California that provides housing support to low-income individuals and families while they are enrolled in job training programs. In 2001, 90 percent of the graduates maintained stable housing and secured employment. The Allied Housing Linkages Program also provides rent subsidies and employment services to individuals coming out of homeless shelters by working with area housing authorities and private sector landlords to obtain transition housing as people move towards self-sufficiency (Welfare Information Network, 2002).

Nonprofit Affordable Housing Organization: In the 1970s, the US Department of Housing and Urban Development provided low-interest loans to encourage construction of affordable housing. Twenty years later, low-income people are losing their subsidized housing as building owners repay these loans and convert apartment buildings to market-rate rents. The Ecumenical Association of Housing is a nonprofit affordable housing organization in San Rafael, California raising financing to purchase many of these apartments before tenants face rent increases. In 1996, the Association used Housing and Urban Development grants and other financial sources to invest $95.1 million to acquire 831 units of affordable housing (Anders, 1997).

Habitat for Humanity: This nonprofit organization has chapters across North America which raise funds (and in-kind contributions) to construct low-cost homes. Mimicking the Amish style of community barn-raising, volunteers work together to construct houses. Some Habitat chapters are building energy-efficient homes so that the new homeowners will not be saddled with high utility bills. Others are experimenting with strawbale or adobe environmentally sound construction materials.

Service-Enriched Housing

Beyond Shelter: Beyond Shelter, a nonprofit affordable housing and social services provider, develops, owns and operates a number of service-enriched affordable housing projects as well as develops family support and childcare centers. At each project, an on-site Services Coordinator helps residents access community resources and services. Tenants participate in Resident Management Committees that manage the building and common areas, and plan program development and activities for tenants of all ages (Brown, 2001).

Self-Help Housing

Urban Homesteading: The Urban Homesteading Assistance Board in New York City began in 1973 by training tenants to own and manage their own buildings. The Board also promotes the conversion of city-owned buildings into limited equity co-ops. The buildings, acquired by the city through tax foreclosures, are sold back to former renters for $250 an

---

Small Steps to Create Neighborhoods

- Learn the names of your neighbors and local merchants. Share ideas and conversation with them.
- Send out postcards suggesting a babysitting or pet-sitting cooperative.
- Invite a few neighbors to dinner or a barbeque, and suggest a meal rotation (one household at a time cooking one day each month).
- Start a neighborhood newsletter or newspaper. This reinforces neighborhood identify.
- Ask the police department to help sponsor a block meeting to discuss safety. Plan a social time afterwards.
- Invite local architects and planners with vision to speak to your community group. Design is a key element in creating a feeling of community.
- Request some city land be made available for citizen planting of trees and community gardens (Shaffer and Anundsen, 1993).

Family-focused community-building

Family-focused community-building is a model of community organizing in response to a lack of organizing efforts from more traditional models such as Community Development Corporations. The family-focused community-building model, as developed by the Community Organizing and Family Issues organization in Chicago, returns to the notion that community empowerment begins from within and is based on the following:

- Prospective leaders are recruited from low-income families, particularly women.
- Leadership training emphasizes continuities between family and community leadership.
- Visioning conversations are framed in terms of what will make the community a better place for families.
- Recognition of many different kinds and levels of leadership.
- Recognition that many of the conditions making communities unsafe and unhealthy are rooted in public policies beyond the local level.

Housing can be designed to accomodate greenery or to grow food by providing set-back terraces and deep flower boxes

apartment, which means the tenants together own the building and share responsibilities (Brozan, 2004). The experience helps build skills, empower people, and reduce crime rates in and around these buildings.

Mutual Housing Associations

Mutual Housing Associations are private, nonprofit corporations created to develop, own, and manage affordable housing. All residents are stockholders and therefore participate in decision-making. Housing Associations unite groups of buildings, such as limited equity co-ops and low- and middle-income dwellings, into larger associations. It is believed that larger associations will improve the delivery of housing services and assist in on-going development. Other benefits are providing resident training and professional property management, and pooling capital and leadership resources.

Financing through Bonds

Municipal Bonds: Essential Function Bonds (EFBs) have been used to finance the construction and rehabilitation of affordable housing or other community facilities. Recognizing the continuing need for affordable housing, cities have increased the use of EFBs to a total of $2.12 billion as of 2002. For example, the City of Chicago used $291 million in bond financing to rehabilitate their portfolio of 12,252 seniors' housing units (Apgar and Whiting, 2003).

Linkage Programs and Partnerships

Linkage programs collect a portion of the value created by investment in neighborhoods undergoing substantial development and direct that value to build affordable housing, to provide job training, and to fund social services in less fortunate neighborhoods. In Boston, for example, in 2001, real estate developers paid a "linkage payment" of $8.62 per square foot of construction over 100,000 square feet, $1.44 of which went to a job training fund and $7.18 for affordable housing purposes (Boston Redevelopment Authority, 2003). Linkage programs could also provide a means for financing investment in environmental protection and restoration. While these programs have operated for several years in US cities such as Boston and San Francisco, they are also becoming more common in Canada.

Daycare Center: In December 1990, Vancouver, BC approved its first agreement with a commercial developer in which the capital costs of a daycare center were financed as a condition of rezoning.

Mixed-Use Complex: In an unusual partnership, Habitat for Humanity teamed up in 1996 with an Equity Housing Cooperative to construct a mixed-use complex in East Vancouver, BC A commercial partner is developing the street level shops, and 29 units of housing make up the second and third stories. Some of the units will be co-op owned, and others will be Habitat homes provided to low-income families. By helping construct the complex, people earn equity toward their new home.

Community Grants

Block Grants: Galion, Ohio used a Community Development Block Grant to leverage $10 million of funding from other private and public sources to refurbish the historic uptown area. As a result of the revitalization, businesses have returned to the area, a walking tour has been developed to promote tourism and the historic movie theatre has reopened. Additionally, a historic hotel on the Main Street has been converted into a seniors' residence, adding to the population in the historic area (Housing and Urban Development, 2004).

Community Land Trusts

Community Land Trusts have acquired or developed several thousand units of permanently affordable housing, and heritage buildings, and have provided land for shelters, health centers, farms and other community social and economic development needs. The land is owned by a nonprofit organization and protected by it for a specific use. (Institute for Community Economics, 1982; Roseland, 1992).

Governments have formed several kinds of partnerships with Community Land Trusts, such as allocating funds or city-owned lands to them. Municipal zoning has the power to negotiate commitments from developers to donate land for Trusts and to build affordable housing. Trusts also manage publicly owned lands, such as bike paths, conservation areas, and community gardens.

Burlington Community Land Trust: In 1987, the affordable housing shortage in northern Vermont inspired the creation of the Burlington Community Land Trust (BCLT). The organization obtains land and places it within the Trust, thereby taking the land out of the speculative market and making the housing perpetually affordable. Since its creation, BCLT has preserved affordability, retained wealth in the community, enhanced residential stability, expanded homeownership opportunities, created individual wealth and enabled residential mobility. It has been able to achieve these results in a real estate market with rising prices, growing demand and a chronic shortage of homes within the reach of persons earning below 80 percent of median income (Davis and Demetrowitz, 2003).

Cooperative Housing Land Trust Foundation: In 1993, the Cooperative Housing Federation of BC formed the Cooperative Housing Land Trust Foundation to ensure access to affordable housing in BC The Foundation works with nonprofit housing co-ops to protect the existing stock of affordable housing. Nonprofit co-ops cannot distribute their assets to residents who buy into the co-ops, yet as agreements with government expire, tenants may lose their homes as prices jump to keep pace with market values. By joining the Foundation and transferring the asset value, the value is held in perpetuity by the land trust (BC Working Group, 1995).

Shared-living Communities

Cohousing: Residents of the Doyle Street co-housing complex in Emeryville, California live in loft-style apartments in a converted brick warehouse. Adaptive reuse of an old building helped to revitalize an economically disadvantaged area; it also encouraged a sprawling community to embrace the neighborhood by, among other things, establishing a community garden nearby.

Cooperative Housing: Recognizing the need for safe, affordable housing options for single-mothers, the nonprofit Entres Nous Femmes Housing Society is helping build co-operative housing units in Vancouver, BC. Primarily occupied by single-parent families, the townhouse-style complexes provide both a home and a community to many people who were previously isolated. Empowerment of the co-op's members is key. Residents sit on the board of directors and make decisions about maintenance and management of the facilities, which provides opportunities to learn management and organizational skills useful in the job market.

Urban Cooperative Block: In a suburb of Davis, California, residents formed an urban cooperative block called N Street Community by removing fences and sharing their lives. Residents of eleven houses merged their backyards to share paths, patios, fruit trees, compost bins, gardens, greenhouses, a chicken pen, and a clothes line. One house was converted into a common house, and the group pooled their resources to purchase two adjacent houses to enable rental tenants to join the community. Efforts toward sustainability include organically managing gardens, growing fruits and vegetables, and installing solar collectors. Neighbors share cars, compost, and reuse and recycle materials.

Community Revitalization Programs

Don't Move, Improve! Campaign: Faced with urban decay and an exodus from the South Bronx in New York, a community-group initiated an urban revitalization program addressing health, daycare, economic education, housing, environment, transportation, and capital development. The "Don't Move, Improve!" campaign has channeled $100 million of investment into the community, rehabilitated and constructed 25,000 units of affordable housing, implemented energy-efficiency retrofits in more than 8,000 units, and provided technical and financial assistance to 125 small businesses (Wheeler, 1996).

Nuisance Alley Program: Residents convert debris-ridden alleys in Los Angeles, California into common gardens and recreational areas. Efforts by the Los Angeles Neighborhood Initiative to revitalize the city's streets also include funding and spearheading renovation of storefronts, tree planting, and other improvements in eight of the city's most rundown neighborhoods. Local residents and businesses recommend improvements, and funds come from a variety of federal, state, and private monies.

Mosaic Park: East Vancouver, BC has fewer parks per capita than any other neighborhood in the city. Modest funding from local grants and city support helped a group of citizens, including an architect and a landscape architect, come together to convert a vacant lot into a playground and park. With no vegetation or streams on the barren lot, the group found another way to create some connection with nature. A meandering stream was designed and built with mosaic tiles, assisted by a local artist who taught school children and community groups how to create ceramic tile mosaics. Large boulders (free byproducts of city excavation work) and logs were brought in for children to climb on, and locals planted trees. Mosaic park is the pride of the community that built it.

HEALTHY COMMUNITIES

A healthy community reflects the health of its citizens. A century ago, municipalities were instrumental in improving public health by preventing the spread of disease through slum clearance, community planning, water treatment, and the provision of certain health services. These initiatives were based on the view of health as the absence of disease, and disease prevention as the main challenge for local government. Yet health is influenced more by our physical and social environments than by interventions of the health care system.

Since the mid-1980s, a broader conception of public health has been adopted by municipal governments in Europe and North America. Although the name "healthy communities" implies a focus on medical care, the Ottawa Charter for Health Promotion (WHO et al., 1986) recognizes that "the fundamental conditions and resources for health are peace, shelter, education, food, income, a stable ecosystem, sustainable resources, social justice, and equity." Local governments play a big role in all these areas through their impact on public hygiene (waste disposal and water systems), food handling and other public health regulations, recreational facilities, education, transportation, economic development, and land-use planning.

The Healthy Communities approach is based on a worldwide Healthy Cities movement, which now numbers over 7,000 cities. Launched with the support of the World Health Organization, the movement had its genesis in Toronto at a 1984 health conference workshop called "Healthy Toronto 2000." The Healthy Communities approach is based on five key action areas at the local level:

- *Create Supportive Environments*: The protection of the natural and built environments and the conservation of natural resources must be addressed in health promotion strategies.
- *Strengthen Community Actions*: The empowerment of communities is a key to generating their ownership and control of their destinies.
- *Develop Personal Skills*: Enabling people to learn, throughout life, to prepare themselves for all its stages and to cope with chronic illness and injuries is essential.
- *Reorient Health Services*: The role of the health sector must move in the direction of health promotion, beyond its responsibility for providing clinical and curative services.
- *Healthy public policy*: Health promotion policy requires the identification of obstacles to the adoption of healthy public policies in non-health sectors, and ways of removing them (Kickbusch, 2002).

TOOLS AND INITIATIVES

Healthy Communities/Healthy City Programs
Healthy Communities Coalition: The Ontario Healthy Community Coalition (OHCC)

Environmental Justice

The 1982 decision to site a PCB landfill in an African American community in North Carolina is recognized as the beginning of the environmental justice movement, and in 1994 President Clinton ordered the federal government to "make achieving environmental justice part of its mission" (Draper and Mitchell, 2001). By 2003, regional offices of the EPA were required to submit an *Environmental Justice Action Plan* to report on progress towards meeting this goal.

The movement traditionally organized around LULUs (Locally Unwanted Land Uses) such as waste facility siting, transfer storage and disposal facilities (TSDFs) and issues such as lead contamination, pesticides, water and air pollution, workplace safety, and transportation. More recently, sprawl and smart growth (Bullard, 2000), sustainability (Agyeman et al., 2003; Agyeman, 2005) and climate change (International Climate Justice Network, 2002; Congressional Black Caucus Foundation, 2004) have engaged environmental justice advocates.

Environmental justice deals with a number of equity issues:

- *Procedural equity:* The way rules, regulations and evaluation criteria are applied and reinforced; privileging certain rights over others.
- *Social, or intra-generational equity:* The way sociological factors like race, ethnicity, class, culture, and political power influence decision-making so that certain groups seem to be systematically disadvantaged in terms of, for example, living in the most polluted neighbourhoods (or countries).
- *Distributional equity:* Refers to inequity that results from some neighbourhoods receiving direct *benefits* (jobs, tax revenues) from industrial production while the costs (burden landfills, toxic waste dumps) are sent to other neighbourhoods.
- *Inter-generational equity:* Refers to the environmental impact of the current, on future generations.
- *Inter-species equity:* Concerns balancing human needs with ecosystem survival.

emerged as an informal group from the "Healthy Toronto 2000" workshop. It was established formally in 1993 as the provincial secretariat to provide a broad range of services and resources to help local Healthy Community coalitions become established and flourish province-wide. Their mission seeks to achieve social, environmental and economic health and well-being for individuals, communities and local governments. OHCC provides support through regional community animators who work closely with community groups and coalitions to identify and provide for their training and development requirements. OHCC also produces educational resources, maintains an educational resource library, produces a biannual newsletter and organizes an annual Healthy Communities Conference (Heidenheim, 2004; OHCC, 2004).

Health and Wellness Programs

Health and Fitness Campaign: Obesity and heart disease require billions of dollars of money spent on medical care each year, and are leading causes of death in Canada and the US With promotional support from the local newspaper, the City of Vancouver developed a huge annual health and fitness campaign that is linked to a charitable fund-raising event. From "couch potatoes" to athletes, the program is helping people join others in improving their health. The three-month program, which includes weekly walking/jogging training and lessons on nutrition and fitness training, culminates in a popular fitness fair and 10-kilometer (6.2-mile) run.

Smoking Ban: Numerous cities, states and provinces have heeded the warning about the hazards of cigarette smoke. In an effort to protect people from second-hand smoke, these jurisdictions have banned cigarette smoking in restaurants and all public buildings.

Junk Food Ban in Schools: The Ontario government has banned the sale of junk food from elementary-school vending machines in an effort to improve the eating habits of students. The ban is covers all sugary drinks, chips and candy-bars, in an effort to promote healthy eating habits among young children (Alphonso, 2004).

Safety Audits

Metro Action Committee: In Toronto, informal groups of people get together and, using a safety audit checklist, evaluate lighting, access to emergency phones, overgrown shrubbery near bus shelters, and so on. Government authorities use the information to guide decisions about safety improvements within their jurisdiction. The organization has since produced a guide for auditing women's safety and it has been translated into numerous languages and adapted for use in European and African cities (Drusine, 2002).

Community Police and Patrol

Community Police: In downtown Vancouver, BC community police centers are opening up in small store-front centers to help bring police closer to citizens. As they walk or bike throughout the neighborhood, police officers get to know local residents and inform "street people" about opportunities for assistance.

Volunteer Park Patrollers: In Vancouver, volunteer park patrollers rollerblade or bicycle around the 15-kilometer (9.3-mile) long seawall path in Stanley Park. In addition to enjoying comradery, the wheeling park patrollers ensure that the many cyclists, joggers, and rollerbladers are safely enjoying the spectacular public park.

Local Food Supplies

Organic Community Garden: Concerned about poor nutrition and health in their community, the Cariboo Health (BC) Unit partnered with the Salvation Army to start an organic community garden. Volunteers grow fruit and vegetables for low-income residents and garden space is also available for people who don't have land of their own.

Edible Schoolyard: The schoolyard of Martin Luther King Jr. Middle School in Berkeley, California, is not your typical concrete playground. The yard has been transformed by students into a garden that produces organically grown fruits and vegetables that are eventually used in the cafeteria, which has been transformed into a classroom kitchen. Every year, the program introduces over 900 students to the finer points of organic gardening and healthy eating (Bogo, 2002).

Community Kitchens

Community Kitchen: The Vancouver Community Kitchen project is an educational resource centre for the development of community kitchens throughout Greater Vancouver. Their goal is to build community around food and create opportunities for people to cook together. Everyone who participates in a community kitchen is expected to take part in menu selection, shopping, preparation and cooking. Members share food and nutrition knowledge and reinforce the importance of good nutrition to healthy community (GVFBS, 2004).

A Loving Spoonful: A volunteer group in Vancouver, BC called A Loving Spoonful delivers prepared meals to people debilitated by AIDS.

Environmental Justice Advocacy Programs

Environmental Benefits Program: Greenpoint-Williamsburg is one of the poorest and most highly industrialized areas in the New York City borough of Brooklyn. Many residents suffer from the risks and consequences of waste, pollution, and odors caused by nearly 1000 industrial firms. The Environmental Benefits Program, a partnership between the city and local citizens, integrated public participation into the process of remediating environmental problems. The state ordered establishment of a benefits fund made up of money collected for non-compliance of environmental regulations; the Citizens' Advisory Committee directs the funds to local environmental initiatives. An Environmental Watchperson contracts with community-based organizations to implement and administer initiatives (ICLEI, 1995).

Labor/Community Watchdog: An environmental justice project of the Labor/Community Strategy Center in Los Angeles, California, Watchdog criticized the equity implications of Metropolitan Transit Authority's (MTA) proposal to increase transit fares to fund rail transit at the expense of bus service, upon which predominantly low-income residents depend. Consequently, the Bus Riders Union (BRU) was created and a lawsuit was brought against MTA on the basis of discriminatory practices of transit funding. The case was eventually settled out of court, transit-dependent bus riders obtained restructured fares and increased service and the MTA now accepts the BRU as a valid stakeholder with legitimate interests (Grengs, 2002).

Neighborhood-Building

Family Reunion: Gerald Mason is a citizen concerned about the rift between the African American and the "white" population in Chattanooga, Tennessee. His perception is that "what's keeping blacks and whites from coming together as a community is our inability to be together socially" (Shaeffer and Anundsen 1993). Mason sent a letter to two or three hundred black and white acquaintances, inviting them to bring a member of the opposite race to Sunday brunch at a restaurant. More than a hundred people showed up, and so began the Chattanooga Family Reunion, which is now a monthly event. There's no agenda — blacks and whites just socialize and friendships are formed. As both races grow to understand each other, the community is flourishing.

Residents Plant Flowers: In an ad hoc organizing effort, residents of one East Vancouver, BC street gathered to plant flowers in their new traffic calming circle. Now their neighborhood is more attractive as well as safer.

Outdoor Volunteers: The small towns of the Roaring Fork Valley in Colorado rely heavily on volunteers for the many social events and social programs offered throughout the community. Roaring Fork Outdoor Volunteers helps to improve the quality of the environment and life in the valley. Outdoor Volunteers build and repair nature trails, plant trees, and help those in need. On designated volunteer days, locals get together to paint the exterior (or interior) of nursing homes or the homes of elderly or lower-income residents. The gatherings always include a big outdoor picnic, and sometimes live music and a camp-out.

Publicity

Act Locally Calendar: The Eco-City Network in Vancouver, BC publishes the "Act Locally" calendar. The calendar, which is distributed in hard copy and through the Internet, features free listings of community activities and initiatives for community improvement and urban revitalization.

Connecting to Other Communities

Mega-Cities Project: A network of professionals and institutions in the world's largest cities is committed to promoting urban innovations for the 21st century. Its focus is reducing poverty and environmental degradation, and encouraging popular participation. Mega-cities are cities with over 10 million inhabitants — by 2000 there will be 23 of them, including New York, Los Angeles, and Mexico City. The project gives particular attention to urban innovations that empower women.

Awards for Community Contributions

Coast Capital Savings and VanCity: Two credit unions in Vancouver, British Columbia help to support and publicly recognize citizens and organizations active in the community. Each year, Coast Capital awards scholarships to students for outstanding contributions to the community. VanCity provides an annual $1 million VanCity Award to a nonprofit organization for a project that supports the social, environmental or economic well-being of the community.

RESOURCES

Institute for Community Economics is a nonprofit corporation providing technical and financial assistance to community land trusts, limited-equity housing co-ops, community loan funds, and other grassroots organizations. The Institute also provides information and educational material to the general public, such as *The Community Land Trust Handbook* (Rodale Press, 1982).

Website: www.iceclt.org

Labor/Community Strategy Center is a multiracial, labour/community "think tank/act tank" located in Los Angeles that is committed to building a democratic, internationalist social movement.

Website: www.thestrategycenter.org

National Environmental Justice Advisory Council is a federal advisory committee that was established to provide independent advice, consultation, and recommendations to the Administrator of the US Environmental Protection Agency (EPA) on matters related to environmental justice.

Website: www.epa.gov/compliance/ environmentaljustice/nejac/index.html

REFERENCES

Agyeman, J., and B. Evans. 1996. "Black on Green: Race, Ethnicity and the Environment." In *Environmental Planning and Sustainability*, S. Buckingham-Hatfield, and B. Evans, eds. Chichester, UK: John Wiley and Sons.

Alphonso, C. 2004. "Ontario bans junk food from school machines." *Globe and Mail* October 21:. A9. Retrieved from www.globeandmail.com

Anders, C. 1997. "Housing Association Preserves Low-Cost Apartments." *San Francisco Examiner and Chronical*, 6 April:. E1, E3.

Apgar, W., & Whiting, E. J. 2003. *Essential function bonds: An emerging tool for affordable housing finance*. Cambridge, MA: Joint Center for Housing Studies, Harvard University.

BC Working Group on Community Economic Development. 1995. *Sharing Our Stories.* September.

Bogo, J. 2002. Hungry for change. *Audubon,* 114(2): 30-34.

Boston Redevelopment Authority. 2003. *The Boston Economy — 2003.* Retrieved from www.ci.boston.ma.us/bra/PDF/Publications//Rpt589.pdf

British Columbia Ministry of Community, Aboriginal and Women's Services (BCMCAWS). 2004. *Planning for housing, 2004: An overview of local government initiatives in British Columbia.* Victoria: Ministry of Community, Aboriginal and Women's Services.

British Columbia Round Table on the Environment and the Economy (BCRTEE). 1993. *Strategic Directions for Community Sustainability.* Victoria, BC: Crown Publications.

Brown, R. 2001. *Preventing homelessness resources.* Retrieved from www.financeprojectinfo.org/Publications/preventinghomelessnessresource.htm

Brozan, N. 2004. "A happy ending for a troubled building." *New York Times.* October 17: 2. Retrieved from www.nytimes.com.

Bullard, R., ed. 1993. *Confronting Environmental Racism: Voices from the Grassroots.* Boston: South End Press.

Cooper-Marcus, C. 1986. "Design as if People Mattered." In *Sustainable Cities,* Sim Van der Ryn, Peter Calthorpe, eds. San Francisco: Sierra Club Books.

Davis, J. E., & Demetrowitz, A. 2003. *Permanently affordable homeownership: Does the community land trust deliver on its promises?* Burlington, VT: Burlington Community Land Trust.

Draper, D., & Mitchell, B. 2001. "Environmental justice considerations in Canada." Canadian Geographer, 45(1): 93-98.

Drusine, H. 2002. "Claiming the night." *Habitat Debate, 8*(2). Retrieved from www.unhabitat.org/hd/hdv8n4/forum6.asp

Fromm, D. 2000. "Introduction to the cohousing issue." *Journal of Architectural and Planning Research, 17*(2): 91-93.

Greater Vancouver Food Bank Society (GVFBS). 2002. *Programs: Community kitchens.* Retrieved from www.foodbank.bc.ca/programs/index.html

Grengs, J. 2002. "Community-based planning as a source of political change: The transit equity movement of Los Angeles' bus riders union." *Journal of the American Planning Association, 68*(2): 165-178.

Hamilton Spectator. 1991. "Hamilton Women's Group Plans to Take Safety Audit of City." Reprinted in Vancouver Sun, 18 September, p. A4.

Haughton, G. 1996. Spheres of Influence and Sustainable Urban Development. Presented to the Annual Conference of the Association of America Geographers, Charlotte, North Carolina, April.

Heidenheim, L. 2004. Insipring change: 2004 OHCC conference. *Update: The Newsletter of Ontario's Healthy Communities.* Fall: 2. Retrieved from www.healthycommunities.on.ca/publications/newsletter/

Housing and Urban Development. 2004. *Community development block grants: Preserving America.* Retrieved from www.hud.gov/offices/cpd/communitydevelopment/library/historicpreservation/historicpreservation.pdf

International Council for Local Environmental Initiatives (ICLEI). 1995. *The Role of Local Authorities in Sustainable Development: 14 Case Studies on the Local Agenda 21 Process.* Nairobi: UN Centre for Human Settlements.

Institute for Community Economics. 1982. The Community Land Trust Handbook. Emmaus, Pa.: Rodale Press.

Kickbusch, I. 2002. "The future value of health." *Perspectives in Health Magazine: The Magazine of the Pan American Health Organization*, 7(2): 1-3.

Los Angeles Daily News. 1990. "L.A. City Council to Vote on Total Restaurant Smoking Ban." Reprinted in *Vancouver Sun*, 16 October: A5.

Ontario Healthy Communities Coalition (OHCC). 2004. *About us.* Retrieved from www.healthycommunities.on.ca/about_us/index.html

Renew America. 1997. *Success Stories.* 1400 16th Street, N.W., Suite 710, Washington, DC <solstice.crest.org/environment/renew_america/>.

Roseland, M. 1992. "Linking Affordable Housing and Environmental Protection: The Community Land Trust as a Sustainable Urban Development Institution." *Canadian Journal of Urban Research* 1(2): 162-80.

Shaffer, C., and K. Anundsen. 1993. *Creating Community Anywhere.* G.P. Putnam's Sons Publishers.

Welfare Information Network. 2002. *Homelessness.* Retrieved from www.financeprojectinfo.org/win/homeless.asp

Wheeler, S. 1996. "Best Practices in Urban Development." *Urban Ecologist* 3.

World Health Organization (WHO), Health and Welfare Canada, and Canadian Public Health Association. 1986. "Ottawa Charter for Health Promotion." *Canadian Journal of Public Health* 77: 425-27.

CHAPTER 12

COMMUNITY ECONOMIC DEVELOPMENT

The social and natural capital of many communities is controlled by outside interests. In recent years, the inadequacies of conventional economic development have been manifested in disparity in distribution of economic benefits, under-employment, and "downsizing" as companies automate or require more work from less employees. But what is the alternative?

DEVELOPMENT REDEFINED

Sustainable community economic development (CED) is a feasible, community-based alternative to the economy we are familiar with — an economy focused on growth rather than development, on global trade and currency rather than people and ecosystems. By placing greater emphasis on sustainability, including social equity and environmental responsibility, citizens and their governments choose economic development that provides opportunities for people of different incomes and skills, promotes a better quality of life, *and* protects the environment.

The Centre for Sustainable Community Development at Simon Fraser University defines CED as "a process by which communities can initiate and generate their own solutions to their common economic problems and there-by build long-term community capacity and foster the integration of economic, social, and environmental objectives" (CSCD, 2004). CED calls for citizens to help shape their local economies by influencing the type of business, industry, and employment opportunities in their own backyards. "Green business" refers to economic activities that avoid harm to the environment, or help protect the ecosystem in some way. By merging the goals and principles of CED and green business, it is possible to move toward sustainable communities.

Many communities pursuing CED focus on social and economic goals, neglecting the environmental agenda, but this is starting to change. The main goal of most CED initiatives is individual and community self-reliance through collaborative action, capacity building, and returning control of business enterprises, capital, labor, and other resources from the global marketplace to communities. It targets job creation and poverty alleviation, and uses economic activity to help improve the quality of life for citizens; it recognizes the value of non-monetary transactions, such as bartering, and non-material transactions such as child- or elder-care offered by friends and neighbors. Development of local, small businesses has been a common goal of many CED initiatives, along with job training and provision of affordable housing.

Local Self-Reliance

Local self-reliance does not mean isolation. It means diversification of local economies to support local needs, encourage cohesiveness, reduce waste and enable more sustainable trade practices with other communities. Local self-reliance strives to strengthen connections between producers and consumers, whether local farmers, clothing manufacturers, furniture builders or travel agents. One way to enhance the self-reliance of a community is to identify the imports and, where possible, substitute local products, in order to invest in the local economy. As communities organize to find substitutes for imports, people become more aware of the social and environmental impacts of economic activities, and the benefits of supporting their local economy through wise investment in local goods and services. Local self-reliance fosters greater responsibility because the costs and benefits of decisions are directly borne by the community in which they are made.

The goal of a self-reliant community is to enhance local wealth by developing the community's existing resource base. Every community has some resources — physical, human, social — which can be harnessed for creating local wealth. The four basic tools communities can use to generate local wealth are:

1. Making more with less — maximizing use of existing resources.
2. Making money go round — circulating dollars within a community.
3. Making things ourselves — replacing imports.
4. Making something new — creating a new product (Nozick, 1992; Kinsley, 2001).

Community Development Organizations

CED may be driven by social entrepreneurs in the community, and municipal governments can help by structuring social services and support systems to enable self-reliance rather than creating dependency (Bruyn, 1987). Chambers of Commerce

CED Principles

In 1991, a group of individuals and community organizations formed to promote community economic development in British Columbia. Over 30 provincial groups endorsed their "Statement of CED Principles," condensed below:

- *Equity*: equitable access to community decision-making processes and resources.
- *Participation*: of all members of the community in planning and decision-making.
- *Community Building*: CED seeks to build a sense of community.
- *Cooperation and Collaboration*: because many problems can't be solved in isolation, CED encourages connections within and between communities.
- *Self-reliance and Community Control*: building on local strength, creativity, and resources to decrease dependency on economic interests outside the community.
- *Integration*: of social, cultural, and ecological dimensions of community well-being.
- *Interdependence*: local community exists within the context of a larger complex web of relationships.
- *Living within Ecological Limits*: CED encourages processes and initiatives that respect ecological limits and helps to sustain, regenerate, and nurture both the community and the Earth.
- *Capacity Building*: self-reliance requires skills development and other supportive structures and institutions.
- *Diversity*: CED encourages diverse economic activities appropriate to each community.
- *Appropriate Indicators*: CED monitors and evaluates progress according to its goals (B.C. Working Group 1995).

promote local business and services, but other kinds of community organizations can help to support and sustain economic development as well.

Community development corporations offer a range of financial and other services for CED, but they are only one source of financing. Other community financing institutions or financing programs provide a variety of means for access to capital for CED. This is especially critical in areas experiencing disinvestment or shortages of conventional sources of investment capital for business and economic development.

Financing Community Economic Development

Financing and support for community development and new business development projects can come from government agencies, foundations, corporations, venture capital, educational institutes (providing research or training), religious investors, and a variety of financing sources organized specifically to support community-based projects:

- *Local Development Corporations*: certified small business administration lenders providing funds for job creation and retention in small and medium-sized businesses.
- *Community Development Corporations*: may provide loans, function as real-estate developers, or invest in local businesses or community development organizations.
- *Downtown Development Authorities*: nonprofits created by local governments to support downtown businesses. They organize special events, marketing campaigns and finance downtown improvements.
- *Credit Unions*: cooperative, nonprofit corporations created by and for people affiliated by a common bond, for the purpose of promoting thrift among their members and of loaning funds to their members at reasonable interest rates.
- *Community Development Credit Unions*: a specific type of credit union, serving low- to moderate-income communities and individuals. The Union's goal is community economic empowerment, and they typically provide financial services (such as loans) to people who need them, but cannot get them readily from banks.
- *Community Loan Funds*: a not-for-profit corporation, or a program within a not-for-profit corporation, that accepts loans from individuals and institutions and uses this capital to make loans for community development projects. Community Loan Funds usually target community-based organizations that are unable to get loans from conventional sources, offering the financial support as well as technical assistance in developing sound financial plans.
- *Revolving Loan Funds*: funds created specifically to provide alternative financing to small businesses and nonprofit organizations. Often administered by community development corporations or other nonprofits, funding may be in the form of loans provided at lower rates than conventional lenders, supporting business start-up, expansion, job creation, or affordable housing.
- *Micro-Enterprise Loan Programs*: a few financial intermediaries are serving

Whether CED . . . is practised in hinterland resource towns, urban ghettos, obsolescent manufacturing cities, or Native communities reserves, the general objective is the same: to take some measure of control of the local economy back from the markets and the state. Within this common objective, CED practice is variously oriented to controlling the local economy for narrow ends (increasing the capacity of a community to make money), for broader purposes (e.g., to increase economic stability and control of resources) or to serve fundamental goals of economic justice. That is to say, CED varies according to whether "economic," "development," or "community" is emphasized (Boothroyd, 1991).

clients who require very small loans for entrepreneurial initiatives. The programs are a way to help low-income people get access to capital for entrepreneurial initiatives. Borrowers may not have any collateral so they are too risky, or the amount is too small, to be acceptable for conventional loan programs. Programs are usually organized as lending circles wherein borrowers receive guidance and support from others who have successfully repaid a micro-loan in the past.

- *Community Land Trusts and Housing Trusts*: strategies to finance affordable housing. (See Chapter 11: Housing and Community Development.)
- *Trust Funds*: permanent endowments, dedicated to the investment of capital assets in housing or other community economic development activities. Endowments may be capitalized by one-time contributions, or by annually renewable revenue sources.
- *Linkage Programs*: provide funds for affordable housing, job development, and daycare. Linkage works by taking a portion of the value created by investment in areas undergoing substantial development, and directing that value to build affordable housing, provide job training, and fund social services in less fortunate neighborhoods.
- *Reinvestment Policies*: The Community Reinvestment Act requires that US depository institutions, such as banks and many insurance companies which extract capital from communities in the form of deposits, have an obligation to reinvest significant portions of their assets in those communities. Community economic stability is largely dependent on the availability of investment capital (Kinsley, 1996).

The Deli Dollar, from Great Barrington, MA, helped to finance the move of a favorite deli to an alternative location, the finance raised by its customers who purchased food ahead of time with these locally-made notes.

TOOLS AND INITIATIVES

Bartering and Local Currencies

Bartering systems and local currencies are becoming increasingly popular in North America. Bartering provides access to goods and services for people who may not otherwise have cash available for transactions, thereby strengthening local economies. Local currencies encourage investment and re-investment in local business and discourage the flow of dollars outside the community.

Ithaca Currency: "In Ithaca We Trust" are the community-minded words printed on the local currency used in Ithaca, New York. More than 3,500 local businesses and entrepreneurs in Ithaca accept "Ithaca Hours" which entitle the bearer to goods or services at participating businesses. About 2,000 people have bartered some $2 million in commerce since the alternative currency first appeared in 1991 (Spayde, 1997; Ithaca, 2002).

Time Traders is a barter program created by ROSE (Revitalize Outer South East) in Portland, Oregon. The network serves four neighborhoods with growing immigrant populations. Participants exchange services rather than goods (Rose, 2003).

Local Exchange Trading System: The LETSystem is a local exchange trading system that originated in Courtenay, BC in 1983. Adopted by hundreds of communities around the world, it uses a computerized accounting system to record transactions instead of alternative paper currency. Each account holder purchases goods and services by transferring credits from their account to a seller. A negative balance does not indicate debt, but a commitment to do work or exchanges goods within the community. LETS uses a dollar as the unit of exchange, so accounting is easy and taxes can be paid accordingly.

"Buy Local" Policy

Examining Purchasing Policy: The Western Australian Government has a Buy Local Policy that applies to all state agencies in the region in recognition of the capacity of government purchasing to impact on local small business and employment. Government agents must consider local content in bids. All projects seeking cabinet approval must be accompanied by a Buy Local Statement and impact assessment on local business (GWA, 2002).

"Fair Trade" Programs

While CED places an emphasis on improving local self-reliance, it also recognizes interdependency with other towns and regions. In North America there are more than 200 local and national organizations working to promote fair trade by supporting and promoting economic exchange (import or export) with groups that produce goods in an equitable manner.

Overseas Partners: The CED Resource Society of Vancouver teamed up with two larger nonprofits to provide fair trade opportunities for worker co-ops, artisans and small entrepreneurs from lesser developed countries, such as in Pakistan, Nicaragua, and Guatemala. OXFAM and CUSO (Canadian University Students Overseas) identify appropriate trade partners and help bring the imports to Vancouver, BC where clothing, jewelry, coffee, and carvings are available in a local shop (staffed mostly by volunteers). Products are also available via mail order, and the shop accepts LETS dollars.

Cooperative Enterprises

Evangeline: The Evangeline region of Prince Edward Island is home to a network of cooperatives that emphasizes decentralization and community control. Despite being a small community, the co-ops have helped residents of Evangeline control their own economy, succeeding where externally-driven development failed (Wilkinson and Quarter, 1996).

Skills Training and Small Business Development

Van Buren County Hospital: The Board of Directors and staff of Van Buren County Hospital in Iowa began an extensive community planning process in 1990. The goal was to find diverse and creative ways to provide quality medical care and contribute to community health. Instead of buying expensive medical technologies, they helped improve community health by creating economic opportunities for the county's high number of single mothers, unemployed people, and low-income residents. With local and state funding, they started a daycare center, computer training program, and job linkage services using hospital facilities and computer equipment. In a vocational training program, they used the hospital kitchen to start up a bakery which now operates at an outside location. By using hospital facilities, the costs of these programs and business start-ups were lower. The hospital generated revenues, local people gained career training and job opportunities, and Van Buren county gained much needed community services.

Community Development Corporations and Foundations

New Dawn Enterprises: Founded in 1976, New Dawn Enterprises in Cape Breton, Nova Scotia is Canada's oldest community development corporation. From modest beginnings, it has grown to encompass nine companies that pursue a range of real estate and health care related enterprises. Today New Dawn employs upwards of 175 people and has over $20 million in assets with a $4-million annual operating budget (Colello, 2001). It operates much like a business in its pursuit of viable economic activities, but the focus of the outcome is not return on equity but benefits to the community. New Dawn creates jobs, affordable housing, and care for the elderly, to name a few social benefits.

Greyston Foundation: For more than 20 years, Greyston Foundation in Yonkers, New York has worked to create jobs and housing opportunities for homeless people. Greyston built a bakery that now sells more than $3.5 million annually. The bakery employs 45 formerly homeless or ex-convict workers. The Foundation has also helped to establish local HIV/AIDS programs, family service programs, job training and life skills programs, housing, a Healing Centre, childcare facilities, community gardens and a Technology Education Centre (Greyston Foundation, 2001).

The fortunes of local economies, communities, and ecosystems go hand in hand (Northwest Report, 1996).

ENVIRONMENTAL RESPONSIBILITY

Community economic development is not just about business creation; it's about creating self-sustaining communities. Citizens who protect their natural resource base and preserve their environment from deterioration contribute to more sustainable economies. Growing public awareness, fear, and intolerance of the pollution and ecological devastation associated with conventional business and industrial growth has prompted some communities to move toward sustainable economic development. Some communities (and businesses within them) are recognizing it is possible, and even advantageous, to support a thriving economy while preserving the quality of the environment in our communities.

Green Business is Good Business

Despite often being viewed as an economic burden, environmental stewardship, pollution control, and resource efficiency offer significant economic opportunities. For businesses, environmental responsibility can mean lower operating costs associated with waste reduction, energy-efficiency, water conservation and reduced pollution, assured regulatory compliance, enhanced public image, and perhaps even new market opportunities. For communities that attract and support environmentally responsible business, the rewards include less burden on local infrastructure (waste disposal, sewage, electric and water utilities, etc.), protection of the ecosystem, and opportunities for jobs and tax revenues without compromising the quality of life for local citizens.

Often short-term economic gains in tax revenues and job creation are accompanied by erosion in the long-term quality of life of the community. Many people believe the choice to be jobs or the environment, yet green businesses and certain policies and initiatives can create more employment opportunities than conventional economic development (Renner, 2000). Mandatory container reuse and recycling policies, energy-efficiency and enhanced public transportation programs have stimulated thousands of new business and employment opportunities in North America. Policy changes sometimes cause dislocations in jobs, but special job training programs and new forms of social safety nets can help people in transition from unsustainable forms of employment (Rees, 1995; Roseland, 1997). Pollution control and other environmental policies and regulations may also serve as economic stimulators. For example, prior to the passage of local government regulations on ozone-depleting compounds, there were few manufacturers and few models available of CFC "vampire" units — machines that remove freon from refrigerators and air conditioners to enable the freon to be recycled. Since local governments started passing CFC regulations in 1989, more manufacturers have begun producing the vampire units, making available a variety of models at lower, competitive prices. (Skinner, 1990).

Many green business and economic development initiatives are market driven. Companies recognize the bounty of opportunities to sell greener products and services, or a more ecologically responsible image, to the growing market of environmentally aware customers. Other businesses identify financial savings or benefits associated with environmental improvements to their operations. Local governments can play a role by supporting, encouraging, or even demanding improvement in the environmental performance of businesses in their communities. Municipal or local governments can also implement policies and strategies to attract and support new ecologically responsible businesses and economic activities in their community.

In addition to lobbying governments for legislation and policies that promote ecologically sound economic development, citizens (and governments) can encourage environmentally responsible corporate behavior by exercising consumer power. By choosing to purchase greener products or goods that are produced by more responsible companies, citizens can influence business decisions and direction. Banks and other financial intermediaries can also get involved by supporting green business development, offering preferred interest rates, and applying environmental standards as criteria for loans. Community policies can also encourage more sustainable business development.

A more sustainable economy promises great environmental and economic benefits, though the transition will not be without pain. It will produce many losers, particularly among extractive and heavy industries. But the evidence is strong that the winners will outnumber the losers: more jobs will be created in energy efficiency, recycling, and public transportation than will be lost in the oil and coal industries, car manufacturing, and waste disposal. In fact, automation is a much more important cause of job loss than environmental protection is. And while extractive industries tend to be geographically concentrated, jobs arising out of energy conservation, renewables, and recycling are likely to be more evenly spread (Renner, 1991).

TOOLS AND INITIATIVES

Local Government Policies, Programs and Regulations

Energy Conservation Program: The Fox River sock company in Osage, Iowa was one of the beneficiaries of the town's energy conservation program that began in 1974 and continues today. In 1984, Fox River was a struggling medium-size textile manufacturer, when an energy audit revealed opportunities to reduce energy costs per unit output by 29 percent. Since implementing the energy-efficiency initiatives, Fox River company is not only thriving, but has expanded production by about 300 percent and almost tripled its workforce. Fox River is not the only beneficiary of the city's programs; the 3,600 residents of Osage, Iowa use 25 percent less electricity than the state average, and the city estimates energy savings amount to more than $1 million per year in savings to residents, local government, and local businesses. The savings, which amount to more than $200

Defining Green Business
There are myriad ways to improve the environmental performance of industry and commerce: • Employ "end of the pipe" strategies to reduce waste and pollution. • Employ "front of the pipe" strategies to avoid waste, pollution, and environmentally harmful materials and processes. • Conserve water, optimize energy efficiency, and/or use renewable energies such as wind power. • Employ strategies to protect or enhance the environment, preserve biodiversity, and protect the ecosystem. • Target environmental issues for business activities. "Environmental businesses" help to improve environmental quality (e.g., soils remediation business).

per year for homeowners (and more for most businesses) translate into enhanced economic activity because energy conservation has an economic multiplier of $2.32 (meaning that every $1 spent conserving energy generates $2.32 in local economic activity). The economic multipliers associated with energy conservation have been shown to be comparable with, and in some studies higher than, the economic multipliers associated with energy consumption (Hubbard and Fong, 1995; Renew America, 1997; Swenson and Eathington, 2002).

Energy-Efficiency Program: In the early 1980s, the City of San Jose, California began an energy-efficiency program that reduced home, business, and agency energy utility bills by a total of $5.5 million annually. The city predicts its programs will produce a county-wide $33 million increase in wages and salaries, with a net gain of 1,753 jobs over a 10-year period (Hubbard and Fong, 1995).

A city plan called for municipal government investment ($645,000) for technical assistance educational campaigns to show consumers how to save energy, and energy reduction in government buildings and transportation. Economic benefits were projected to spur nearly $20 million in private spending in San Jose, while the program paid for itself in two-and-a-half years (Flavin and Lenssen, 1991). In 2001, the City of San Jose adopted a Smart Energy Plan committed to cutting energy consumption by a further 10 percent, a program that has resulted in energy cost savings for the municipal government of hundreds of thousands of dollars (City of San Jose, 2002). (See Chapter 7: Energy Efficiency and Renewables for more discussion of tools and initiatives.)

Mandated Recycling Rate: Compared with incineration and landfilling, recycling offers more long-term employment and is a cheaper alternative due to its lower capital requirements. In New York City, the cost of building an incinerator (about $500 million) is three times that of recycling facilities that can handle the same amount of trash (Renner, 1991). Boosting the city's mandated recycling rate from 18 percent to 25 percent in 1994 created jobs in collection and sorting, and stimulated remanufacturing business activity.

Business and NGO Programs and Policies

Benefits from Environmental Protection: Under US environmental regulations, 3M manufacturing facilities earns pollution credits by exceeding targets for reducing air emissions. The company can sell these credits or give them away. In 1997, the company donated credits earned by a Chicago facility to the State of Illinois who in turn donated them to a community foundation run by the Centre for Neighborhood Technology. The foundation sold the credits and used the millions of dollars realized for local sustainability initiatives, including environmental literacy programs, energy conservation, and local job creation. Truly a win-win, 3M gained community recognition and tax write-offs, while creating a new capacity to transfer wealth to local citizens (Johnson Foundation, 1997).

Good Neighbor Agreements: The Good Neighbor Project trains community activists to engage in negotiations with corporations to establish Good Neighbor Agreements that address the community's needs and concerns, especially related to pollution control. The Project worked with the West County Toxics Coalition and several community groups concerned about pollution from a Chevron oil refinery in Richmond, California. The groups negotiated with Chevron to convince the multinational corporation to upgrade and improve pollution controls, and spend $100,000 to restore native vegetation, provide skilled job training to 100 local residents, contribute $2 million to a local health center, and contribute $5 million in philanthropic support to the predominantly poor African-American neighborhood.

Green Maps and Directories

Green Maps: The Green Map System started in 1992 with New York City's Green Apple Map, a tool for residents and visitors seeking green businesses and environmentally sound tourist opportunities. The New York based nonprofit Green Map System now produces green maps in over 250 cities worldwide. In addition to identifying eco-friendly ways to spend money, the maps often include educational information for consumers such as definitions for environmental terms like "organic" or "biodynamic" (Green Apple Map, 2004).

Green Business Directory: With funding from local foundations, an entrepreneur published a green business directory for Vancouver, BC. In addition to addresses of companies providing environmentally sound products or services, the directory included clip-out coupons for discounts, and the text explained the environmental benefits of recycled paper, washable diapers, and other such products.

Local Currencies

Prairie Bucks: In 1988, the local Energy Commission in Lester Prairie, Minnesota (with a population of 1,229) developed an innovative way to invest state energy grant money for long-term local development: the "Prairie Buck." Residents and businesses who signed up for an energy audit received 15 Prairie Bucks, good for the purchase of a compact fluorescent lamp at local hardware stores. Instead of flowing out to distant energy suppliers, local dollars stay in town and bolster the local economy. To encourage carpooling to nearby towns, Lester Prairie began offering "Rideshare Bucks" according to the number of passengers in the car and the number of gallons required for their commute (Rocky Mountain Institute, 1991).

Government Funding for Green Business and Jobs

Environ: Peter's Community Development Corporation and the City of St. Peter (Minnesota) helped finance business start-up and construction of a manufacturing plant for Phenix Biocomposites. The company's product is an environmentally-friendly biocomposite material made of recycled newsprint fibers mixed with soy flour. The new product, "Environ," keeps 50 people busy manufacturing materials suitable for furniture, cabinetry, flooring, and other products.

SunLine: In Thousand Palms, California, the suburban bus company SunLine joined forces with a local gas company to purchase and operate 40 alternative-fuel buses. Financing came from federal, state, and county grants, and a local guarantee was issued. SunLine converted its fleet of cars and trucks to compressed natural gas, and Southern California Gas utility also got involved, constructing a compressed natural gas fueling station. A local college created the first US training facility for maintaining alternative-fuel vehicles, and Sunline's switch to alternative-fuel vehicles created at least 28 jobs while saving the company thousands of dollars in fuel costs (Makower, 1995). In 2000, Sunline opened the Clean Fuels Mall where natural gas, hydrogen and other alternative fuels are available to the public 24-hours and where visitors come from around the world to see first hand how hydrogen is generated from solar power (APTA, 2004; Sunline, 2004).

Funding Energy Efficiency and Recycling

All over North America, electric utilities, municipal, state/provincial, and federal government programs have helped businesses and industry improve energy performance of buildings and manufacturing operations, conserve water, and reduce waste and pollution. Rebates, tax breaks or grants to "green" their operations provide the push needed and close the "payback gap."

Post Office Retrofit: The Reno (Nevada) Main Post Office received federal government funds to finance an energy-efficiency retrofit. The goal was to reduce operating costs by saving energy, yet the $300,000 retrofit yielded unexpected dividends in worker productivity. The energy-efficient lighting and better acoustics improved working conditions so much that in 1986, Reno's mail sorters became the most productive sorters in the western US, and operators of the mail sorting machines achieved the lowest error rate. In addition to savings in energy costs of about $22,400, the Post Office yielded productivity gains worth $400,000 to $500,000 per year (Browning and Romm, 1995).

Economic Network: St. Paul, Minnesota's "Home-Grown Economy" project experimented with a number of attempts to establish closed-loop, self-sustaining economic networks. Rubber tires, for example, are ordinarily a disposal nuisance. St. Paul learned that tires can be recycled by freezing them in liquid nitrogen, pulverizing them, and using them as a filler for repairing potholes, another nuisance for which the city is responsible. The recycling costs were $1 per tire; the disposal costs were $3.25 per tire (Meehan, 1987).

Financial Institution Support

Shore Trust: Ecotrust, a Portland-based conservation organization partnered with Shorebank Corporation, the oldest community development banking institute in the US, to support conservation-based economic development in the Pacific Northwest. The bank holding company, "Shore Trust, the First Environmental Bancorporation," offers financing, technical assistance, marketing, and brokering services for entrepreneurs and business to support local innovation and help individual businesses develop sound ways to manage their land and resources. Their long-term goal is "to create a remarkably different economy, one that can restore and protect the environment, while bringing forth innovation, prosperity, meaningful work, and true security" (Von Hagen and Kellog, 1996). Between 1999 and 2004, Ecotrust Canada invested over $5 million into companies whose businesses incorporate socially and environmentally sustainable practices, including an organic farm, a First Nations owned saw-mill, an employee-owed fish plant, a green office supply company, and shellfish aquaculture operations, among others (*Business Examiner*, 2004).

Revolving Loan: Revolving Loan: The Cascadia Revolving Loan Fund in Seattle, Washington is a private nonprofit organization providing loans to under-served entrepreneurs, small businesses and community-building organizations. Over 80 percent of the money for loans comes from private investors who receive a market-rate return on their investment. In 18 years of operation the fund has lent $29 million, lost less than 1 percent of money lent, and no investor has lost money on their investment. Loans are targeted to businesses owned by low-income people, women, minorities, and immigrants; child care businesses; businesses that create family-wage jobs in low-income communities; businesses in rural communities; nonprofit community building organizations; cooperatives; and businesses that work to preserve or restore the environment. Borrowers have included five drycleaning shops who borrowed funds to purchase closed-loop drycleaning machines (reducing the use of chemicals and water, operating costs and environmental impact), recycled wood sellers, a hemp clothing retailer, a Community Cycling Centre, and a bison ranch (Cascadia, 2004).

Technical Support and Education

Stay in the Black Guide: The Boulder Energy Conservation Center, sponsored by the Colorado Small Business Development Centers, Chamber of Commerce and others produced the guide, *Stay in the Black by Being Green*. The book covers energy, waste, water and transportation issues, as well as support for businesses going green (State of Colorado, 2004)

US Department of Energy Support: A business park in Soldiers Grove, Wisconsin is heated by solar energy, thanks to the Department of Energy's Argonne National Lab. In 1978, Argonne was doing research on solar thermal energy, so they offered the service to the business park and continued to study the solar energy in use. Argonne has also assisted groups in Chicago in designing affordable housing. In Chattanooga, Tennessee, Oak Ridge National Labs is helping an electric-bus manufacturer to design improvements for city buses.

A farmers' market in the city.

Job Training

Casa Verde Builders: In Austin, Texas, Casa Verde Builders helps high school drop-outs (17- to 25-year-old men and women) learn carpentry and construction skills while completing course work to earn a high school diploma and certificate of mastery. Participants earn a salary for spending 40-hours per week doing studies and working in crews building environmentally responsible housing. They learn sustainable construction techniques by building affordable housing that is sold to low-income families. A private lender and federal funding provide financing for home purchases and mortgages, and proceeds from the sale of these houses is returned to Casa Verde to build more houses.

Micro-entrepreneurial Training: The Nuestra Communidad Development Corporation in Boston runs two micro-enterprise training programs for inner-city residents who lack the experience and capital to set up their own business. Through the Village Pushcarts Program, individuals are assisted with a street vending operation — books, plants, jewelry, T-shirts, incense and much more — through which they gain enough knowledge and experience to open their own neighborhood storefront or obtain a higher paying, skilled position, such as retail management. Nuestra Culinary Ventures is a kitchen incubator that helps small-scale food entrepreneurs succeed by providing a large shared kitchen facility and commissary that small business people can rent as needed (Nuestra, 2004).

Community Forestry, Fisheries, and Agriculture

Community Supported Agriculture: In hundreds of North American towns and cities, Community Supported Agriculture is gaining popularity as a way for urbanites to supply themselves with fresh vegetables while supporting small local organic farms. Urban families or individuals pay yearly fees for shares that entitle them to weekly shipments of locally grown fruits and vegetables. Purchasers share the risks of farming with farmers — they may receive less of one vegetable than expected, but more of another. In addition to supporting sustainable agriculture, city folk gain connection with local farmers and the bioregion. (See Chapter 4: Greening the City for more discussion.)

Adding Value to Forestry

"To explore the potential of community-based, value-added manufacturing, a single cedar tree was cut and a variety of products were manufactured by a group of Slocan Valley, British Columbia, residents in their spare time. Products were made from all parts of the tree, even those that would have otherwise become wood waste, such as bark, branches, leaves, top and stump. The result was over 50 different items (over 275 value-added wood objects, including drums, baskets, coasters, and games), amounting to a potential sale value of $4,052 for the local economy. Even without accounting for the avoided disposal impacts and associated costs, valley volunteers generated 80 times the amount of revenue to the local economy than the timber company would have using the same tree" (Martineau, 1997).

Menominee Forest: A community forest is "a tree-dominated ecosystem managed for multiple community values and benefits to the community" (Duinker et al. 1994). Managed by the community, this type of forestry lends itself to more sustainable practices that preserve the resource base and provide long-term sustainable employment in forestry and related activities. In 1890, the Menominee Tribe obtained authorization for commercial logging in Wisconsin. The Tribe pioneered sustained yield management including selection harvest methods that balanced annual growth with timber production. The Tribe lost control of the land for a time, but when they regained reservation privileges, they continued their sound forestry practices. Sawmill profits have funded social services, such as medical programs, education and law enforcement activities (Bernard and Young, 1996; Warnock, 2003).

Natural Balance Forestry Cooperative: The for-profit worker cooperative, Natural Balance Forestry Cooperative, is establishing criteria for sustainable forest management in western Washington State. The Cooperative seeks small- and large-scale forest owners to help develop forest management plans that produce economic yields while protecting the long-term survival and health of the forest ecosystem.

Fishing Quotas: The current system of fisheries management separates conservation responsibilities from fishing rights, pits individual fishers against one another, and promotes short-term individual profit over community cooperation and shared responsibility for resource management. A proposed alternative is to establish community quotas whereby fishing rights are allocated to communities, and distributed in turn to local fishers, just as timber-cutting rights are distributed in community forests. By providing the opportunity for long-term economic benefits to a community, quotas may foster community stewardship of resources.

Alliances and Partnerships

Green Business Alliance: Architects, publishers, booksellers, builders, consultants, educators, nonprofits, retailers, and wholesalers in the San Francisco Bay area committed to a sustainable economy formed the Green Business Alliance. Among their goals, they aim to foster an understanding by the business community of the importance of sustainable business practice and develop networks of businesses where the public can be assured that the companies are attempting to follow sustainable practices. They conduct forums and seminars for education and to discuss challenges of green business.

Technology Transfer: Bethel New Life, a community development corporation in Chicago partnered with the US Department of Energy's Argonne National Laboratories to create a technology transfer program designed to support environmentally-sound job creation programs and community development initiatives. Projects include training of local residents in environmental analysis and clean-up of abandoned industrial facilities. The initiative provides job opportunities and training in site restoration. As hazardous sites in the community are cleaned up and refurbished they are made available for new tenancy (Renew America, 1997; Bethel New Life, 2004).

A community garden within the city.

Environmental Business Clusters and Incubators

Environmental Business Cluster: The Thousand Oaks Environmental Business Cluster is the first business park in California that caters specifically to start-up companies with products, technologies, or services that are environmentally responsible. The nonprofit public-private initiative, sponsored by local government and large established corporations provides 15 companies in the Cluster with below-market rental rates, furnishings, and management services. The emerging environmental technologies and service companies share offices equipment and services, such as photocopiers, conference rooms, and kitchens to minimize costs. Companies support each other's business activities and seek synergies. Sponsoring organizations are encouraged to engage in technology transfer and licensing agreement opportunities with the smaller firms. The maximum period for a business to stay is two years, and acceptance into the Cluster is based on potential economic impact on the community, such as job creation and sales tax revenue, as well as business potential and evaluation of the management team.

       Greenmarkets: New York City's Council on the Environment, a citizen's organization based in the Mayor's office, initiated a system of Greenmarkets in 1976. Operating at 23 sites year-round and 47 in the summertime, Greenmarkets aim to preserve farmland, and help struggling upstate farmers while making fresh fruits and vegetables available in city neighborhoods. Greenmarkets donate some 500,000 lbs. of fresh produce to hunger relief organizations annually. The markets offer many New Yorkers their only chance to get local produce without journeying to the suburbs (Lowe, 1991; CENYC, 2004).

Eco-Industrial Parks

Eco-industrial parks are a burgeoning sustainable business concept in North America. Businesses in these parks are interdependent because one business' byproduct or waste is the feedstock or energy source for other businesses. Collaboration in redesigning the industrial food chain enables industries to achieve higher standards of environmental performance while improving operating efficiencies and profit margins as well. Planning is underway for Eco-Industrial Parks in several North American cities such as Baltimore, Maryland; Burlington, Vermont; Brownsville, Texas; and in Nova Scotia.

<table>
<tr><td>

Building an Environmental Economy in Berkeley, California

Berkeley has come to be known as the "green valley" (in comparison to the nearby "silicon valley") because of its policies and programs promoting sustainable economic development. Recognizing economic development opportunities associated with protecting the environment and supporting the emerging environmental business sector, city council, the Community Development Department, local citizens, and consultants worked together to develop strategies for building an "environmental economy." The following are some of the strategies proposed or adopted by the city:

- policies, guidelines, zoning bylaws to attract and retain green businesses;
- regulatory streamlining;
- innovative financing opportunities;
- technical assistance and support;
- public/private partnerships (government or universities with private businesses) for research, financing and business development;
- environmental business incubator and value adding networks (flexible networks) to help small businesses team up (virtually or physically) for research, development, operations, or marketing of products and services;
- environmental business directory;
- export trade shows, eco-fairs and conferences;
- media strategies to attract and promote the green valley; and
- programs, committees, and task forces to develop and support the above initiatives (Friend, 1993; Skinner, 1997).

</td></tr>
</table>

Burlington, Vermont: Developers in Burlington, Vermont are planning an eco-industrial park that will use excess heat from a municipal power plant to grow food and flowers in a greenhouse, and provide heat and energy for other park businesses. The University of Vermont helped form the nonprofit Partnership of Environmental Technologies and Science to encourage Vermont universities to partner with private and public sectors on projects such as this one. A federal community development block grant through the City of Burlington provided the funds for a feasibility study on the park. The site will include the production and processing of organic food, as well as environmental research and education (UHDG, 2004).

Chattanooga, Tennessee: In the 1960s, Chattanooga, Tennessee had one of the worst air pollution problems in the US Today it is one of the few cities to meet the federal Environmental Protection Agency's clean air standards. A program to make Chattanooga a model of sustainability is the reason for the improvements and the driver behind four eco-industrial parks under development in the city. Parks are planned at a 2,834-hectare (7,000-acre) army munitions facility being converted to civilian use, on a brownfield site of an abandoned manufacturing facility, and at two other sites.

RETHINKING ECONOMIC DEVELOPMENT

Just as sustainability has prompted a shift in our transportation and energy planning away from the traditional focus on increasing supply to a focus on managing demand, so too can the emphasis of economic development shift from growth (increase in supply of products and services) to sustainable economic development, or economic demand management (EDM). EDM should seek to satisfy our economic needs without requiring endless growth. The outdoor goods chain store, Patagonia, defied conventional marketing practices a few years ago when they claimed they didn't intend to keep expanding and their hope was that people would buy less, but buy quality (of course, they felt their product represented that quality). Individuals perceive that growth is synonymous with success and very often that is measured by gross income. Yet economic demand management redefines values to acknowledge contributions, such as unpaid work, that enhance the community and indirectly help strengthen the economy.

Calculating the true cost of work will enable people to better evaluate economic costs and benefits. Unemployment and job security threaten many Canadians and

Americans in the 1990s, and yet those who are employed work longer hours than people in past decades. This is taking its toll on individuals and their families. Many households spend a significant portion of their income on transportation costs to and from work, childcare services, and take-out meals because parents are too tired to cook. What is the financial cost to support this work-oriented lifestyle, and what is the cost to quality of life? In a 1991 survey conducted by *Time* magazine and CNN, 61 percent of the respondents agreed that "earning a living today requires so much effort that it's difficult to find time to enjoy life" (Elgin, 1996). The true cost of economic growth cannot be measured by new cars, big houses, and the latest computer games.

In a commodity-intensive economy, people are compelled to seek full-time employment and an increasing income, but some people are making a shift. By re-evaluating their needs and wants and realizing that their true demands are for comfort, security, health, and happiness, some people are finding alternative ways to satisfy these demands.

The Living Wall Garden project in Vancouver, BC.

TOOLS AND INITIATIVES

Voluntary Simplicity: Programs such as Voluntary Simplicity, named after the book by Duane Elgin (1993), provide the rationale and framework for people seeking a return to the simple life. People are making choices that reduce their costs and give them time to enjoy their families, friends, and the world around them. Voluntary Simplicity calls for living in a way that is "outwardly more simple and inwardly more rich." By living a more conserving lifestyle, people are moving toward sustainability and reducing dependence on financial and material affluence for their quality of life (Elgin, 1993; Burch, 1996; Merkel, 2003).

Buy Nothing Day: November 29 is "Buy Nothing Day," thanks to the Media Foundation, publisher of *Adbusters* magazine. The purpose is to demonstrate the power of consumers so that business responds to consumer demands for greater corporate environmental and social responsibility. The impact of non-consumption — even for a day — would reduce waste and output of pollution by staggering amounts. Imagine what a conserver society could achieve!

There is no getting around the fact that material consumption is at the heart of the sustainability crisis (Rees, 1995).

RESOURCES

Centre for Community Enterprise is a nonprofit organization committed to building the capacity of community-controlled organizations to generate durable social and economic benefits. Their journal is must reading: *Making Waves: Canada's Community Economic Development Quarterly.*
Website: www.island.net/~ccelewis/index.html

Centre for Sustainable Community Development at Simon Fraser University supports the sustainable development of communities through education, research and community mobilization programs in British Columbia, Canada, and internationally.
Website: www.sfu.ca/cscd

Ecoforestry (formerly known as the *International Journal of Ecoforestry*) is devoted to the practices, science and philosophy of ecologically responsible forest use, and is an important forum for community forestry.
Website: www.ecoforestry.ca/default.htm

Ecotrust / Ecotrust Canada are private, nonprofit organizations developing creative and innovative approaches to conservation-based development in the coastal rainforests of British Columbia, Washington and Alaska. They work to help communities "get rich slow".
Vancouver :
Website: www.ecotrustcan.org/index.shtml
Portland:
Website: www.ecotrust.org

Green Maps are locally created maps that chart the natural and cultural environment. Using adaptable tools and shared visual language of icons to highlight green living resources, Green Maps cultivate citizen participation and community sustainability.
Website: www.greenmap.com

Institute for Community Economics is a national nonprofit organization providing technical assistance and financing to community land trusts and organizations committed to affordable housing, land preservation, and green economic development. Their journal, *Community Economics*, is a source of inspiration.
Website: www.iceclt.org/

Landsman Community Services Ltd. offers information on LETS.
Website: www.u-net.com/gmlets

COMMUNITY ECONOMIC DEVELOPMENT

REFERENCES

American Public Transportation Association (APTA). 2004. Retrieved from http://www.apta.com/services/intnatl/intfocus/sunline.cfm

Bernard, T, and J. Young. 1996. *The Ecology of Hope: Communities Collaborate for Sustainability*. Gabriola Island, BC: New Society Publishers.

Bethel New Life. 2004. from http://www.bethelnewlife.org

Boothroyd, P. 1991. *Community Economic Development: An Introduction for Planners*. Vancouver: UBC Centre for Human Settlements.

Browning, W.D. and J. Romm. 1995. *Greening Business and the Bottom Line*. Rocky Mountain Institute.

Bruyn, S.T. 1987. "Beyond the Market and the State." In *Beyond the Market and the State: New Directions in Community Development*, S.T. Bruyn and J. Meehan, eds. Philadelphia: Temple University Press.

Burch, M. 1996. *Simplicity: Notes, Stories and Exercises for Developing Unimaginable Wealth*. Gabriola Island, BC: New Society Publishers.

Business Examiner. 2004. "Five years, $5 million, 500 jobs spells success for Ecotrust". July. Victoria, BC

Cascadia Revolving Fund. 2004. from http://www.cascadiafund.org

City of San Jose. 2002. Environmental Services. Retrieved from http://www.ci.san-jose.ca.us/esd/ER-SanJose.htm

Colello, T. 2001. "New Dawn Marks 25th Anniversary". New Breton Post, July 28: 26.

Council on the Environment of New York City (CENYC). 2004. Retrieved from http://www.cenyc.org

Duinker, P. et al. "Community Forests in Canada: An Overview." *The Forestry Chronicle* 70(6).

Elgin, D. 1993. *Voluntary Simplicity*. New York: William Morrow.

Flavin, C., and N. Lenssen. 1991. "Designing a Sustainable Energy System." In *State of the World 1991: A Worldwatch Institute Report on Progress Toward a Sustainable Society*. New York/London: W.W. Norton and Company: 21-38.

Friend, G., and Associates. 1993. *Building an Environmental Economy*. Berkeley, Calif.

Government of Western Australia (GWA). 2002. "Buy Local Policy" Retrieved from http://www.ssc.wa.gov.au/files/guidelines/Buy%20Local%20Policy%20Web%20version.pdf

Green Apple Map. 2004. Retrieved from http://greenapplemap.org/page/home

Greyston Foundation. 2001. Retrieved from http://www.greyston.org/index.html

Harris, L. 1995. "Banana Kelly's Toughest Fight." *The New Yorker*, 24 July.

Hubbard, A, and C. Fong. 1995. *Community Energy Workbook*. Rocky Mountain Institute.

Ithaca Hours Online. 2002. Retrieved from http://www.ithacahours.com/home.html

Johnson Foundation. 1997. "Tradable Assets for Sustainable Communities." *Wingspread Journal* 19(2).

Kinsley, M. 2001. "Building Community Prosperity through Natural Capitalism." Rocky Mountain Institute. Retrieved from http://www.rmi.org/images/other/EconRenew/ER01-23_BldCommProsp.pdf

Lowe, M.D. 1991. "Shaping Cities: The Environmental and Human Dimensions." *Worldwatch* 105. Washington DC: Worldwatch Institute.

Makower, J. 1995. *Good, Green Jobs: How Business is Putting the Environment to Work for California.* California: California Department of Conservation.

Martineau, S., and M. Martineau. 1997. "Slocan Valley Residents Ask for Community-Based Forestry." *International Journal of Ecoforestry* 12(3): 267-70.

Meehan, J. 1987. "Working Toward Local Self-Reliance." In *Beyond the Market and the State: New Directions in Community Development*, S.T. Bruyn and J. Meehan, eds. Philadelphia: Temple University Press.

Merkel, J. 2003. *Radical Simplicity: Small Footprints on a Finite Earth.* Gabriola Island, BC (Canada): New Society Publishers

Northwest Report. 1996. "Special Issue on Sustainable Development and Culture." January: 19.

Nozick, M. 1992. *No Place Like Home: Building Sustainable Communities.* Ottawa: Canadian Council on Social Development.

Nuestra Communidad Development Corporation. 2004. Retrieved from http://www.nuestra.org

Rees, W.E. 1995. "More Jobs, Less Damage: A Framework for Sustainability, Growth and Employment." *Alternatives* 21:4:24-30.

Renew America. 1997. *Success Stories.* 1400 16th Street, N.W., Suite 710, Washington, DC <solstice.crest.org/environment/renew_america/>.

Renner, M. 2000. "Working for the Environment: A Growing Source of Jobs." Worldwatch Institute Paper #152

Rocky Mountain Institute. 1991. *Newsletter* VII(1). Spring.

Rose Community Development Corporation. 2003. 222.rosecdc.org.

Roseland, M. 1997. *Eco-City Dimensions: Healthy Communities, Healthy Planet.* Gabriola Island, BC: New Society Publishers.

Skinner, N. 1990. "Ecocity Legislation." In *Report of the First International Ecological City Conference.* Berkeley, Calif.: Urban Ecology.

Skinner, N. 1997. "Economic Development as a Path to Sustainability: The Berkeley Experience." In *Eco-City Dimensions: Healthy Communities, Healthy Planet*, M. Roseland, ed. Gabriola Island, BC: New Society Publishers.

Spayde, J. 1997. "Our Kind of Town (Ithaca, NY)." *Utne Reader* May/June.

Swenson, D. and Eathington, E. 2002. "Statewide Economic Values of Alternative Energy Sources and Energy Conservation". Mt. Vernon, Iowa: The Iowa Policy Project. Retrieved from www.iowapolicyproject.org/reports_press_releases/020222-energysum.pdf

State of Colorado. 2004. Office of Energy, Management and Conservation.

Sunline. 2004. Retrieved from http://www.sunline.org

University of Hull, Department of Geography (UHDG). 2004. Eco-Industrial Development. Retrieved from http://www.hull.ac.uk/geog/research/EcoInd/html/resources.html

Wilkinson, P., and J. Quarter. 1996. *Building a Community-Controlled Economy: The Evangeline Cooperative Experience*. Toronto: University of Toronto Press.

Von Hagen, B., and E. Kellogg. 1996. "Entrepreneurs and Ecosystems." *Northwest Report*, Northwest Area Foundation (January): 10-15.

Warnock, J. 2003. "Sustainable forestry is possible." *Briar Patch Magazine*, February.

Part 3

Mobilizing Citizens and Their Governments

*M*obilizing citizens and their governments to strengthen all forms of community capital is required to apply the concept of sustainable development to North American communities. Community mobilization is necessary to coordinate, balance and catalyse community capital. Part 3 focuses on how to mobilize citizens and their governments to achieve this goal.

CHAPTER 13

GOVERNING SUSTAINABLE COMMUNITIES

Governance and government are not the same. *Government* is about "doing" things, and delivering services, whereas *governance* is "leading" society, convincing its various interest groups to embrace common goals and strategies (Osborne and Gaebler, 1993).

This chapter is about governing sustainable communities, and explores both governance and government in this context. In particular, it focuses on public participation, decision-making, the role of local government, and planning for action.

PUBLIC PARTICIPATION

In the last several years there has been an enormous shift toward the "politics of inclusion." These new politics are here to stay, not only because they are demanded, but also because they ensure results that better fulfil the broad public interest than decisions that are shaped by the lobbying of powerful and vocal interests. For some categories of decisions that affect a broad spectrum of interests, a fair hearing is no longer sufficient to achieve a lasting and equitable result. Direct participation in the decision-making process is necessary (Owen, 1994).

The traditional approach to public demand for greater participation has been described as "decide, educate, announce, defend," otherwise known as DEAD. Collaborative processes are an alternative which can lead to better communication and understanding. Quite different perspectives can find common ground and agree to recommendations regarding particularly difficult issues. This does not necessarily mean that everyone comes to full agreement, but rather that there is no substantial disagreement; participants can live with the outcome.

Democratic decision-making, where decision-making power is shared in reality if not in name, has been effective in some contexts and some regions. Community development corporations in the Maritimes, community land trusts in the United States, and the Mondragon system of industrial cooperatives in the Basque region of Spain are all examples of the potential of democratic decision-making.

Shared Decision-Making

The primary rationale for enhanced stakeholder participation in community planning and governance is based on the democratic maxim that those affected by a decision should participate directly in the decision-making process. Within the broader framework of representative democracy, participatory democracy provides a system of checks and balances against the limitations of a purely representative system (Duffy, Roseland and Gunton, 1996).

The benefits of participatory democratic structures have far-reaching implications for community planning. So-called "consultation" of stakeholders is no longer adequate (Arnstein, 1969). Stakeholders often demand genuinely cooperative decision-making, if not outright control over decision-making. In response, formal recognition has been provided at some levels of government through legislation legitimizing public participation initiatives. Policy statements supporting stakeholder participation are inadequate, however, if they are not backed by sufficient resources, staff, and commitment to implement meaningful participation. Truly meaningful participation requires that all concerned and affected stakeholders are provided the information and resources they require to influence and contribute to the decision-making process, and that planning and decision-making processes must be designed and implemented to foster comprehensive stakeholder participation. The issues of who participates, when they participate and how they participate are critical to achieving fairness, efficiency, and stability in decision-making.

The essential difference between conventional and collaborative, or "shared decision-making," is the level of true collaboration and involvement of those not traditionally involved in decision-making (Crowfoot and Wondolleck, 1990). Specifically, shared decision-making involves planning *with* stakeholders rather than *for* stakeholders. Shared decision-making processes depend on the explicit recognition that all stakeholder values and interests are legitimate.

Consensus Decision-Making

Consensus is a process for making group decisions without voting. Agreement is reached through a process of gathering information and viewpoints, discussion, persuasion, a combination of synthesis of proposals and/or the development of totally new ones. Consensus does not necessarily mean unanimity. Rather, the goal of the consensus process is to reach a decision with which everyone can agree. Consensus at its best relies upon persuasion rather than pressure for reaching group unity.

The consensus method is most useful for groups whose members value their association highly. Consensus decision-making sometimes requires a great deal of patience. It is necessary to listen carefully to opposing viewpoints to reach the best decision. In spite of this drawback, the consensus method has the following advantages over a voting method (Beer and Stief, 1997; Coover et al., 1977; Kaner et al., 1996): it produces more intelligent decisions, by incorporating the best thinking of everyone; it keeps people from getting into adversary attitudes where individual egos are tied to

The processes that occur in our [societies] are not arcane, capable of being understood only by experts. They can be understood by almost anybody. Many ordinary people already understand this; they simply have not considered that by understanding these ordinary arrangements of cause and effect, we can also direct them, if we want to (Jacobs, 1961).

The President's Council on Sustainable Development recommended that all levels of government, especially local government, should identify barriers to greater citizen involvement in decision-making — such as lack of child care or transportation — and develop strategies to overcome them. Employers should give employees flexibility and incentives to increase the time they and their families can devote to community activities (PCSD, 1996).

a proposal that will win or lose; it increases the likelihood of new and better ideas being thought up; everyone has a stake in implementing a decision, because all have participated in its formation (participants have more energy for working in groups with which they are fully in agreement); and it lessens significantly the possibility that a minority will feel that an unacceptable decision has been imposed on them.

Canada's National Round Table on the Environment and the Economy, in conjunction with several provincial and local Round Tables, has articulated some of the guiding principles that characterize consensus processes:

- *Purpose Driven*: People need a reason to participate in the process.
- *Inclusive*: All parties with a significant interest in the issue should be involved in the consensus process.
- *Voluntary*: The parties who are affected or interested participate voluntarily.
- *Self-Designed*: The parties design the consensus process.
- *Flexible*: Flexibility should be designed into the process.
- *Fair*: All parties must have equal access to relevant information and the opportunity to participate effectively throughout the process.
- *Respectful of Diverse Interests*: Acceptance of the diverse values, interests, and knowledge of the parties involved in the consensus process is essential.
- *Accountable*: The parties are accountable both to their constituencies and to the process that they have agreed to establish.
- *Time Limited*: Realistic deadlines are necessary throughout the process.
- *Implemented*: Commitment to implementation and effective monitoring are essential parts of any agreement (NRTEE ,1993) .

Alternative Dispute Resolution

Consensus is also used in the context of conflict management. Alternative dispute resolution is a form of shared decision-making. Two key strategies are negotiation and mediation. These processes are "alternative" in the sense that they are outside the conventional judicial, litigious route of problem-solving. Conventional legal channels are often criticized for being excessively costly and slow in resolving disputes (and therefore favoring those with time and money), for contributing to a climate of uncertainty in decision-making, and for emphasizing win/lose over win/win solutions. In response, interest in alternative dispute resolution has grown significantly.

Interest in consensus-based dispute resolution strategies is also increasing. In the context of dispute resolution, consensus generally refers to a situation in which all parties agree to a decision. This outcome may have been arrived at by one party being persuaded by arguments of another, or by both parties finding a new common goal (Minnery, 1985). Reaching a consensus may involve bargaining, negotiation, consultation, facilitation, fact-finding and/or mediation in order to resolve conflicts. In contrast to a decision resulting from a vote or made unilaterally by a decision-making authority, a consensus process is qualitatively different in that each participant has an effective veto. This veto "levels the playing field" and provides each stakeholder with equal authority in reaching the decision. The power of consensus as a dispute resolution tool lies in its ability to protect the minority or single party from the "tyranny of the major-ity" (Cormick, 1989).

THE ROLE OF LOCAL GOVERNMENT

All of us play many roles in our society, such as worker, employer, parent, child, con-sumer, student, teacher, and so on, and all of these roles are important for moving toward sustainable communities. However, it is primarily in our role as citizens (and to a lesser extent, as consumers) that we can create sustainable communities and a sus-tainable economy. It is through participating in the governance of our communities that we can take the necessary measures to create a sustainable society. Sustainability will be adopted through active pressure on governments (for example, from citizen organizations and voluntary environmental groups) and through the power of the electoral system. Individual actions and lifestyle choices, such as recycling or bicycle commuting, are important personal contributions, but sustainability requires a *collec-tive* shift in individual actions and political choices, which governments can only gain the authority to call for if people have voted for sustainability (Jacobs, 1993). Democracy is fundamental to sustainability.

Local government provides one of the best ways to demonstrate the necessity, the desirability, and the practicality of moving toward sustainable communities. Although local governments are not the only agencies charged with community planning and development, they are locally elected, representative, and accountable bodies respon-sible for community decision-making. This makes them critical players in the move-ment toward sustainable communities. In the words of Peterborough, Ontario Mayor Sylvia Sutherland (1991):

> We in local government are closest to our communities. We are closest to the peo-ple who must participate in a very direct and active way if the transition to sustain-ability is to have any hope of success. We are uniquely situated to assist in the evolution of new social values and practices. We can encourage cooperation between the sectors of the community with a stake in the environment and in development and sustainability. We can act as a catalyst for local action beyond the boundaries of our own jurisdiction.

Local governments are also important actors in their local economies. They build and maintain infrastructure that is essential for economic activity, and set standards, regulations, taxes, and fees that determine the parameters for economic development. Local governments procure large numbers of services and products and can influence markets for goods and services. These products include environmental services (e.g., water, waste management, and land-use control), economic services (e.g. transporta-tion infrastructure), and social services (e.g., health and education) (ICLEI, 1996; MEMSW, 2003). Burlington, Ontario Alderman Jim Ryan (1992) notes that:

> [Sustainable development] requires that communities protect and enhance the environment upon which their future depends by changing the way they make decisions and by developing an ecological framework for planning sustainable com-munities. Translating the concept of sustainable development into action at the

municipal level will require far-reaching institutional changes, changes in thinking, decision making, policy and process. . . .

Sustainable development is a global imperative with an urban focus, because that is where the greatest growth is occurring and where the majority of our global and regional environmental problems originate. It calls for a fundamental change in the way we plan and manage our urban centers. Municipal officials as stewards of local communities have a vital role to play in effecting the necessary change.

There are a variety of ways that local governments can respond to sustainable development and global environmental concerns. For example, Gilbert (1991) characterized eight styles of local government response with respect to potential climate change and global warming (Table 1).

Governments are formed to preserve and protect the general good. Protecting the environment, safeguarding human health and preserving the national habitat should be an integral part of every government's environmental responsibilities. Local governments, in their own operations and in their regulation and monitoring of actions by others, should be model environmental citizens (New York City Environmental Charter, 1990).

Table 1: Local Government Styles of Response Regarding Global Warming

Style	*Examples*
1. Flout the law.	Use illegally polluting vehicles.
2. Merely obey the law.	Do no more, or less, than is required.
3. Set a good example within the administration	Intra-office recycling; use natural gas vehicles.
4. Advocate within jurisdiction.	Encourage reduction, reuse, and recycling; promote transit and district heating.
5. Legislate within jurisdiction.	Ban certain materials at landfill sites; local restrictions on automobile use.
6. Advocate outside jurisdiction.	Push for tighter automobile pollution standards; promote inter-city rail.
7. Seek new legislative authority.	Tax automobile ownership; ban sale of items made with CFCs.
8. Legislate outside jurisdiction.	Ban sale of items made with CFCs; ban use of many kinds of packaging.

Local governments also operate under the considerable constraints of most public agencies: limited resources, jurisdiction, imagination, courage, time, and so on. For local governments to fulfill their potential in moving toward sustainable communities, they need citizen organizations as community partners.

Citizen organizations provide many innovative programs and concepts, and furnish whole new paradigms for problem definition, because they are able to tap and organize information laterally. They can network across borders as well as across corporate and government boundaries, enabling rapid syntheses of overlooked and new information into fresh approaches and paradigms. Today, the most creative, energetic forces addressing the planetary problems of poverty, social inequity, pollution, resource depletion, violence, and war are grassroots citizens' movements. Hazel

Henderson calls this "grassroots globalism" — pragmatic, local solutions that keep the planet in mind. These approaches "bubble up" rather than "trickle down," and they are often innovative, stressing positive action and role models (Henderson, 1996).

A good example of grassroots globalism is the overwhelming interest and participation of all kinds of organizations in the UN global conferences organized in the 1990s. This is not accidental, but rather the "tip of the iceberg" in a wide social process affecting all the continents: the emergence of organized civil society (ICPQL, 1996).

Civil society groups vary in the causes they stand for and in their goals. Some are structured, capable of action with a sense of continuity; others are more "prophetic" in nature, likely to act intensively in a more episodic way. Still others endure changes from outside or within, intervening with forms of action that are permanent or else change during the entity's lifetime. Once empowered, citizens are quite capable of turning to those forms of organized action allowing them to apply pressure where they themselves are affected. The multiplicity of these forms of action, their cross-fertilization and their potential for confrontation create an enormous vitality within the social fabric (ICPQL, 1996).

Leadership by Example

Local government is an influential employer and consumer in most communities. A key step toward making our communities sustainable is leadership by example, particularly "greening" city hall. We need to insist that our local officials lead by example. As described throughout this book, a variety of tools are available for this purpose. Every community member has a legitimate interest in knowing what measures their local government is, could, or should be taking to make their community more sustainable.

Unfortunately, energy-efficient light bulbs and reusable china in the city hall cafeteria will not in themselves achieve sustainable development or slow global climate change. These kind of well-intentioned initiatives are but small steps toward creating sustainable communities.

Environmental Administration

Another key step toward sustainable communities is conceptual and organizational. One of the greatest obstacles to sustainability is the reductionist administrative mindset that subdivides problems and prevents the left hand of government from understanding what the right hand is doing. For example, despite considerable trumpeting of environmental protection programs (which are sometimes themselves endangered species), most sober analyses of public budgets and spending estimates conclude that governments spend billions of dollars more on programs and policies that *create* pollution and *encourage* environmental degradation. Such bureaucratic schizophrenia is perpetrated at all levels of government as well as throughout academia.

Sustainable communities cannot be achieved through the kind of fragmented and bureaucratized administration that characterizes senior government. At the commu-

The terms non-governmental organization (NGO) and nonprofit don't explain what these organizations do or stand for, only what they are not. A new acronym has been coined to describe those organizations and activities sometimes referred to as civil society or the social economy. CSO stands for civil society organization. From this perspective many governments and corporations are NCOs, or non-civil organizations (Henderson, 1996).

nity level, such issues as transportation, land use, economic development, public health, environmental protection, and housing affordability cannot be successfully managed as separate problems by separate agencies using separate strategies.

Conventional wisdom considers the environment as an administrative problem, to be solved by better management — understood as cutting the environment into bite-size pieces. This approach seems increasingly unable to deal effectively, sensitively, and comprehensively with environmental complexities.

Rather than the environment as an administrative problem, it would appear that administration is itself an environmental problem. One alternative to conventional municipal administration is an emerging form of what has been called "environmental administration." It can be characterized as non-compartmentalized, open, decentralized, anti-technocratic, and flexible (Paehlke and Torgerson, 1990). Environmental administration provides a holistic way of addressing both "environmental" issues and a whole range of community issues. Some examples of this approach are discussed below.

It will take a great effort over a long time to turn the system of local government into a paragon of environmental administration, though try we must. In these transition decades, however, an effective and popular way to implement sustainable community development is urgently required.

Beyond Local Government

A third key step toward sustainable communities is improving the context for sustainable community planning and governance. This requires looking beyond the local level toward regional, state/provincial, and federal policies and programs. These programs encourage, enable, and empower those communities that have already started to plan local initiatives for a sustainable future, and require the rest to begin.

PLANNING FOR ACTION

We can only develop community sustainability if we plan for it. A citizen's group planning process for community sustainability can be organized in six steps (ORTEE, 1995). First, develop a widely shared *vision* of the type of community the group would like to work towards. Second, *develop plans* on how to achieve this vision. This involves several sub-steps, including formulating a clear mission statement, analyzing the strengths and weakness of the group and the community, and assessing the many opportunities and obstacles that may be encountered. Then realistic goals and objectives can be set, and an action plan outlining specific tasks and activities should be developed. Third, *get city hall onside*. Fourth, d*evelop the resources* necessary to implement the plans. Fifth, prepare a strategy for *communicating* ideas and activities to the community. Sixth, be sure to *evaluate* your efforts regularly (see Chapter 14). This will help you to assess the degree to which your actions are helping the group move toward its stated goal, identify and keep track of successes, and communicate your successes to the community.

Getting City Hall Onside

One of the barriers encountered by many community groups intent on promoting sustainability in their community is the reluctance of city hall to be part of the quest and process. Yet the understanding and cooperation of both elected officials and professional staff are essential to making progress along the path to sustainability, for they must support the changes that must occur for things to be done differently. Here's some "how-to" advice obtained from both politicians and professional staff (ORTEE 1995):

1. Crucial to being taken seriously by city hall is having truly broad, multi-sectoral community representation at your "sustainability" table from the outset.

2. Obtain up-to-date information about the community that will provide you with a baseline picture of current community management.

3. Educate yourselves about the civic process. Administration is part of the town or city corporation. Council acts like a board of directors. Knowing how ideas get considered and subsequently translated into policy and programs can be very helpful when trying to promote new ideas. Understand the budget process as well.

4. When you feel you have an idea of the state of affairs in your community, develop a vision of where you want to go. But don't try to do too much at once. Choose one, two or three key issues to focus on. Avoid trying to sell the big sustainable picture at the outset. Action will not result from sustainability principles or ideals on their own. The approach should always be proposed on a smaller scale, in practical and "doable" terms.

5. Build allies for your initiative:
- Look for allies within the community at large. Develop constituencies of support. Politicians and staff respect such support.
- Approach the bureaucracy before the politicians.

Research the work already underway by municipal departments. Look for allies on staff who can speak in support of your initiative. Explain the initiative to them in practical terms. See if it is possible to build on municipal initiatives that are in the planning stages. Could a pilot program be developed? Sell specific targets which can later be used as a springboard to larger programs.
- In terms of city council, look for a possible political champion for your initiative. Consider who on council has the ability to communicate the need for change in a non-intimidating manner. Work with these councillors to bring them onside. Demonstrate the extent of community support you have for the initiative.

6. Don't go to city council until you have everything lined up, including:
- a committed steering group made up of individuals from the community who command some respect and represent key sectors;
- baseline facts and figures that are pertinent to your initiative;
- goals and objectives that fit with any stated municipal priorities;
- allies and champions on council and in the municipal departments;
- sound community support for the initiative; and
- a sound proposal for financing the sustainability measures being recommended.

7. When change is underway, develop a set of indicators that will show/measure progress being made. People must see and feel the results of the initiative. Tie the indicators into community goals where possible.

Community Visioning

Most communities that have created sustainable development plans have used some form of community involvement process. For example, Racine, Wisconsin (with a population of 85,000) developed the following principles in order to assure that its "visioning" process is productive and open:

"We believe the community visioning process must:

- Be equitable and just, so that *all* residents become fully engaged in it.
- Generate resident and organization ideas throughout the process that reflect the overall demographics of the community.
- Provide multiple ways for ideas and suggestions to be brought forward and for residents to become engaged.
- Be simple, understandable, positive, open, transparent, trustworthy, and flexible in order to generate widespread community buy-in and ownership.
- Nurture a culture of full participation and commitment of community residents *and* organizations in the development and implementation of the vision.
- Appeal to the self-interest of individuals and organizations by showing them how their individual lives as well as the life of the community will be better as a result.
- Recognize that youth need to be a driving force in the development of a community vision and its implementation.
- Run on as short a timetable as possible in recognition of the community's pent-up desire to begin working on solutions.
- Put the visioning process in the context of the overall community effort. This will demonstrate that visioning is only the *first* step in an ongoing movement towards a sustainable community.
- Encourage the community to become a learning community — one in which learning leads to continuous improvement" (Johnson Foundation, 1997).

Co-Management

The term co-management has been used in a broad sense to designate a wide array of arrangements for shared decision-making between government resource management agencies and community-based parties. Co-management has now been widely recognized as contributing to solutions in the problematic management of "common property" or common pool resources such as fish, water, wildlife, forests and rangelands.

Co-management arrangements typically involve participatory decision-making by one or more government agencies working cooperatively with one or more community-based groups and involving one or more management functions. As long as there is significant overlap in management objectives (for example, sustainable harvest rates) and some commitment to joint problem-solving, it is not necessary for all of the community-based groups or parties to have the same level of power, rights, or management authority. Planning is more successfully implemented when all affected parties have a voice in decisions (Pinkerton, 1996).

Examples of co-management include an agreement between the treaty tribes of western Washington State and the Washington Department of Fisheries, which share management authority over salmon, and do important aspects of joint harvest planning; the Gwaii Haanas Agreement for a national protected area in western Canada; and the Wendaban Stewardship Authority agreement for the Temegami area of Ontario (Duffy, Roseland and Gunton, 1996; Parks Canada, 2003; WDFW, 2004)

Local Round Tables

The aim of a local round table is to be a fully representative body, comprising many interests, seeking consensus on ways to achieve sustainability, and providing advice on local developments. These goals are met through a variety of methods and initiatives. To achieve multi-sectoral representation, for example, local round table members come from a wide variety of community sectors in order to build consensus and promote sustainability in the region. Membership seeks to achieve geographic representation, a mix of knowledge and skills, gender balance, and ethnocultural variety.

Local round tables provide advice and comments on local governments activities by conducting research, offering critiques, recommending new policies, plans and initiatives and monitoring reports and data. Another crucial element of their activities is educating the public about environmental and economic issues through speakers, special events and publications. These activities, in combination with networking with local action groups, assist in ensuring community input and involvement in local sustainability issues (ORTREE, 1995). Round table initiatives on sustainability have been initiated in communities across North America and are also being used at the national, state and provincial levels (NRTEE, 2004).

Neighborhood Councils

At the community level, shared decision-making can take various forms. Neighbourhood councils are an example of a participatory planning approach to community development (CANC, 2004; City of Quebec, 2004; UNCHS, 2000; Clague, 1993).

Neighborhood councils may be an informal association of neighbors or may be registered as a nonprofit society and charity; they also may be established by and officially connected to city hall. Generally they operate with nominal funds, although they may receive grant money for special projects or a small operating grant from the municipality.

Neighborhood councils are structured to have representation from each block in the neighborhood and/or other local organizations. They elect an executive, which is small enough that all members can meet regularly, to provide coordination and support to activities. The executive may also have the assistance of a social planner from the municipality or planning council.

Neighborhood councils foster information and communication on neighborhood issues/activities and on city activities that affect the neighborhood. They bring people together for planning and problem-solving on local interests, including advocacy to city hall. They facilitate good inter-group and inter-family relations in the neighborhood, and can address all issues of local concern, whether they concern social, educational, economic, land, environmental, or cultural dimensions of the community. Neighborhood councils also propose and act on projects and activities that strengthen community life.

Participation in neighborhood councils provides an opportunity for people to build their skills in democratic participation. Neighborhood councils offer an openness of agenda and flexibility, and maximum impact for minimum financial resources. They also can provide valuable sounding boards for municipal politicians on issues.

The limitations of neighborhood councils are that they require a core of very dedicated volunteers prepared to invest large amounts of personal time in their neighborhood for work that is not always appreciated. They also risk being dominated by a single issue group, or group that is not representative of the neighborhood. As well, they may require assistance in developing the skills for democratic community participation and decision-making.

Despite their limitations, neighborhood councils are very successful at promoting leadership, responsibility, and collaboration among community members. Seattle's neighborhood associations get deeply involved in economic development and neighborhood revitalization projects (City of Seattle, 2004). Neighborhood associations initiated Education Summit, which resulted in a package for a levy seeking $65 million for the city to establish family support centres, health clinics, etc. The levy won overwhelming support.

Portland's 95 neighbourhood associations and neighbourhood district coalitions represent all areas of Portland and participate in local government decision-making on virtually every aspect of civil business (City of Portland, 2004).

Neighbourhood organizations improve quality of community life. They keep the streets clean, fight crime, tutor children, organize recreation programs, plant community gardens, build housing, and more. They are by nature geographically based, volunteer driven, problem solving, empowering, multi-purpose and flexible (Dobson, 1995).

Goal-Oriented Planning

Sustainable community planning works best in the context of a supportive regional, provincial or state planning framework. The key is goal-oriented planning — that is, planning *for* sustainable community development. Governance systems in some regions have been relatively successful in planning and managing for a healthy environment.

Supportive national planning programs exist in France, Norway, Finland, and Holland. In North America, provincial or state legislation can require each town's land use to be compatible with specified regional interests, but leave the actual planning process up to the local community. In Canada, British Columbia enacted growth strategies legislation in the mid-1990s. In the US, such legislation has given new force to urban planning in eight states: Florida, Georgia, Maine, New Jersey, Oregon, Rhode Island, Vermont and Washington. All cities and counties in these states are required to plan their own development according to stipulated goals such as energy conservation, protection of open space, and provision of affordable housing. These statewide planning requirements not only enhance regional cooperation, but they also give cities the backing they need to apply a comprehensive, long-term vision to their land-use planning (Lowe, 1992; Florida, 2004; Georgia, 2003; New Jersey, 2004; Oregon, 2004; Rhode Island, 2004; Vermont, 2002; Washington, 2004).

Sustainable Community Planning

Citizen organizations and local governments all over North America are engaging in sustainable community planning processes. Some notable initiatives are those of

Chattanooga and the San Francisco Bay Area in the U.S,. Ottawa, Hamilton-Wentworth, and Greater Toronto in Canada, and Curitiba in Brazil.

In 1969, Chattanooga, Tennessee was the most polluted city in the US In 1990 it was recognized as the country's best turn-around story. How did it happen? In 1984, the entire community was invited to envision what they wanted their community to be like by 2000. The shared vision of sustainable community development that emerged put affordable housing, public education, transportation alternatives, better urban design, parks and greenways and neighborhood vitality at the top of the community's agenda. Energetic collaboration of government agencies, manufacturers and citizens resulted in successful initiatives to clean up the air and revitalize a city in decline. Several eco-industrial parks were established to rebuild the city's economic base, proving that economic development and environmental stewardship can be achieved together. Most importantly, all participants determined to set in motion a comprehensive, interrelated and strategic process for sustainable community development (Bernard and Young, 1996; Gilbert et al., 1996).

Urban Ecology organized a five-year participatory process to develop their *Blueprint for A Sustainable Bay Area*. It was based on providing residents with new choices for a prosperous life; protecting, restoring and integrating nature into people's lives; working toward social, environmental and economic justice; promoting development and transportation alternatives that connect the region; encouraging resource conservation and reuses; designing with respect for local and historical uniqueness; and enabling residents to nurture a strong sense of place, community and responsibility (Urban Ecology, 1996). The reports 95 recommendations reflect the range of tools and initiatives in this book. Sustainable community planning continues to be an integral part of community development in San Francisco (San Francisco, 2002).

The Health, Family, and Environment Committee of the San Francisco Board of Supervisors, with the support of the Mayor, unanimously endorsed in 1997 a Sustainability Plan that would guide decisions of all city commissions and departments. Air quality, solid waste, biodiversity, and food and agriculture are among the 10 major topics of the 150-page plan. The plan's transportation suggestions include creating 10 auto-free zones over the next four years, increasing the city parking tax, raising gasoline taxes and bridge tolls, and introducing "congestion pricing" charges for driving at rush hour. Critics such as right-wing radio talk-show host Rush Limbaugh and the conservative magazine *National Review* have called it "eco-totalitarianism." San Francisco joins Santa Monica, California and Chattanooga as American cities with extensive environmental plans (*GreenClips*, 1997; Langton, 1997).

Ottawa, Ontario's 1992 Official Plan, developed through an elaborate public consultation process with solid community support, is based on the concept of sustainable urban development. The city's commitment to sustainable development is manifested in the Mission Statement, Guiding Principles, and the Vision for Ottawa found at the beginning of the Plan. Specific policies contained in the Plan are designed to reflect this commitment. For example, the housing policies promote affordable housing, infilling and intensification, which reflect the guiding principles of adequate shelter, and conservation and enhancement of the resource base. The transportation policies encourage increased use of public transportation, cycling, and walking, which reflect the guiding principle of increasing non-automobile transportation. In addition, the plan outlines the city's environmental impact assessment process, which is designed to address the cumulative impact of everyday practices and development projects on the environment (ORTREE, 1995; Ottawa, 2003).

The Sustainable Community Initiative is an ongoing collaborative process in which the Hamilton-Wentworth regional government, 75 kilometers (46.5 miles) west of Toronto, is working with thousands of citizens to turn a jointly-developed community vision into a reality. Since Vision 2020 was formally adopted in 1993, the regional government has devised an implementation strategy outlining the major policy shifts needed to achieve the vision, along with over 400 recommendations for specific action and a unique approach for monitoring progress. Twenty-eight sustainability indicators are compiled into the Annual Report Card, which is the basis of an Annual Sustainable Community Day and forum to assess progress in relation to the goals of Vision 2020. The Sustainable Community Initiative has had a profound impact on the way the local government operates and is leading toward significant improvements to the local environment, including development of a bicycle commuter network, creation of habitat corridors for wildlife protection, and a home-energy and waste-auditing program (Hamilton, 2003; ICLEI, 1995).

In 1988, a Royal Commission on the Future of the Toronto Waterfront was created to examine matters related to the use, enjoyment and development of the area. By the mid-1980s, the Toronto waterfront had become an embarrassment. Pollution had closed the beaches; expressways and condominium towers blocked public access; contaminated and abandoned industrial lands degraded the harbor area; and rehabilitation efforts were frustrated by jurisdictional squabbling among federal, provincial, regional, and municipal authorities. The Commission, headed by former Toronto Mayor David Crombie, initiated broad public discussion of waterfront issues and quickly saw that the conventional, fragmented, waterfront-specific approach would not work, so they expanded its scope from the waterfront to the watershed. This larger area, which the Commission called the Greater Toronto bioregion, is home to four million people as well as innumerable other creatures in complex social as well as ecological relations. Before the Crombie Commission, the notion of bioregional or ecosystem planning was little known outside professional and citizen planning circles, and did not seem likely to play a major role in guiding practical efforts to reunite economy, community, and ecology. Now it is a real possibility that has begun to be tested in practice (Gibson et al., 1997). The draft Toronto Sustainability Charter incorporates many of these principles (Toronto, 2004).

Curitiba, Brazil has received international acclaim as a city that works for its integrated transportation and land-use planning, and for its waste management programs. Both are good examples of sustainable community planning. But how did Curitiba manage to become a positive example for cities in both developed and developing countries? In part, the city's success can be attributed to strong leadership — city officials focused on developing simple, flexible, and affordable solutions that could be realized at the local level and adapted to changing conditions. In addition, "the government promoted a strong sense of public participation. Officials were encouraged to look at problems, talk to the people, discuss the main issues, and only then reach for the pen" (Rabinovitch, 1996).

Cities are now banding together under the auspices of various regional associations and partnerships concerning approaches and solutions to common urban problems. The CO_2 Reduction Program is a partnership coordinated by the International Council for Local Environmental Initiatives (ICLEI). More than 100 local governments from 27 countries have joined an International Cities for Climate Protection Campaign. Participants pledge to meet and exceed the requirements of the Framework Convention on Climate Change by reducing carbon dioxide emissions by up to 20 percent by 2005. As part of this initiative, ICLEI worked with 14 cities to develop comprehensive local action plans to reduce carbon dioxide emissions (Brugmann, 1996).

Jonas Rabinovitch, a long-time advisor to Curitiba Mayor Jaime Lerner, believes the lesson to be learned from Curitiba is that creativity can substitute for financial resources. Any city, rich or poor, can draw on the skills of its residents to tackle urban environmental problems (Rabinovitch, 1996). All these examples confirm the importance, discussed in Chapter 1, of multiplying social capital as a key to moving toward sustainable communities.

REFERENCES

Arnstein, S.R. 1969. "A Ladder of Citizen Participation." *Journal of American Institute of Planners* July: 216-24.

Beer, J, and E. Stief. 1997. *The Mediator's Handbook*. Gabriola Island, BC: New Society Publishers.

Bernard, T., and J. Young. 1996. *The Ecology of Hope: Communities Collaborate for Sustainability*. Gabriola Island, BC: New Society Publishers.

Brugmann, J. 1996. "Cities Take Action: Local Environmental Initiatives." In *World Resources 1996-97: The Urban Environment*, World Resources Institute, United Nations Environment Program, United Nations Development Program, World Bank. New York: Oxford University Press.

City of Hamilton. 2003. Retrieved from http://www.vision2020.hamilton.ca/default.asp

City of Ottawa. 2003. "Ottawa 2020: Official Plan." Retrieved from http://ottawa.ca/city_services/planningzoning/2020/op/

City of Portland. 2004. Office of Neighbourhood Involvement. Retrieved from www.portlandonline.com/oni/index.cfm?c=28380

City of Quebec. 2004. Retrieved from: http://www.ville.quebec.qc.ca

City of San Francisco. 2002. "Profiles of Community Planning Areas." Retrieved from: http://sfgov.org/site/planning_index.asp?id=25367

City of Seattle. 2004. Department of Neighborhoods. Retrieved from. http://www.seattle.gov/neighborhoods/

City of Toronto. 2004. "Toronto's Sustainability Charter." Retrieved from: http://www.toronto.ca/sustainability/sustainability_charter.htm

City Wide Alliance of Neighborhood Councils (CANC). 2004. Retrieved from http://www.allncs.org/

Clague, M.. 1993. *A Citizen's Guide to Community Social Planning*. Vancouver: Social Planning and Research Council of BC

Coover, V., et al. 1977. *Resource Manual for a Living Revolution*. Philadelphia: New Society Publishers.

Cormick, G. 1989. "Strategic Issues in Structuring Multi-party Public Policy Negotiations." *Negotiation Journal* 5(2): 125-32.

Crowfoot, J. E., and J. M. Wondolleck. 1990. *Environmental Disputes: Community Involvement in Conflict Resolution*. Washington, DC/Covelo, Calif.: Island Press.

Dobson, C., ed. 1995. *The Citizen's Handbook: A Guide to Building Community in Vancouver*. Vancouver: Vancouver Citizen's Committee.

Duffy, D., M. Roseland, and T. I. Gunton. 1996. "A Preliminary Assessment of Shared Decision-Making in Land Use and Natural Resource Planning." *Environments: A Journal of Interdisciplinary Studies* 23(2): 1-16.

Gibson, R.B., D.H.M. Alexander, and R. Tomalty. 1997. "Putting Cities in Their Place: Ecosystem-Based Planning for Canadian Urban Regions." In *Eco-City Dimensions: Healthy Communities, Healthy Planet*, M. Roseland, ed. Gabriola Island, BC: New Society Publishers.

Gilbert, R. 1991. *Cities and Global Warming*. Toronto: Canadian Urban Institute.

Gilbert, R., D. Stevenson, H. Giradet, and R. Stren. 1996. *Making Cities Work: The Role of Local Authorities in the Urban Environment*. London: Earthscan.

GreenClips. 1997. 76, 16 July. <GreenClips@aol.com>.

Henderson, H. 1996. *Building a Win-Win World: Life Beyond Global Economic Warfare*. San Francisco: Berrett-Koehler Publishers.

Independent Commission on Population and Quality of Life (ICPQL). 1996. *Caring for the Future*. New York: Oxford University Press.

International Council for Local Environmental Initiatives (ICLEI). 1995. *The Role of Local Authorities in Sustainable Development: 14 Case Studies on the Local Agenda 21 Process*. Nairobi: U.N. Centre for Human Settlements.

International Council for Local Environmental Initiatives (ICLEI), International Development Research Centre (IDRC), and United Nations Environment Program. 1996. *The Local Agenda 21 Planning Guide*. Toronto: ICLEI and Ottawa: IDRC.

Jacobs, J. 1961. *The Death and Life of Great American Cities*. New York: Vintage Books.

Jacobs, M. 1993. *The Green Economy: Environment, Sustainable Development and the Politics of the Future*. Vancouver: University of British Columbia Press.

Johnson Foundation. 1997. "Visioning Principles." *Wingspread Journal* 19(2).

Kaner, S., et al. 1996. *The Facilitator's Guide to Participatory Decision-Making*. Gabriola Island, BC: New Society Publishers.

Langton, J. 1997. "City's Plan to Kill Stray Cats Raises a Howl." *Vancouver Sun*, 11 August: A8.

Lowe, M.D. 1992. "City Limits." *Worldwatch* 5(1) Jan./Feb.: 18-25.

Minnery, J. R. 1985. *Conflict Management in Urban Planning*. Brookfield, Vt.: Gower Publishing.Municipal Environmental Management System Workshop (MEMSW). 2003. Workshop Notes from The Globe Biennial Conference and Trade Fair, Vancouver, BC, Canada. Retrieved from http://www.c2p2online.com/documents/IndustryCanada-EMS.pdf

National Round Table on the Environment and the Economy (NRTEE). 2004. Retrieved from: http://www.nrtee-trnee.ca

New York City. 1990. *The Environmental Charter for New York City.* New York: City of New York, Office of the Comptroller.

National Round Table on the Environment and the Economy (NRTEE). 1993. *Building Consensus for a Sustainable Future: Guiding Principles.* Ottawa: NRTEE.

Ontario Round Table on the Environment and the Economy (ORTEE). 1995. *Sustainable Communities Resource Package.* Toronto: ORTEE.

Osborne, D., and T. Gaebler. 1993. *Reinventing Government.* New York: Plume.

Owen, S. 1994. "Introduction." *From Conflict to Consensus: Shared Decision-making in British Columbia.* M. Roseland, ed. Burnaby, BC: Simon Fraser University, School of Resource and Environmental management.

Paehlke, R., and D. Torgerson, eds. 1990. *Managing Leviathan: Environmental Politics and the Administrative State.* Peterborough: Broad View Press.

Parks Canada. 2003. "Gwaii Haanas National Reserve and Heritage Site." Retrieved from: http://www.pc.gc.ca/pn-np/bc/gwaiihaanas/plan/plan2_e.asp

Pinkerton, E. 1996. "The Contribution of Watershed-Based Multi-Party Co-Management Agreements to Dispute Resolution: The Skeena Watershed Committee." *Environments* 23(2): 51-68.

President's Council on Sustainable Development (PCSD). 1996. *Sustainable America: A New Consensus for Prosperity, Opportunity, and a Healthy Environment for the Future.* Washington, DC: US Government Printing.

Rabinovitch, J. 1996. "Integrated Transportation and Land Use Planning Channel Curitiba's Growth." In *World Resources* 1996-97: *The Urban Environment*, World Resources Institute, United Nations Environment Program, United Nations Development Program, World Bank. New York: Oxford University Press.

Ryan, J. 1992. "Sustainable Development: An Agenda for Change for Municipalities." *Municipal World* 102(3): 3-6.

State of Florida. 2004. "Comprehensive Planning." Retrieved fromhttp://www.dca.state.fl.us/fdcp/dcp/compplanning/comprehensiveplanning.htm

State of Georgia. 2003. "Comprehensive Planning Program" from http://www.dca.state.ga.us/planning/

State of Maine. 2004. Department of Land Use & Planning Resources. Retrieved from http://www.maine.gov/spo/landuse/resources/landuse.php

State of New Jersey. 2004. Office of Smart Growth. Retrieved from http://www.nj.gov/dca/osg/plan/index.shtml

State of Oregon. 2004. Department of Land Conservation and Development. Retrieved from http://www.oregon.gov/LCD/goals.shtml

State of Rhode Island. 2004. Rhode Island Statewide Planning Program. Retrieved from http://www.planning.state.ri.us/

State of Vermont. 2002. Department of Housing and Community Affairs. Retrieved from http://www.dhca.state.vt.us/Planning/index.htm

State of Washington. 2004. Department of Community, Trade and Economic Development. Retrieved from http://www.cted.wa.gov/DesktopDefault.aspx?tabid=715

Sutherland, S. 1991. Remarks to Association of Municipal Clerks and Treasurers of Ontario (AMCTO) and Intergovernmental Committee on Urban and Regional Research (ICURR) Management Symposium, "Implementing Sustainable Development in Municipalities." Hockley Valley, Ontario. May.

United Nations Commission on Human Settlements. 2000. "Special Themes: Urban Governance." Retrieved from http://www.unchs.org/chs18/English/HSC187.htm

Urban Ecology. 1996. *Blueprint for A Sustainable Bay Area.* Oakland, Calif.: Urban Ecology.

Van Thijn, E. 1991. Mayor of Amsterdam, Remarks to World Cities and Their Environment Congress of Municipal Leaders, Toronto, 25-28 August.

Washington Department of Fish and Wildlife (WDFW). 2004. "Fact Sheet: How tribes and state co-manage salmon and steelhead." Retrieved from http://wdfw.wa.gov/factshts/comgrs.htm

TOOLS FOR COMMUNITY SUSTAINABILITY

M oving toward sustainable communities is a long-term goal, so it is important that the incremental steps we take in the short-term are leading us in the right direction. This chapter surveys some of the many tools available to citizens and their governments for managing community sustainability, and then discusses one of these tools, sustainability indicators, in more detail.

The tools described below (adapted from ICLEI et al., 1996 and Levett, 1997, unless otherwise indicated) are organized into two categories: planning tools and assessment tools. Community planning and assessment tools can sometimes be conducted by citizen groups with little training, whereas technical planning and assessment tools more often require the involvement of trained staff or consultants. The latter may not lend themselves readily to public participation, but citizens can participate more effectively in decision-making if they know about many of the tools available to their communities. These tools can be complementary and used in parallel (Robért et al., 2002).

PLANNING

Community Tools

Several community planning tools are useful for awareness building, problem diagnosis, and dialogue and participation in decision-making. These tools can be used from the pre-planning through to the evaluation stages of the planning process. Relatively familiar or self-explanatory tools include brainstorming, community meetings, field trips, media campaigns, open houses, public hearings, public meetings, role playing, vision building, and workshops. Popular education and search conferences are less well known.

Popular Education: The tools of theater, sculpturing, puppet shows, and storytelling have developed in communities where development practitioners and educators have worked. Popular techniques engage the community in the identification and critical analysis of issues, information gathering related to these issues, and problem-solving and decision-making methods. Popular education can enhance people's capacity to participate in decisions and actions affecting their lives.

CHAPTER 14

Search Conferences: These are two- to three-day strategic community planning conferences designed to engage stakeholders in planning and managing the future. A search conference entails building consensus on a vision of the future as a basis for planning within and among all sectors. Future possibilities and trends rather than current problems or risks are the focus of subsequent action planning. The elements of a search conference include a review of past and current trends, an analysis of external and internal forces, the creation of a future vision, and development of an action plan.

Technical Tools

The following technical planning tools are used to establish environmental carrying-capacity limits and human impacts on them, and to guide policy.

Ecological Footprint Analysis: This tool estimates the land area required by any human activity, both directly — the land occupied by buildings or infrastructure — and indirectly — including the land needed to grow crops and assimilate pollutants. The ecological footprint may offer a meaningful single measure of all global ecological impacts of human activities, at household, municipal, national, or global levels. The degree to which the footprint of human activities exceeds the total productive area is a measure of unsustainability (Wackernagel and Rees, 1996).

Environmental Space: The maximum sustainable rates of human use of key resources (energy, selected non-renewable resources, land, wood) are estimated, and then the resources are divided evenly among the world's population to give each individual's entitlement. The extent to which any country (or household) exceeds this is a measure of unsustainability. The calculations support calls for a ten-fold "dematerialization" of Western lifestyles.

Community-based State-of-the-Environment Reporting: The intention is to develop broad perceptions of ecosystems and our relationships with them, and to identify ecological approaches to planning and designing urban areas, on which residents and governments can ponder and act. As with all state-of-the-environment reporting, the question of appropriate indicators presents a major challenge, especially at the local government level. Ideally, state-of-the-environment indicators should be key measures that most represent the state of the environment and that collectively provide a comprehensive profile of environmental quality, natural resource assets, and agents of environmental change.

Sustainability Reporting: This is state-of-the-environment reporting broadened to include quality of life as well as aspects of sustainability; it is focused on information needed to guide decisions and action.

Environmental Budgeting: Local carrying capacities are used to set budgets for the maximum amount of environmental impact permissible in the municipal area. For example, the water extraction budget would be based on replenishment rates. The municipality works with all environmental consumers to keep impacts within budget. More consumption of water by households, for example, would have to be offset by less consumption by industry, or by more recovery/treatment of wastewater.

ASSESSMENT

Community Tools

Assessment tools are used for figuring out where we're at, and for monitoring and evaluating where we're going. Some familiar or self-explanatory community assessment tools include risk assessment, focus groups, periodic monitoring reports, ranking, and surveys. Some less familiar assessment tools are described below.

Community Case Studies: These are collective descriptions and analyses of the community and its problems, documented in a local language or medium (e.g., drawing, storytelling, role playing, audio-visual). They can be used to promote awareness and discussion among community members, and to gather baseline information for assessment.

Community Environmental Assessment: Stakeholders can be involved in gathering information and analyzing the environmental and social impacts of proposed activities to predict their positive and negative effects. Designed for group observation and value judgment, the importance of any impact is determined by the community and given numerical value, such as environmental and social scores. Although not useful in themselves, these scores can be used to facilitate priority setting and to identify indicators for monitoring and evaluation.

Community Interviews: Interviews are a form of surveying in which all members of a community are invited to a meeting to answer specific pre-set questions. Discussion is restricted because the meeting size is large, so this tool is not useful for consensus-building; but it gathers preliminary information on community perspectives or solicits feedback on proposed strategies and actions.

Force Field Analysis: This is a facilitated and structured exercise in which participants identify specific hindering and facilitating forces affecting the functioning of any situation, assess the relative strength of each force, and plan alternative actions to overcome or promote these forces. It is useful for achieving a shared understanding of opportunities and constraints that can influence a desired goal, which helps participants determine effective strategies and priorities.

Geographic Information Systems: GIS is a computer-based data system for the storage, easy retrieval, manipulation, transformation, comparison, and graphic display of data. Intensive (and perhaps expensive) data gathering is often required, but once established, GIS can provide a user-friendly source of information that can be manipulated by non-experts as well as experts. In some communities, GIS systems have been used by community "watch-dogs" to monitor local environmental situations.

Community-Based Mapping: Mapping involves residents in the pictorial construction of information about their community. During a mapping exercise, maps are constructed from local knowledge and observation, and provide an excellent starting point for discussion about community-based issue identification, analysis, and problem-solving.

Oral History: This is a participatory technique for information sharing during the analysis of local issues. Historical accounts can be compared with present information to generate an analysis of underlying trends and structural problems in a community, and can be used to inform residents about the history of changes and development in their community.

Service Issues Mapping: This facilitated group brainstorming and analysis technique helps stakeholders "map" the diverse issues that must be considered in order to address a single priority issue. This exercise helps people see the systemic nature of local problems by highlighting complex sets of relationships among issues and by identifying different stakeholders who need to be involved in problem-solving.

SWOT Analysis: Strengths, Weaknesses, Opportunities, and Threats (SWOT) Analysis is a strategic planning tool that aids in the formulation of attainable long-range goals, action programs, and policies. Strengths and weaknesses refer to internal factors in the community, such as resources or declining budgets. Opportunities and threats refer to outside influences that could benefit or damage the community.

Technical Tools

Environmental Impact Assessment and Social Impact Assessment: These comprehensive tools integrate environmental and social considerations into project planning, development, and implementation. To be effective, assessment must be a decision-making tool. The application of an effective assessment process ensures that potential environmental and social effects are identified and mitigative measures put in place to minimize or eliminate these impacts. Effective assessment requires that the environmental and social implications of a proposal be considered prior to taking or making irrevocable decisions and as early in the planning process as possible. The assessment of a proposal should include the concerns of the public with regard to both environmental and social evaluation (City of Ottawa, 1990).

Sustainability Appraisal: Appraisal of activities, projects, programs, plans and/or policies applies to social and economic sustainability criteria as well as environmental ones, and considers their integration and reconciliation.

Environmental Audit: Such an audit is based on an assessment of the environmental impacts of a government's policies and practices. In some cases these will be known or easily identifiable, while in others, it will be possible only to indicate the likely consequences. The policy review should encompass all activities of the government, and all departments and arms of its service. It should not be restricted to official or approved policy, because much local government practice has evolved through tradition, or results from informal decisions of staff.

Environmental Action Planning and Management: This tool is a variation of an environmental audit; it involves setting environmental objectives, implementing environmental improvement actions, and monitoring and reporting on their effectiveness

— in other words, applying familiar "management by objectives" to environmental effects.

Eco-Management and Audit System: Another variation of an environmental audit, an eco-management and audit system is a formal management systems standard for environmental "management by objectives." Originally designed for the manufacturing industry, it has been adopted for municipal use in the UK A proposed update is "sustainability management and audit system," which includes social and economic aspects of sustainability, and strengthens involvement of stakeholders in setting criteria and assessing performance, according to social audit principles.

Social Auditing: Just as financial accounting measures financial performance, social auditing measures social performance by better understanding its relation to the goals and key stakeholders of an organization. Social auditing is increasingly popular with large private institutions such as Ben and Jerry's Ice Cream, The Body Shop International, and VanCity Savings Credit Union. It can also be applied to smaller businesses, community enterprises, cooperatives, non-governmental organizations and public bodies (Pearce et al., 1997).

Sustainability Indicators: This effective tool for communities and governments to evaluate their progress toward sustainability is discussed below.

TOOLS IN ACTION

In June, 1992, the United Nations Conference on Environment and Development established Agenda 21, a sustainable development action plan for the 21st century. That plan includes a proposal made by the International Council for Local Environmental Initiatives (ICLEI) to support local governments in the development of their own Local Agenda 21s. ICLEI's Local Agenda 21 Initiative (ICLEI, 1993) provides a common vehicle for local governments to strengthen local environmental planning. From 1992 to 1996, approximately 1,200 local governments in 33 countries established Local Agenda 21 campaigns (Brugmann, 1996).

A Local Agenda 21 campaign can be any participatory, local effort to establish a comprehensive action strategy for sustainable development in that local jurisdiction or area. All local governments are urged to complete their campaigns and strategies and to report their results to both the United Nations Commission on Sustainable Development and to ICLEI. The proposed planning framework is based on the following four elements:

- *Community consultation processes*, such as round tables, to achieve input and participation from every sector;
- *Sustainable development auditing*, to provide sound information about current conditions;
- *Setting sustainable development targets*, both near and long-term, for quality of life, environmental quality, resource consumption, and human development; and
- *Development and use of indicators*, to inform the community about the impact

The indicators a society chooses to report to itself about itself are surprisingly powerful. They reflect collective values and inform collective decisions. A nation that keeps a watchful eye on its salmon runs or the safety of its streets makes different choices than does a nation that is only paying attention to its GNP. The idea of citizens choosing their own indicators is something new under the sun — something intensely democratic (Meadows, 1972)

of its programs and investments upon the sustainable development of the community.

Sustainability Indicators

Why are sustainability indicators important? According to Osborne and Gaebler (1993), what gets measured tends to get done. If you don't measure results, you can't tell success from failure. If you can't recognize success, you can't reward it. And if you can't recognize failure, you can't learn from it.

The steps involved in developing sustainability indicators are: clarify goals — the aim of the evaluation and the type of desired outcome; determine who will lead the process; invite participation — the process of evaluation may be as valuable as the eventual application of the indicators themselves; decide how to choose indicators; collect data by which to measure the indicators; report on the indicators; and update and revise the indicators. (For details on these steps and related issues, see Azar et al., 1996; Brugmann, 1997; Forss et al., 1994; Kline, 1997; Maclaren, 1996; McLemore and Neumann, 1987; Papineau, 1996; Parker, 1995; Schön and Rein, 1994; Schwandt, 1997; Waddell, 1995.)

The following initiatives are a small sample of ongoing and emerging projects to design and use sustainability indicators. They represent the spectrum of aims for which sustainability indicators can be used — from the Sustainable Seattle Project, with a focus primarily on community education and empowerment, to the Oregon Benchmarks project, with a greater focus on providing feedback to government agencies.

Sustainable Seattle Project : The Sustainable Seattle Project began in 1992 with a meeting of 150 citizens. During this gathering, 99 indicators were proposed and 40 key indicators were selected; the first 20 of these indicators were assessed in 1993, and in 1995, the remaining 20 were assessed. Indicators ranged from total water consumption, per capita waste generation, and recycling rates to volunteering in schools and household incomes. The Sustainable Seattle Project plans to update and improve their indicators on an annual basis.

The people behind the Sustainable Seattle Project believe that "measuring progress is not the same as making it." The project promotes action by encouraging Seattle-area citizens to:

- employ local media to spread indicator results and analysis;
- use the political process to promote change in public policy;
- broaden the information base used for economic decision-making;
- use indicators in schools for education and as a basis for additional research;
- form a basis for linking local nonprofit and volunteer groups; and
- question personal lifestyle choices.

Willapa Bay Indicators: In southwest Washington State, the Willapa Bay Indicators Project is evaluating the environmental, social, and economic sustainability of a rural watershed. The Willapa indicators explicitly tie the health of the environment to the vitality of the local economy and community. Environmental indicators are divided

Goals, Targets, and Indicators

In 1994, the Santa Monica Task Force on the Environment developed a Sustainable City Program in partnership with the City of Santa Monica Environmental Programs Division. Each of the program's policy areas has clear goals reflecting the city's current and future programs. Specific targets were established for each goal, and an indicator was established for each target, as in the example below (ICLEI et al., 1996):

Policy Area: Community and Economic Development

Goals

- Encourage the development of compact, mixed-use, pedestrian-oriented projects.
- Promote the growth of local businesses that provide employment opportunities for Santa Monica residents.
- Facilitate education programs that enrich the lives of all members of the community.

Targets

- Provide 750 additional affordable housing units.
- Create three new community gardens.
- Establish partnership with local schools to create and complement a Sustainable Schools program.
- Increase total public open space by 15 acres.

Indicators:	1990 (Actual)	1993 (Actual)	2000 (Target)
Deed-restricted affordable housing units	1,172 units	1,313 units	1,922 units
Community gardens	2 gardens	2 gardens	5 gardens
Creation of a Sustainable Schools program	n/a	n/a	implemented
Public open space	164 acres	164.8 acres	180 acres

into three categories: water resource quality, land-use/vegetation patterns, and species populations. Economic indicators are included under the categories of productivity, opportunity, diversity, and equity. Finally, community measures fall under life-long learning, health, citizenship, and stewardship.

The Willapa Project links with other community groups and organizations. A joint effort by the Willapa Alliance and Ecotrust, the *Willapa Indicators for a Sustainable Community* report is intended to promote discussion of sustainability issues in the local communities. Published as a companion volume to the indicators report is *The Directory of Organizations and Services in Pacific County, Including Key Government Officials*. And among other projects, the Alliance formed the Willapa Science Group, a group of local and regional scientists and educators who encourage scientific research that is meaningful to local people.

Hamilton-Wentworth's Sustainable Community Indicators Project: In Ontario, Hamilton-Wentworth's Sustainable Community Indicators Project arose out of the regional municipality's Vision 2020 initiative. This vision of a sustainable future was developed by a citizens' Task Force on Sustainable Development appointed by the regional council; over 400 individuals and 50 community groups took part in the visioning process (Maclaren, 1996). The Indicators Project measured progress toward the goals outlined in the Vision 2020 document, and drew on participation of the community throughout the process. While the final set of indicators are intended for decision-makers, the prime goal was developing a set of indicators which were understandable and useful to local citizens.

Oregon Benchmarks Program

The Oregon Benchmarks process resulted from the State of Oregon's strategic plan, *Oregon Shines*. A multi-stakeholder organization supporting the plan, the Oregon Progress Board, presented a reporting framework to the state legislature after extensive consultation, and the benchmarks process was officially adopted in 1991.

The framework for reporting consists of 269 indicators. Rather than simply present indicators to measure and report trends, however, the Oregon process defines targets, known as benchmarks. The benchmarks cover a diverse range of issues around sustainability, including categories such as children and families, education and work force, health and health care, clean natural environment, equal opportunity and social harmony, and economic prosperity. The Board publishes a report card every two years to report on progress toward the stated targets.

While the Oregon Benchmarks program has drawn on public consultation and aims to inform the public, its main strength is its ability to promote action and accountability in the state government. Rational and clear sustainability goals have formed the basis for strategic planning throughout government agencies. The legislature even passed several bills directing agencies to work toward benchmarks. On a smaller scale, the Oregon Benchmarks are being applied by municipal governments and community organizations, and several cities and counties are adopting strategies to complement the state program.

The Need for National Indicators

It is too early to judge the impact of local and regional projects on community sustainability over the long-term, but they seem to be helping communities move in the right direction. Many researchers have also recognized the importance of developing sustainability indicators at the national scale. Currently, much national policy is driven by trends in GNP, which only considers narrow economic measures of a country's well-being; sustainability, including

---

Redefining Wealth

"In September 1995 the World Bank introduced a preliminary new index of national wealth which includes natural capital (environmental resources), produced assets (factories, infrastructure, financial assets — what is usually measured by the GNP), human resources (educated, healthy, productive people) and social capital (families, communities, institutions). Moreover, the World Bank acknowledges that 'produced assets' account for only some 20% of national wealth, while natural capital accounts for another 20% and human resources and social capital between them account for the remaining 60%. From this perspective the wealthiest nation in the world is Australia (with 70% of its wealth based on its land and natural resources) followed by Canada (also rich in natural resources) in second place. Luxembourg, Japan and Sweden (3rd-6th place) owe their wealth mainly to human capital, as does the USA which ranks 12th on this scale" (Henderson, 1996).

trends in natural and social capital, is not considered. Effective indicators of national sustainability would provide important information for citizens and governments supporting initiatives at the local and regional level.

RESOURCES

The **Community Based Environmental Protection** division of the EPA provides publications and toolkits to help communities develop locally unique multiple-stakeholder processes for environmental problem solving.
    Website: www.epa.gov/ecocommunity

Community Indicators Project is an initiative of Redefining Progress with the goal of linking existing and emerging indicator projects, and facilitating the development of more initiatives. The main products being developed by CINet include the *Community Indicators Handbook*, the CINet web site, and an e-mail discussion group, RP-CINET, for the exchange of information. These products promise to be a significant contribution to providing accessible and relevant information to groups interested in sustainability indicators.
    Website: www.redefiningprogress.org

Guide to Sustainable Community Indicators by M. Hart (Ipswich, Mass.: QLF/Atlantic Center for the Environment, 1999) is a useful guidebook describing the entire process of developing and implementing sustainability indicators at the community level. The guide includes sample indicators, list of projects, and references. The author has also developed an excellent website.
    Website: www.sustainablemeasures.com

The International Institute for Sustainable Development has compiled *Compendium: A Global Directory to Indicator Initiatives*, the best place to start.
    Website: www.iisd.org/measure/compendium/.

Life in Jacksonville: Quality Indicators for Progress is available from:
    Website:www.jcci.org/statistics/statistics.aspx

New Economics Foundation is a leading organization in the field of social auditing. The Foundation has contributed both to the development of a practical methodology and its increasingly widespread use through a combination of research and publications, training, and direct social auditing activities. The Foundation aims to promote social responsibility in the corporate, not-for-profit, and public sectors. Publications include *Social Auditing for Small Organizations*, and *Building Corporate Accountability*.
    Website: www.neweconomics.org

Oregon Benchmarks reports are available from the Oregon Progress Board.
    Website: http://egov.oregon.gov/DAS/OPB/

Sustainable Seattle is a resource and a catalyst for urban sustainability. Their indicators report is on their website.
    Website: www.sustainableseattle.org

Vision 2020 is Hamilton's long term vision of a vibrant, healthy, sustainable future shared by local government, citizens, business, groups and organizations. Vision 2020's Sustainability Indictor's Report is available on-line.

Website: www.vision2020.hamilton.ca/

REFERENCES

Azar, C., J. Holmberg, and K. Lindgren. 1996. "Socio-ecological Indicators for Sustainability." *Ecological Economics* 18:89-112.

Brugmann, J. 1996. "Cities Take Action: Local Environmental Initiatives." In *World Resources 1996-97: The Urban Environment*, World Resources Institute, United Nations Environment Program, United Nations Development Program, World Bank. New York: Oxford University Press.

Brugmann, J. 1997. "Is There a Method in Our Measurement? The Use of Indicators in Local Sustainable Development Planning." *Local Environment* 2(1): 59-72.

City of Ottawa. 1990. Urban Environmental Conservation Strategy: Framework Document, discussion paper. Ottawa: City of Ottawa, Department of Engineering and Public Works.

Forss, K., B.Cracknell, and K. Samset. 1994. "Can Evaluation Help an Organization to Learn?" *Evaluation Review* 18(5): 574-91.

Henderson, H. 1996. *Building a Win-Win World: Life Beyond Global Economic Warfare.* San Francisco: Berrett-Koehler Publishers.

International Council for Local Environmental Initiatives (ICLEI). 1993. "The Local Agenda 21 Initiative: ICLEI Guidelines for Local and National Local Agenda 21 Campaigns." Toronto: ICLEI.

International Council for Local Environmental Initiatives (ICLEI), International Development Research Centre (IDRC), and United Nations Environment Program. 1996. *The Local Agenda 21 Planning Guide.* Toronto: ICLEI and Ottawa: IDRC.

Kline, E. 1997. "Sustainable Community Indicators." In *Eco-City Dimensions: Healthy Communities, Healthy Planet*, M. Roseland, ed. Gabriola Island, BC: New Society Publishers.

Levett, R. 1997. "Tools, Techniques and Processes for Municipal Environmental Management." *Local Environment* 2(2): 189-202.

Maclaren, V.W. 1996. "Developing Indicators of Urban Sustainability: A Focus on the Canadian Experience." Toronto: Intergovernmental Committee on Urban and Regional Research Press.

McLemore, J.R., and J.E. Neumann. 1987. "The Inherently Political Nature of Program Evaluators and Evaluation Research." *Evaluation and Program Planning* 10: 83-93.

Meadows, D.H., et al. 1972. *The Limits to Growth* . New York: Signet.

Osborne, D., and T. Gaebler. 1993. *Reinventing Government* . New York: Plume.

Papineau, D. 1996. "Participatory Evaluation in a Community Organization: Fostering Stakeholder Empowerment and Utilization." *Evaluation and Program Planning* 19(1): 79-93.

Parker, P. 1995. "From Sustainable Development Objectives to Indicators of Progress: Options for New Zealand Communities." *New Zealand Geographer* 51(2): 50-57.

Pearce, J., P. Raynard, and S. Zadek. 1997. *Social Auditing for Small Organisations: A Workbook for Trainers and Practitioners.* London: New Economics Foundation.

Robért, K.-H., B. Schmidt-Bleek, J. Aloisi de Larderel, G. Basile. J.L. Jansen, R. Kuehr, P. Price Thomas, M. Auzuki, P. Hawken, and M. Wackernagel. 2002. "Strategic Sustainable Development — Selection, Design and Synergies of Applied Tools," *Journal of Cleaner Production* 10: 197-214.

Schön, D.A., and M. Rein. 1994. *Frame Reflection: Toward the Resolution of Intractable Policy*

Controversies. New York: Basic Books.

Schwandt, T.A. 1997. "Evaluation as Practical Hermeneutics." *Program Evaluation* 3(1): 69-83.

Wackernagel, M., and W.E. Rees. 1996. *Our Ecological Footprint: Reducing Human Impact on the Earth* . Gabriola Island, BC: New Society Publishers.

Waddell, S. 1995. "Lessons from the Healthy Cities Movement for Social Indicator Development." *Social Indicators Research* 34: 213-35.

LESSONS AND CHALLENGES

O ne might believe today that sustainable development has finally come of age. Born — publicly, at least — in the 1987 report of the UN's (Brundtland) Commission on Environment and Development, a child of the global agenda at the Rio "Earth Summit" in 1992, stumbling toward maturity with the Johannesburg World Summit on Sustainable Development (ICLEI, 2002; Otto-Zimmerman, 2002) and the Kyoto Accord on climate change, sustainable development seems to have survived even the shift to a "post-September 11" world.

More people are using the term "sustainable" today than ever before, but most often they use it to simply mean "surviving," "staying afloat," or "not going out of business," rather than any lofty notion of integrating economic, social and environmental objectives.

Some in the environmental movement might look askance upon equating sustainability with economic survival, but with the end of the Cold War and the absence of any credible alternative to capitalism, it is clear that serious attempts to promote sustainable development must honour this basic capitalist and biophysical reality: nothing is sustainable if it's not here next year. For better or worse, this has not changed since Adam Smith first published the *Wealth of Nations* in 1776.

What has changed, however, is an emerging recognition that a contemporary view of sustainable development has to blend this basic desire for economic prosperity (or at least survival) with multiple bottom-line objectives. Staying in business is undoubtedly necessary, but it is no longer enough. We have obligations to the planet and to each other and to future generations. Business depends upon our commitment to these obligations (e.g., environmental stewardship; a healthy, educated, and peaceful population), and fulfilling these obligations depends upon our ability to create and distribute wealth such that society and nature become more stable and secure, not less so.

Gated communities within gated countries will not lead to long-term global stability and security. Genuine "homeland security" requires us to "do development differently." As discussed in Chapter 1, this means:

1. learning to live on our natural income rather than depleting our natural capital;
2. finding ways to live more lightly on the planet, including increasing the efficiency of our resource and energy use, and reducing our present (not to speak of projected) levels of materials and energy consumption;

CHAPTER 15

3. enhancing our quality of life and the public domain by strengthening our community capital; and
4. fostering the critical resources for strengthening community capital: trust, imagination, courage, commitment, the relations between individuals and groups, and time.

We must therefore explicitly aim to nurture and strengthen community capital in order to improve our economic and social well-being. Government and corporate decisions should be reviewed for their effects on all forms of community capital. Programs and policies need to be effected at every level to ensure that community capital is properly considered.

No single person can raise the wind that might blow us into a sustainable future. But we can all help put up the sail so that when the wind comes, we can catch it. If we can create now the possibility of a sustainable future, we can genuinely breathe some hope into our communities for ourselves and for our children.

Our communities provide enormous, largely untapped opportunities for making our society more sustainable. This final chapter reviews some lessons for policy-making that emerge from the foregoing chapters, and explores the challenges ahead.

LESSONS FOR POLICY-MAKING

Communities are coming to recognize their responsibility to develop sustainably. The community capital approach to sustainable community development requires some relatively new thinking about broad questions of community sustainability and self-reliance, and more specific innovations concerning community ownership, management, finance, organization, capacity, and learning. Taken together, the initiatives described in this book begin to delineate a strategy for encouraging a globally conscious culture of sustainability in our communities. They also indicate some practical suggestions on how to design effective sustainable community development policies. The key features of any sustainable development policy framework should recognize the following:

Sustainable development requires sustainable communities. Global sustainable development requires local authority and capacity for sustainable community management and development. Despite the concentration of population in urban areas, many city and local governments do not have the regulatory and financial authority required to effectively contribute to sustainable urban development. Other levels of government must provide resources and support for the financing, management, and policy-making authority necessary for local governments to achieve sustainable development in their communities.

To make wise decisions about key aspects of their communities, particularly land use, local governments need more generous national funding for infrastructure, education, and social services. The experience of recent years has demonstrated that placing the burden of all these costs on property taxes can lead local governments to act irresponsibly — for example, allowing ecologically destructive development of valuable open space, or excluding low-taxpaying land uses such as affordable housing. Deteriorating municipal services, along with failing roads, bridges and sewerage systems in major urban areas worldwide also testify to the need for giving more financial resources to communities (Muro and Puentes, 2004).

Rules can and must be changed. Many community policy-makers are stuck in the paralyzing belief that our market society and our bureaucratic nation-state system cannot be changed in any basic sense. To play by those rules means that both the environment and the less fortunate members of society always lose until eventually everything is lost.

Sustainability can mean "less" as well as "more." So long as sustainable development is conceived merely as "environmental protection," it will be understood as an "added" cost to be "traded" against. Once sustainable development is conceived as *doing development differently*, such trade-offs become less critical: the new focus is instead on finding ways to *stop* much of what we are already doing, and use the resources thus freed for socially and ecologically sustainable activities.

Where the market works, use it. As one utility executive explained his sudden interest in energy conservation, "the rat has to smell the cheese." Create and promote incentives for ecologically sound practices. Well-designed ecological incentive programs are also cost-effective, since larger expenditures for clean-up and restoration are avoided.

Where the market fails, don't be afraid to mandate changes. The prevailing economic orthodoxy is that we must have a political and economic environment that welcomes foreign-owned companies and supports business through a reduction in regulations to become globally competitive, no matter what the consequences in our society and in our communities.

Yet the evidence may suggest otherwise. For example, Rainey et al (2003) note that productive local economic development policy seeks to provide high-quality infrastructure and attract highly skilled labour, rather than engaging in a tax- and wage-cutting race to the bottom, in which localities compete with one another by reducing their standard of living. They also observe that, "Holding everything else constant, higher taxes will tend to have a negative impact on capital investment. However, if higher taxes are used to make investments in public services that improve the productivity of private capital, the negative impact of the high taxes may be diminished or overcome by the positive productivity benefits."

Polluters should pay for the costs of remediation, but it is even more important to prevent pollution and the waste of resources in the first place. This principle is particularly significant in the debate over "green" taxes. Governments can reflect new priorities without increasing the total tax burden by shifting taxes away from income and toward environmentally damaging activities. If governments substituted taxes on pollution, waste and resource depletion for a large portion of current levies on employment and income, both the environment and the economy would benefit. The Worldwatch Institute estimated that a set of potential US green taxes (particularly on carbon content of fuels and on generation of hazardous wastes) could substitute for *reducing income taxes* by nearly 30 percent (Postel, 1991), and more recent work (e.g., see Robért et al., 2002) supports this. Citizens, corporations and the environment could all come out ahead.

Social equity is not only desirable but essential. Inequities undermine sustainable development, making it essential to consider the distributive effects of actions intended to advance sustainable development. During times of tight budgets, more efficient and beneficial growth strategies make more sense than ever. No less a source than The Brookings Institution finds that compact development patterns and investing in projects to improve urban cores would save taxpayers' money and improve the overall economic performance of regions (Muro and Puentes, 2004). The most common image of sprawl is usually the farm paved over for a subdivision, but the more insidious images are the blocks and blocks of abandoned neighborhoods scattered throughout urban America. Divisions by income and race have allowed some areas to prosper while others languish. As basic needs such as jobs, education and health care become less plentiful in some communities, residents have diminishing opportunities to participate in their regional economy. Sustainable community development expands opportunities by expanding transportation connections to jobs and steering economic development toward existing communities (Smart Growth America, 2004).

Public participation is itself a sustainable development strategy. To a considerable extent, the environmental crisis is a creativity crisis. By soliciting the bare minimum of public "input," rather than actively seeking community participation from agenda-setting through to implementation and evaluation, local and senior decision-makers have failed to tap the well of human ingenuity. They have failed to recognize that *only* from this well can the myriad challenges to redevelop our communities be met successfully. Effective and acceptable local solutions require local decisions, which in turn require the extensive knowledge and participation of the people most affected by those decisions, in their workplaces and in their communities.

THE CHALLENGES AHEAD

Sustainable communities will not come easily — they require significant change in our structures, attitudes, and values. Sustainable development implies a shift in the capacity of individuals, companies, and nations to use resources which they have the right to use — and are encouraged to use — under present legal and economic arrangements. Although even the most conventional analyses recognize the need for changing these arrangements, few openly acknowledge that moving toward a sustainable society requires more than minor adjustments to existing practices.

The key to a sustainable future lies not in making us more competitive, but rather in making us more perceptive, more able to realize what we have, what we need, and what are the long-term consequences of the short-term choices we are making (Wachtel, 1989). Many North Americans intuitively understand that the reason why economic growth no longer brings a sense of greater well-being, why the pleasures of our new possessions swiftly melt away is that "what really matters is not one's material possessions but one's psychological economy, one's richness of human relations and freedom from the conflicts and constrictions that prevent us from enjoying what we

The enduring legacy of the environmental movement is that it has taught us the distinction between price and cost. Price is what the individual pays. Cost is what the community pays. The marketplace works efficiently only when guided by accurate price signals (Morris, 1990).

have." Indeed, we have attempted "to use economics to solve what are really psychological problems" (Wachtel, 1989).

Like others writing in the growing sociological literature on the "communitarian approach" (e.g., Bellah, 1991; Lasch, 1991), Wachtel (1989) argues that our societal focus on productivity and economic efficiency as defining values leads to greater emphasis on competition, the pursuit of self-interest, and the stimulation of demand:

> This in turn means still more decline in the security to be gained via shared ties and a stable, securely rooted place and way of life, still more need to compensate by organizing everything around what enables us to have "more," still more decline of traditional sources of security, and so forth. Thus, the more fully we have committed ourselves to increasing material abundance as our ultimate societal value, the more we have undermined older sources of security and made ourselves dependent on material goods for our sense of well-being to an unprecedented degree.

The challenge ahead is to explore the implications of a sustainable future and to find a new set of guiding images and metaphors suited for it. Sustainable communities are the next steps in suggesting an alternative vision of the future that is not just a bitter necessity (for example, the need to reduce materials and energy consumption), but promises a genuinely better life. Sustainable communities do not mean settling for less, but rather thinking of new opportunities along a different, and likely more satisfying, dimension.

With their relatively wealthy and well-educated populations, North American communities have a moral obligation to demonstrate leadership (and consequently benefit from) developing the knowledge, technologies, and processes the world requires for sustainability in the coming decades. Citizens and their governments have the ability to frame issues, assume leadership, champion initiatives, and demonstrate sustainable alternatives in their everyday practice. With creative leadership, we may yet be proud of the legacy left for our children.

Sustainable community development requires mobilizing citizens and their governments to strengthen all forms of community capital. This includes minimizing consumption of essential natural capital and improving physical capital, which in turn require the more efficient use of urban space. It also includes strengthening economic capital, increasing human capital, multiplying social capital, and enhancing cultural capital. Community mobilization is necessary to coordinate, balance and catalyze community capital.

In the century ahead, those communities, enterprises, cities and nations that learn how to strengthen all six forms of capital simultaneously are likely to be the ones that will thrive.

"It is important to recognize that this process of change will take much time to accomplish. There are no quick-fix solutions to the creation of healthier cities and communities, instead a long-term commitment to multiple small steps must be taken. In essence, a healthy community and a healthy city is created one household at a time, one street at a time, one block at a time, one neighborhood at a time and one day at a time. Multiple small strategies provide multiple opportunities to learn and also provide a margin for failure, because failure will occur and is a learning experience that needs to be accepted, not penalized. The challenge for cities is to learn how to create community capital as a fundamental strategy for creating a healthy city" (Hancock, 2001).

This synergistic approach will enable our communities to be cleaner, healthier, and less expensive; to have greater accessibility and cohesion; and to be more self-reliant in energy, food, and economic security than they are now. Sustainable communities will not, therefore, merely "sustain" the quality of our lives — they will dramatically *improve* it.

REFERENCES

Bellah, R.N., et al. 1991. *The Good Society.* New York: Knopf.

City of Toronto. 1989. *The Changing Atmosphere: A Call To Action.* Toronto: City of Toronto.

Hancock, T. 2001. "People, Partnerships and human Progress: Building Community Capital." *Health Promotion International* 16 (3) Sept: 275-280.

International Council for Local Environmental Initiatives (ICLEI). (2002). *Accelerating sustainable development: Local action moves the world.* New York: United Nations Economic and Social Council.

Lasch, C. 1991. *The True and Only Heaven: Progress and Its Critics.* New York: W.W. Norton.

Morris, D. 1990. *An Environmental Policy for the 1990s: Fashioning the Molecular Basis for a Green Economy.* Washington, DC: Institute for Local Self-Reliance.

Muro, M. and R. Puentes. "Investing in a Better Future: A Review of the Fiscal and Competitive Advantages of Smarter Growth Development Patterns." Cities and Suburbs, The Brookings Institution, November 20, 2004. Retrieved from http://brookings.edu/urban/publications/200403_smartgrowth.htm

Otto-Zimmermann, K. 2002. "Local action 21: Motto-mandate-movement in the post-Johannesburg decade." *Local Environment*, 7(4), 465-469.

Postel, S. 1991. "Accounting for Nature." *Worldwatch* 4(2) March/April: 28-33.

Rainey, D. V., Robinson, K. L., Allen, I., & Christy, R. D. 2003. "Essential forms of capital for sustainable community development." *American Journal of Agricultural Economics*, 85(3): 708-715.

Robért, K.-H.., B. Schmidt-Bleek, J. Aloisi de Larderel, G. Basile. J.L. Jansen, R. Kuehr, P. Price Thomas, M. Auzuki, P. Hawken, and M. Wackernagel. 2002. "Strategic Sustainable Development — Selection, Design and Synergies of Applied Tools." *Journal of Cleaner Production* 10: 197-214.

Smart Growth America, 2004. "Social Equity." Retrieved from www.smartgrowthamerica.org/

van Vliet, W. 1990. "Human Settlements in the US: Questions of Even and Sustainable Development." Prepared for the Colloquium on Human Settlements and Sustainable Development, Toronto, 21-23 June.

Wachtel, P. 1989. *The Poverty of Affluence: A Psychological Portrait of the American Way of Life.* Gabriola Island, BC: New Society Publishers.

SUSTAINABLE COMMUNITY RESOURCES

T he previous edition of this book contained an extensive appendix of useful sustainable community resources for citizens and their governments. The sustainable communities movement is growing so fast that it is no longer possible to
publish a resource book that will not quickly be obsolete. Therefore, the Resources section of this volume is now available and regularly updated, with many important links,
on the web site of the Centre for Sustainable Community Development at Simon Fraser
University, in Vancouver, Canada. Please visit www.sfu.ca/cscd and click on *Toward
Sustainable Communities*.

APPENDIX

Index — General

numbers in **bold** indicate illustrations

and local government, 194
and the poor, 162, 163-164
and renewable energy, 94
technical planning tools for, 208-209. *see also* pollution
Environmental Protection Agency (EPA), 100-101, 106, 108
environmental space, 208
Environmentally Preferable Purchasing (EPP), 82
Environmentally Sensitive Area (ESA) studies, 48
Enwave, 96
EPA (Environmental Protection Agency), 100-101, 106, 108
EPP (Environmentally Preferable Purchasing), 82
EPUD (Emerald People's Utility District), 97
Equity Housing Cooperative, 158
Equity Trust, 149
Essential Function Bonds (EFBs), 158
Eugene, OR, 90-91, 93, 97, 100, 121
Europe, 109
Evangeline, PEI, 172
Everett, WA, 62

F
fair trade programs, 172
Fannie Mae, 143
Federal Energy Management Program (FEMP), 91
FEMP (Federal Energy Management Program), 91
fertilizers, 66
fishing quotas, 180, 198
Florida, 49, 70, 110, 123, 142-143
Food Share, 53-54
food systems and urban agriculture, 51-54
force field analysis, 209
forestry, community, 180
fossil fuels and greenhouse gases, 106
Fox River sock company, 175
Framework Convention on Climate Change, 203
Freiburg, Germany, 38
From the Ground Up, 54

G
Gaebler, T., 212
Galion, OH, 159
Galt House, 96
Gardening Angels, 52-53
geoexchange systems, 96
Geographic Information Systems (GIS), 209
George, Henry, 138
Geothermal Heat Pump Consortium (GHPC), 96

geothermal systems, 95
Germany
New Urbanism initiatives, 146, 147
sustainable community initiatives, 49, 82, 96
traffic experiments, 121-122, 122
GGC (Go Green Choices), 124
GHPC (Geothermal Heat Pump Consortium), 96
Gilbert, R., 194
GIS (Geographic Information Systems), 209
Glendale, AZ, 62
Global ReLeaf Program, 50
global warming, 104, 106
Go Green Choices (GGC), 124
golf courses, 46
Good Neighbor Project, 176
GoodCents utility marketing and certification program, 92
Goodland, R., 8
government, 190-203
and bureaucracy, 195-196
and decision making, 191-193
importance of mobilizing, 26, 27, 190
planning process, 196-200
role of local government, 193-195 (*see also* local government)
state and provincial land-use legislation, 200, 214
sustainable community planning initiatives, 200-203
grants, 39, 62-63, 93, 157, 159
grass paving, 69
grassroots citizens' movements, 194-195
Great River Greening, 51
Green Builder Program, 90
green business, 168
Green Business Alliance, 180
Green Guerrillas, 50
Green Map System, 176, 185
Green power programs, 97
green projects/funds, 39
greenfields, 139
greenhouse effect, 104
greenhouse gasses
causes, 104-105, 106-107
initiatives to reduce, 108-111
greening the city, 44-56
aquatic systems, 54-56
benefits of, 44-45, 47-48
initiatives for, 48-51
opens spaces and parks, 45-46

ABOUT THE AUTHOR

Mark Roseland, Ph.D., MCIP, is Director of the Centre for Sustainable Community Development (www.sfu.ca/cscd) at Simon Fraser University in Vancouver, Canada and is a professor in SFU's Department of Geography. In 1990, as Research Director for the City of Vancouver's Clouds of Change Task Force, he orchestrated one of the first comprehensive municipal responses to global atmospheric change and local air-quality problems. A former Editor of RAIN magazine, he was the North American Editor of the international journal *Local Environment*, published in association with ICLEI — Local Governments for Sustainability, from its inception in 1995 until 2002, and continues to serve on its Editorial Advisory Board. His numerous publications include *Eco-City Dimensions: Healthy Communities, Healthy Planet* (New Society Publishers, 1997). He lectures internationally, advises communities and governments on sustainable development policy and planning, and participates actively in sustainable community development projects in Vancouver and elsewhere.

If you have enjoyed *Toward Sustainable Communities*,
you might also enjoy other

BOOKS TO BUILD A NEW SOCIETY

Our books provide positive solutions for people who want to
make a difference. We specialize in:

**Environment and Justice • Conscientious Commerce
Sustainable Living • Ecological Design and Planning
Natural Building & Appropriate Technology • New Forestry
Educational and Parenting Resources • Nonviolence
Progressive Leadership • Resistance and Community**

New Society Publishers

ENVIRONMENTAL BENEFITS STATEMENT

New Society Publishers has chosen to produce this book on Enviro 100, recycled
paper made with **100% post consumer waste**, processed chlorine free, and old
growth free.

For every 5,000 books printed, New Society saves the following resources:[1]

39	Trees
3,533	Pounds of Solid Waste
3,887	Gallons of Water
5,070	Kilowatt Hours of Electricity
6,422	Pounds of Greenhouse Gases
28	Pounds of HAPs, VOCs, and AOX Combined
10	Cubic Yards of Landfill Space

[1]Environmental benefits are calculated based on research done by the Environmental Defense Fund and
other members of the Paper Task Force who study the environmental impacts of the paper industry.

For more information on this environmental benefits statement, or to inquire about environmentally
friendly papers, please contact New Leaf Paper – info@newleafpaper.com Tel: 888 • 989 • 5323.

For a full list of NSP's titles, please call **1-800-567-6772** *or check out our web site at:*

www.newsociety.com

NEW SOCIETY PUBLISHERS